Series on International Taxation

VOLUME 82

Series Editors

Prof. Ruth Mason, University of Virginia School of Law
Prof. Dr Ekkehart Reimer, University of Heidelberg

Introduction & Contents

The Series on International Taxation deals with a wide variety of topics in the global tax arena. The authors include many of the field's leading experts as well as talented newcomers. Their expert views and incisive commentary have proven highly useful to practitioners and academics alike.

Objective

The volumes published in this series are aimed at offering high-quality analytical information and practical solutions to international tax practitioners.

Readership

Practitioners, academics and policy makers in international tax law.

Frequency of Publication

2-3 new volumes published each year.

The titles published in this series are listed at the end of this volume.

The Role of Tax Law in Mergers and Acquisitions

A Chinese Perspective

Chunyang Zhang

Wolters Kluwer

Published by:
Kluwer Law International B.V.
PO Box 316
2400 AH Alphen aan den Rijn
The Netherlands
E-mail: lrs-sales@wolterskluwer.com
Website: www.wolterskluwer.com/en/solutions/kluwerlawinternational

Sold and distributed by:
Wolters Kluwer Legal & Regulatory U.S.
7201 McKinney Circle
Frederick, MD 21704
United States of America
E-mail: customer.service@wolterskluwer.com

Printed on acid-free paper.

ISBN 978-94-035-3741-2

e-Book: ISBN 978-94-035-3762-7
web-PDF: ISBN 978-94-035-3783-2

Printed in the United Kingdom.

This is dedicated to my dear wife, Jun

Table of Contents

List of Abbreviations

ALL	Administrative Licensing Law of the PRC
COE	Collectively Owned Enterprise
CNY	Chinese Yuan
CPC	Communist Party of China
CSRC	China Securities Regulatory Commission
EITL	Enterprise Income Tax Law of the PRC
EITLIR	Enterprise Income Tax Law Implementation Regulations of the PRC
FDI	Foreign Direct Investment
FIE	Foreign-Invested Enterprise
GDP	Gross Domestic Product
IITL	Individual Income Tax Law of the PRC
IRC	Internal Revenue Code of the US
MOF	Ministry of Finance of the PRC
MOFTEC	Ministry of Foreign Trade and Economic Cooperation of the PRC
NDRC	National Development and Reform Commission of the PRC
NPC	National People's Congress of the PRC
SCNPC	Standing Committee of the NPC
OECD	Organization for Economic Co-operation and Development
PRC	The People's Republic of China
STA	State Taxation Administration of the PRC
SOE	State-Owned Enterprise
TVE	Township and Village Enterprise
US	United States
WTO	World Trade Organization

Acknowledgements

There are many people who I would like to acknowledge and thank for their aid during the completion of this book.

I owe the greatest thanks to my supervisors, Professor Robin Hui Huang and Professor Yan Xu, for their enlightening guidance. I am grateful to Professor David C. Donald, Professor Nolan Sharkey, and Professor Noam Noked, who very kindly read an early draft of this work and provided insightful comments.

My gratitude also extends to the Faculty of Law of the Chinese University of Hong Kong and the Melbourne Law School, both of which provide me with not only facilitates to access to a wealth of academic resources but opportunities to develop an international perspective for the work.

Finally, I must thank my family. My parents have always been a source of inspiration for me. My dear wife, Jun, put up with me and provided constant support throughout this entire process. This book would not exist without their tremendous understanding and encouragement.

CHAPTER 1
Introduction

Most mergers and acquisitions (M&A) transactions are an extremely complex process influenced by many factors, out of which taxation stands out for its significance in the decision-making of investors over whether to enter into an M&A transaction and the selection of transaction structure. Researchers from different markets have confirmed through empirical studies that taxation can have a profound effect on the occurrence of M&A transactions.[1]

The impact of taxation on the M&A market is constantly growing, as tax is more and more cherished as a measure for implementing macroeconomic regulation and control rather than a mere tool for raising fiscal revenue. Taxation policy appears to be a convenient instrument for steering the M&A market towards desired economic objectives; however, due to the complexity and diversity of M&A transactions, policymakers always have to walk a difficult tightrope in wanting to promote the desired policy goals without inducing unintended consequences such as tax avoidance or even evasion, severe market distortion, and so on.

Indeed, the question of what kind of role the tax law has in the M&A market and the derivative tax design issues has become a globally debated topic, and income tax – among various forms of taxes imposed on M&A transactions[2] – has long received the most attention. As of 2004, almost all members of the Organization for Economic

1. *See e.g.*, Myron S. Scholes & Mark A. Wolfson, *The Effects of Changes in Tax Laws on Corporate Reorganization Activity*, 63 The Journal of Business S141(1990) (arguing that in the 1980s tax considerations had a first order effect on M&A activities in the US); Lei Yin, *A Research on the Effects of the Enterprise Income Tax Policies on Mergers and Acquisitions in China: An Empirical Test Based on A-share Listed Companies*, Shuiwu Yanjiu [Taxation Research], no. 7, 2021, at 104 (arguing that the effective tax burden has a significant negative impact on the occurrence of M&A transactions in China).
2. The tax consequences of M&A transactions are not limited to income tax. An M&A transaction typically involves transfers of various kinds of assets and thus may trigger other taxes. For example, in China, acquisitions of real property may give rise to large amounts of value-added tax, and stock acquisitions usually result in stamp duty charges. Nevertheless, there is no doubt that income tax treatments are a matter of the utmost concern for taxpayers and tax authorities.

Co-operation and Development (OECD) have established certain special income tax rules for M&A transactions, which seem rather anomalous in the tradition of realization-based income taxation.[3]

The People's Republic of China (PRC) has followed this international trend. The M&A market in China generally emerged in the late 1980s, and ever since, it has experienced exponential growth. According to the China Securities Regulatory Commission (CSRC), the value of M&A transactions involving listed companies increased at an average annual rate of 41.14% from 2013 to 2016, and 2016 alone has witnessed M&A transactions with an aggregate value of around Chinese Yuan (CNY) 2.39 trillion.[4] In 2021, the Chairman of CSRC disclosed that the cumulative total value of M&A transactions involving listed companies was CNY 11.2 trillion between 2016 and 2020 – making China the world's second-largest M&A market behind the US.[5] Alongside the unprecedented growth in the M&A market, China has been endeavouring to modernize its income tax regime for M&A.

With the benefit of overseas experience, in a relatively short period of time, China has set up and developed its income tax regime for M&A in a remarkable manner. China introduced the first specific income tax rule governing M&A transactions in 1993. In the following fifteen years, the fledgling income tax regime for M&A was widely criticized for placing an unfair burden on different types of taxpayers and inducing tax avoidance.[6] Shortly after the enactment of the Enterprise Income Tax Law of the PRC (EITL) that overhauled China's corporate income tax system,[7] the Ministry of Finance of the PRC (MOF) and the State Taxation Administration of the PRC (STA) jointly issued Caishui (2009) No. 59[8] in 2009 to consolidate the different tax treatments for various types of enterprises participating in M&A transactions, heralding a new era of the development of China's taxation of M&A.

However, the task of taxing M&A transactions in a consistent and prudent manner is difficult for China in its climate of rapid and somewhat chaotic economic transformation. Even though the Chinese law has made a quantum leap in the area of

3. *See* OECD, *Taxation of Capital Gains of Individuals: Policy Considerations and Approaches* 108 (2006).
4. CSRC, *Shangshi Gongsi Binggou Chongzu Fuwu Shiti Jingji Zhuanfanshi Tiaojiegou Qude Mingxian Chengxiao [Listed Company M&A Transactions Help Restructure the Economy]*, CSRC (5 October 2021), http://www.csrc.gov.cn/pub/newsite/gjb/dyxc/201708/t20170815_322153.html.
5. Huiman Yi, Yi Huiman Zai 2021 Jinrongjie Luntan Nianhui Shang de Zhuti Yanjiang [Keynote Speech by Chairman Yi Huiman at the 2021 Annual Meeting of Financial Street Forum] (20 October 2021), (transcript available at http://www.csrc.gov.cn/csrc/c100028/c1492450/content.shtml).
6. *See e.g.*, Guo Feng, *Rethinking and Reconstruction: Tax Aspects of Corporate M&A in China*, Gansu Zhengfa Xueyuan Xuebao [Journal of Gansu Institute of Political Science and Law], no. 4, 2007, at 105, 107-110.
7. Zhonghua Renmin Gongheguo Qiye Suodeshui Fa [Enterprise Income Tax Law of the People's Republic of China] (promulgated 16 March 2007, effective 1 January 2008, amended 2017) (PRC) (hereinafter EITL).
8. Caishui (2009) No. 59, Guanyu Qiye Chongzu Yewu Qiye Suodeshui Chuli Ruogan Wenti de Tongzhi [Notice on Several Issues on the Enterprise Income Tax Treatment of Enterprise Restructurings] (promulgated by the MOF and the STA on 30 April 2009, effective retrospectively 1 January 2008) (PRC).

taxing M&A transactions, there have been many flaws and inherent contradictions that need to be addressed. China's income tax regime for M&A is not sustained by a single consistent ideology or issue point. The Chinese government appears to have chosen to continue refurbishing the flawed system in a piecemeal rather than a systematic way, which has led to a patchwork of fragmented rules that are hard to grasp not only for taxpayers but even for tax authorities. Of course, there are a number of reasons behind this unsatisfactory situation. One of the most important reasons, among others, is that China has been too ready to rely on foreign experience in designing its tax rules without assessing whether it fits well in the Chinese context.[9]

The purpose of this book is therefore to deal with the income taxation of M&A transactions in China within its context, critically examine China's income tax regime for M&A and, based upon this examination, set out reform proposals. This book will explore in detail the issue of taxing income derived from M&A transactions in China, based on a careful investigation of the appropriate role that the income tax law shall play in China's M&A market. Moreover, empirical studies of China's M&A market were conducted in order to gain a first-hand understanding of the context in which the tax law operates.

This book consists of eight chapters. Chapter 1 introduces the topic and states the objectives of the book. Chapter 2 presents the historical development of the taxation of M&A transactions in China, including an overview of China's M&A market and a discussion of the historical development of China's M&A taxation. Chapter 3 gives a comprehensive review of the current tax rules for M&A transactions in China, disclosing how they are both divergent from and convergent with that of some other major economies. Chapter 4 analyses widely recognized principles of taxation, identifies the overarching guiding principle underpinning the income tax regime for M&A transactions and sets up the criteria for evaluation of China's tax rules for M&A transactions.

The following chapters, including Chapters 5, 6, and 7, move on to discuss how to better tax M&A transactions in China. Chapters 5 and 6 deal with a prominent aspect of China's M&A taxation system, namely, the special tax treatment for M&A transactions. These two chapters employ an empirical study to reveal the fundamental problems encountered by the current regime of the special tax treatment in China and conduct an examination of the rules and theories on tax-deferred reorganizations in the US to answer the question of whether and how the law should provide exceptional tax treatments for M&A transactions. Based on the results of the empirical study and overseas experience, a blueprint for improving the special tax treatment is proposed. Chapter 7 focuses on another critical issue in M&A taxation, which is how to address the disparity in the tax treatment of different forms of M&A transactions. Chapter 8 contains a concluding remark.

Before moving into the substantive discussion, I would like to explain the meaning and scope of 'tax law' used in this book.

---

9. *See* Wei Cui, *'Ultra Special' Tax Treatment for Restructuring of SOEs: Legal Background and Comments*, Zhongwai Faxue [Peking University Law Journal], no. 6, 2010, at 944, 944-945.

According to the *Constitution of the People's Republic of China* (China's Constitution) and the *Legislation Law of the People's Republic of China* (Legislation Law), China's tax legislation at the state level can be into a three-tiered hierarchy. Primary tax legislation includes all tax statutes (*falv*) enacted by the National People's Congress of the PRC (NPC) and the Standing Committee of the NPC (SCNPC); secondary tax legislation includes tax administrative regulations (*xingzheng fagui*) issued by the State Council, and tertiary tax legislation includes the ministerial regulations (*bumen guizhang*) issued by the central tax agencies, namely the MOF and STA.

The Legislation Law requires 'institution of tax, tax rate, tax administration, and other fundamental tax affairs' to be governed by statutes,[10] and only in cases where statutes are yet to be enacted the State Council may promulgate administrative regulations on those issues with the authorization of the NPC or the SCNPC.[11] Such delegations of legislative power are subject to strict conditions under the Legislation Law. First, each delegation of legislative power shall have specified purpose, scope, items, and timescale, as well as the principles with which the State Council shall comply.[12] Second, the State Council shall not pass the delegated power to other administrative agencies.[13]

China's Constitution and the Legislation Law have established a seemingly clear tax legislation framework, based on which most of the income tax rules shall be prescribed in either statutes or administrative regulations. Unfortunately, this framework has not yet been followed, resulting in an income tax system comprised of numerous rules that exist outside of the formal legal order. Take the corporate income tax regime as an example. From 2008 until now, the NPC and the SCNPC have only slightly amended the EITL, and the *Enterprise Income Tax Law Implementation Regulations*[14] promulgated by the State Council has remained unchanged. The MOF and the STA, meanwhile, have issued plenty of tax rules on corporate income tax and effectively led almost all of the reforms in this area.

The fact that the MOF and the STA tend to make rules in the form of so-called normative documents (*guifanxing wenjian*, commonly referred to as circulars) rather than ministerial regulations further leads China's income tax legislation astray from the formal legal order. The ministerial regulations issued by the MOF and the STA shall take the formats of 'MOF Decree' (*caizhengbu ling*) and 'STA Decree' (*guojia shuiwu zongju ling*) respectively.[15] However, up until now, most income tax rules issued by the two central tax agencies are 'normative documents' that take a format other than

10. Zhonghua Renmin Gongheguo Lifa Fa [Legislation Law of the People's Republic of China] (promulgated on 15 March 2000 and effective from 1 July 2000, amended in 2015) (PRC) (hereinafter Legislation Law), Art. 8(6).
11. Legislation Law, Art. 9.
12. Legislation Law, Art. 10.
13. Legislation Law, Art. 12.
14. Zhonghua Renmin Gongheguo Qiye Suodeshui Fa Shishi Tiaoli [Enterprise Income Tax Law Implementation Regulations of the People's Republic of China] (promulgated 6 December 2007, effective 1 January 2008) (PRC) (hereinafter EITLIR).
15. Caibanfa (2000) No. 68, Caizhengbu Guanche Shishi Lifa Fa de Yijian [Opinions of the MOF on the Implementation of the Legislation Law] (promulgated by the MOF on 4 December 2000, and effective from the date of promulgation) (PRC), Art. 8; STA Decree No. 1, Shuiwu Bumen

decree. The most common formats include 'Finance and Taxation Announcement' (*caishui*), 'STA Issuance' (*guoshui fa*), 'STA Correspondence' (*guoshui han*), and 'STA Announcement' (*guojia shuiwu zongju gonggao*).[16]

The differences between ministerial regulations and normative documents are not merely formalistic. The enactment, revision as well as nullification of ministerial regulations shall accord with strict substantive and procedural requirements provided by the Legislation Law and the *Regulations on Procedures for the Formulation of Ministerial Regulations*.[17] Ministerial regulations cannot have a retrospective effect except where they have the effect of better protecting the rights and interests of taxpayers.[18] Normative documents, which are in fact inter-agency communications issued by the MOF and the STA specifically to local public finance bureaus and local tax bureaus,[19] neither need to go through the strict rule-making procedure under the Legislation Law nor to be published,[20] and some of them are retrospectively effective although to the detriment of taxpayers.[21] It is therefore clear that the normative documents issued by the MOF and the STA in no way come close to the common understanding of 'law' that conforms to the constitutional standard.[22]

While tax rules outside the formal legal order permeate every aspect of China's income tax system, their prevalence in the income tax regime for M&A represents an extreme case. As will be shown in more detail in this book, since China started to develop its income tax regime for M&A, all the important rules in this area are provided

---

Guizhang Zhiding Shishi Banfa [Implementation Measures for Regulation-Making by the STA] (promulgated by the STA on 1 Febuary 2002, and effective from 1 March 2002) (PRC), Art. 2.

16. According to Wei Cui, the number of STA Correspondences may exceed 1,300 a year. *See* Wei Cui, *What is the 'Law' in Chinese Tax Administration?*, 19 Asia Pacific Law Review 73, 86 (2011).
17. Legislation Law, Arts. 83, 65-71; State Council Decree No. 322, Guizhang Zhiding Chengxu Tiaoli [Regulations on the Procedures for the Formulation of Ministerial Regulations] (promulgated by the State Council on 16 November 2001, effective from 1 January 2002, and amended in 2017) (PRC).
18. Legislation Law, Art. 93.
19. To take one example, the addressees of Caishui (2009) No. 59 are 'local public finance bureaus, STA's local branches, and local tax bureaus in all provinces, autonomous regions, centrally administered municipalities, and specifically designated cities'.
20. According to Wei Cui, in the first half of 2010, fewer than 60 out of over 300 STA Correspondences were published. *See* Cui, *supra* note 16, at 86.
21. For example, Guoshuihan (2009) No. 698 requires non-residents to report their gains on the transfer the stock of an offshore holding company. This circular was promulgated on 10 December 2009 and has a retrospective effect from 1 January 2008. Guoshuihan (2009) No. 698, Guanyu Jiaqiang Feijumin Qiye Guquan Zhuanrang Suode Qiye Suodeshui Guanli de Tongzhi [Notice on Strengthening the Administration of Enterprise Income Tax on Income from the Transfer of Shares by Non-resident Enterprises] (promulgated by the STA on 10 December 2009, and effective retrospectively from 1 January 2008) (PRC), Art. 6.
22. It should be noted that the STA has kept putting efforts in improving the clarity, transparency, predictability, and quality of the normative documents in these years. *See* STA Decree No. 41, Shuishou Guifanxing Wenjian Zhiding Guanli Banfa [New Measures for the Administration of Tax Normative Documents] (promulgated by the STA on 16 May 2017, effective 1 July 2017) (PRC). In STA Decree No. 41, the STA requires that all tax normative documents with general binding effect on taxpayers must adopt the form of STA Announcement, all the documents except those beneficial to taxpayers cannot apply retrospectively, and the draft documents must go through substantive review by the STA's legal department. Nevertheless, the progress cannot cure the fundamental constitutional defects of the informal rule-making.

in the normative documents issued by the MOF and the STA. Because of the fundamental defects associated with such informal rule-making, it is fair to say that China imposes income tax on M&A transactions without law. Nevertheless, viewed from a functional point of view, those normative documents constitute the de facto income tax law governing M&A transactions in China. As a work dealing with tax policy issues, this book takes a functional definition of 'tax law' so that rules of equal functional importance for the purpose of imposing income tax on M&A transactions in China receive equal attention, regardless of the format they take.

CHAPTER 2

Historical Development of China's M&A Taxation

§2.01 INTRODUCTION

China's income tax regime for M&A has evolved in tandem with the gradual development of the M&A market. Facing a strong wave of M&A transactions in 1993, the STA promulgated China's first piece of tax law concerning the taxation of M&A transactions.[1] In the following years, the Chinese tax authorities were busy promulgating, amending, or replacing tax rules to address tax issues popping up in the rocketing M&A market, and the income tax treatment of M&A transactions has been the subject of more than sixty tax circulars issued as of 2010.[2] It is remarkable that China could develop a sophisticated income tax regime for M&A within less than two decades.

What is interesting, though, is the way that despite such intensive revamping of the tax rules, China not only failed to reduce but rather increased the contractions within the M&A taxation regime. What are the reasons for this failure? From the study of the history of China's M&A taxation, we can observe that the long-term conflicts between tax policy objectives have foreshadowed the continuous difficulties in improving China's M&A taxation regime to the present day. This chapter offers a survey of the history of China's M&A taxation. Section §2.02 gives an overview of China's M&A market from the late 1970s to the 2000s, which sets the context for understanding the income taxation of M&A. Sections §2.03-§2.05 focus on the pre-2008 development of China's M&A taxation, the period of 1993 to 2007, discussing the evolvement of the regime. This is followed by a brief analysis of the fifteen-year zigzagging progress in §2.06.

1. Guoshuifa (1993) No. 139, Guanyu Gufenzhi Shidian Qiye Ruogan Shewai Shuishou Zhengce de Tongzhi [Notice Regarding Some Policies of Taxation Involving Foreign Parties for Joint-Stock Pilot Enterprises] (promulgated by the STA and effective 3 December 1993) (PRC).
2. Wei Cui & Richard Krever, *The Tax Consequences of Corporate Reorganisations in China*, British Tax Review, no. 3, 2011, at 340, 340.

§2.02 OVERVIEW OF CHINA'S M&A MARKET

Since the late 1970s, China has started to transform its centrally planned economy into a market-oriented one. The reform first began in rural areas. Before 1978, the agricultural sector was organized according to the commune system: rural residents worked in cooperatives known as production teams (*shengchan dui*), collectively owned all capital goods including lands, and received an evenly divided share of the cooperative's income.[3] As a part of economic reform, the commune system was replaced by the household responsibility system,[4] which allows rural households to contract land from the collective, independently make operating decisions, and take responsibility for their profits and losses.[5]

This decollectivization of the rural economy unleashed peasants' energies, leading to a dramatic increase in agricultural outputs and a significant improvement in peasants' living standards.[6] The surge in agricultural productivity released agricultural labour to non-farm sectors, fuelling the proliferation of township and village enterprises (TVEs) in the 1980s. In 1984, the number of TVEs rocketed from less than 1.5 million to more than 6 million.[7]

The booming of TVEs greatly contributed to the development of China's M&A activities. First, TVEs are important participants in the fledgling M&A market. Second and more profoundly, since TVEs were financed by pro rata contributions from rural residents, they represented an 'embryonic model' of China's joint-stock system,[8] which forms the institutional basis for the development of the M&A market. In 1984, the first joint-stock company Beijing Tianqiao General Merchandise Joint-Stock Company was established in Beijing, and since then, joint-stock companies have mushroomed nationwide.[9] The introduction of the joint-stock system expedites the development of the M&A market as it is much easier to transfer ownership of companies by selling stocks.

While TVEs became a great success, many state-owned enterprises (SOEs) suffered from the problem of inefficiency. In the 1980s, the Chinese government rolled out reform measures aiming to improve the performance of SOEs. Apart from well-known reform measures such as devolving rights to the managers of SOEs in the mid-1980s, some local governments started to arrange mergers of the unprofitable SOEs with the profitable ones. On 5 July 1984, under the mandate of the Baoding

3. Mai Lu & Mingliang Feng, *The Evolution of China's Reform and Development Process, in Thirty Years of China's Reform* 28, 28 (Mengkui Wang ed., 2012).
4. More than 93% of production teams have adopted the household responsibility system by 1983, *see* Justin Yifu Lin, *The Household Responsibility System Reform in China: A Peasant's Institutional Choice*, 69 American Journal of Agricultural Economics 410, 411 (1987).
5. Lu & Feng, *supra* note 3, at 28-29.
6. Peasants' income almost tripled from CNY 133.6 in 1978 to CNY 355 in 1984. *See ibid.*, at 28.
7. Editorial Board of China Township and Village Enterprises Yearbook, *Zhongguo Xiangzhen Qiye Nianjian 1978-1987 [China Township and Village Enterprises Yearbook 1978-1987]* 5 (1989).
8. Ru-yin Hu, *The Evolution of China's Capital Markets* 46 (2012).
9. For a review of the development of the joint-stock system in the 1980s, *see* Jianfu Chen, *Securitisation of State-Owned Enterprises and the Ownership Controversy in the PRC*, 15 Sydney L. Rev. 59, 60-62 (1993).

Municipal Government, Baoding Knitting Equipment Factory transferred all of its assets and liabilities to Baoding Textile Machinery Factory and ceased to exist. This merger is widely regarded as the first M&A transaction in post-reform China. After that, reorganizations led by local governments spread across the country.[10]

At around the same time, the central government promulgated some policies conducive to the development of the M&A market. In 1987, the Thirteenth National Congress of the Communist Party of China (CPC) announced that the joint-stock system is 'one means of organizing property for socialist enterprises and should be further implemented on a trial basis'. It also allowed the transfer of ownership of certain small-scale SOEs to collectives or individuals.[11] One year later, in the Report on the Work of the Government to the First Session of the Seventh National People's Congress (NPC), the then acting Premier Li Peng stated that the government would 'actively promote horizontal mergers and vigorously develop enterprise groups'.[12] In 1989, four departments of the State Council jointed issued the *Interim Measures on Enterprise Mergers and Acquisitions*, which was the first national regulation on M&A activities generally.[13] Those policies effectively promoted M&A activities, and in 1989, 2,559 enterprises became targets for M&A.[14]

In 1990 and 1991, a wave of M&A transactions took place after Deng Xiaoping's 1992 'southern tour' (*nanxun*), which revitalized the economic reform of China.[15] During the tour, Deng emphasized that the market economy not be incompatible with socialism.[16] Following Deng's southern tour, at the Fourteenth National Congress of the CPC, the then Party General Secretary Jiang Zemin announced the aim of establishing a socialist market economy. To achieve the aim, the CPC decided to formulate laws and regulations on the joint-stock system and to 'foster the development of financial markets, including markets for bonds, stocks, and other negotiable securities'.[17]

---

10. Huai Kou, *Zhongguo Guoyou Qiye Binggou Qushi yu Zhanlue Yanjiu [China's SOE Reorganization: Trend and Strategy]* 113-120 (2008).
11. Ziyang Zhao, Zhao Ziyang Zai Zhongguo Gongchandang Di Shisan Ci Quanguo Daibiao Dahui Shang de Baogao [Zhao Ziyang's Report to the 13th National Congress of the CPC] (25 October 1987), (transcript available at http://www.gov.cn/test/2008-07/01/content_1032279.htm).
12. Peng Li, Zhengfu Gongzuo Baogao [Report on the Work of the Government] (25 March 1988), (transcript available at http://www.people.com.cn/zgrdxw/zlk/rd/7jie/newfiles/a1310.html).
13. Tigaijing (1989) No. 38, Guanyu Qiye Jianbing de Zanxing Banfa [Interim Measures on Enterprise Mergers and Acquisitions] (promulgated by the MOF et al. on 19 February 1989, and effective from the date of promulgation) (PRC).
14. Anonymous, *Woguo Qiye Jianbing You Xinfazhan [An Update on China's Enterprise Mergers and Acquisitions]*, Remin Ribao [People's Daily], 15 June 1990, at 1.
15. China's economic reform had largely stalled in the early 1990s.
16. Xiaoping Deng, *Zai Wuchang, Shenzhen, Zhuhai, Shanghai Dengdi de Tanhua Yaodian [Excerpts from Talks Given in Wuchang, Shenzhen, Zhuhai and Shanghai]*, in 3 *The Selected Works of Deng Xiaoping* 370, 373 (1993).
17. Zemin Jiang, Jiang Zemin Zai Zhongguo Gongchandang Di Shisi Ci Quanguo Daibiao Dahui Shang de Baogao [Jiang Zemin's Report to the 14th National Congress of the CPC] (12 October 1992), (transcript available at http://www.gov.cn/govweb/test/2008-07/04/content_1035850.htm).

The Standing Committee of the NPC (SCNPC) enacted the *Company Law of the PRC* (Company Law) at the end of 1993.[18] The Company Law has, for the first time, established a comprehensive corporate law framework for the PRC and thus bred a growth in corporate restructurings. Many unincorporated enterprises were restructured into incorporated companies in accordance with the Company Law, and meanwhile, mergers flourished as numerous unincorporated enterprises were absorbed by incorporated companies. Moreover, the Chinese government in the early 1990s established two national stock exchanges – the Shanghai and Shenzhen Stock Exchanges, which later served as platforms for share trading and thus provided a marketplace for enterprises. September 1993 saw the first acquisition of a listed company in the secondary stock market of China.[19]

Another significant change in China's M&A market in the 1990s was the rise of participation by foreign investors. Foreign direct investment (FDI) started to flow into China in 1979, but it grew at a relatively low speed before 1992. Between 1985 and 1991, the annual growth rate of FDI was 14%, and the amount of annual FDI was less than USD 4.5 billion. In 1992, FDI surged by over 150% and reached the amount of USD 11 billion.[20] China's economic development in the 1990s was characterized by manufacturing and export-led growth, with foreign investment as a critical driving force.[21] The exponential growth of FDI created the need for revamping the foreign investment regulatory regime. On 4 April 1995, the Ministry of Foreign Trade and Economic Cooperation (MOFTEC, replaced by the Ministry of Commerce in 2003) issued the *Interim Regulations on the Establishment of Investment Companies by Foreign Investors*,[22] allowing foreign investors to set up onshore investment companies that can engage in direct investments in China. Instead of having to manage different projects through separate foreign-invested enterprises, foreign investors could now establish an investment company as the holding company of different investments in China. This relaxation of foreign investment control induced foreign investors to restructure their existing investments in China through mergers, spin-offs, and so forth, stimulating the number of M&A transactions.

Foreign investors also started to enter the Chinese market through cross-border M&A. In 1996, the acquisition of Beijing Tourist Coach Co. by Itochu Corp. and Suzuki Motor Corp. marked the first foreign purchase of the legal person shares in a listed

18. Zhonghua Renmin Gongheguo Gongsi Fa [Company Law of the People's Republic of China] (promulgated on 29 December 1993, effective from 1 July 1993, and amended in 1999, 2004, 2005, and 2013) (PRC).
19. For a detailed account of this takeover between China Bao'an Group and Shanghai Yanzhong Industrial, *see* Yong Zhen, *China's Capital Markets* 207-209 (2013).
20. John Whalley & Xian Xin, *China's FDI and Non-FDI Economies and the Sustainability of Future High Chinese Growth*, 21 China Economic Review 123, 124 (2010).
21. John Whalley & Weimin Zhou, *Technology Upgrading and China's Growth Strategy to 2020, in China's Integration into the World Economy* 35, 36 (John Whalley ed., 2011).
22. MOFTEC Order (1995) No. 4, Guanyu Waishang Touzi Juban Touzixing Gongsi de Zanxing Guiding [Interim Regulations on the Establishment of Investment Companies by Foreign Investors] (promulgated by the MOFTEC and effective 4 April 1995) (PRC).

Chinese company.[23] China's accession to the World Trade Organization (WTO) in 2001 accelerated this change. In the wake of the WTO accession, more and more foreign investments took place through M&A.[24]

M&A transactions developed into an essential feature of China's economic landscape in the 2000s. From 2001 to 2005, China's M&A value set a new record every year. In 2005, there were USD 46 billion worth of domestic and inbound deals – up 34% from 2004.[25] The surge in transaction value was partly due to China's efforts to restructure the economy by retaining the dominance of SOEs in strategic industries such as national defence while retreating state capital from other sectors. During this period, numerous SOEs got consolidated into large conglomerates, and lots of them were available for private capital. According to one estimation, 4,000 to 5,000 out of 135,000 SOEs were privatized each year around 2005.[26]

Throughout the following years, the government keeps encouraging M&A activities to restructure the economy. In 2010, the State Council issued the *Opinions on Promoting Corporate Mergers and Restructuring*, stating that 'in order to accelerate the transformation of economic development mode and the adjustment of economic structure ... we should promote corporate mergers and restructuring'.[27] Four years later, the State Council reaffirmed its stance in the *Opinions on Further Optimizing the Market Environment for Corporate Mergers and Restructuring*.[28] Thanks to those policies, the momentum in China's M&A market continues to this day. According to the China Securities Regulatory Commission (CSRC), the value of M&A transactions involving listed companies increased at an average annual rate of 41.14% from 2013 to 2016, and 2016 alone has witnessed M&A transactions with an aggregate value of around Chinese Yuan (CNY) 2.39 trillion.[29] In 2021, the Chairman of CSRC disclosed that the cumulative total value of M&A transactions involving listed companies was CNY 11.2 trillion between 2016 and 2020 – making China the world's second-largest M&A market behind the US.[30]

---

23. Kim Woodard, *Acquisitions in China: A View of the Field*, 31 China Business Review 34, 35 (2004).
24. Hui Huang, *The New Takeover Regulation in China: Evolution and Enhancement*, 42 The International Lawyer 153, 155 (2008).
25. Tyrrell Levine & Kim Woodard, *The New Face of Chinese M&A*, 169 Far Eastern Economic Review 18, 18 (2006).
26. *Ibid.*, at 19.
27. Guofa (2010) No. 27, Guanyu Cujin Qiye Jianbing Chongzu de Yijian [Opinions on Promoting Corporate Mergers and Restructurings] (promulgated by the State Council on 28 August 2010) (PRC).
28. Guofa (2014) No. 14, Guanyu Jinyibu Youhua Qiye Jianbing Chongzu Shichang Huanjing de Yijian [Opinions on Further Optimizing the Market Environment for Corporate Mergers and Restructurings] (promulgated by the State Council on 7 March 2014) (PRC).
29. CSRC, *Shangshi Gongsi Binggou Chongzu Fuwu Shiti Jingji Zhuanfanshi Tiaojiegou Qude Mingxian Chengxiao [Listed Company M&A Transactions Help Restructure the Economy]*, CSRC (5 October 2021), http://www.csrc.gov.cn/pub/newsite/gjb/dyxc/201708/t20170815_322153.html.
30. Huiman Yi, Yi Huiman Zai 2021 Jinrongjie Luntan Nianhui Shang de Zhuti Yanjiang [Keynote Speech by Chairman Yi Huiman at the 2021 Annual Meeting of Financial Street Forum]. 20 October 2021.

§2.03 ORIGIN OF M&A TAXATION: 1993-1996

In the wake of the promulgation of the Company Law in 1993, many investors sought to incorporate their investments or transform the enterprises already established into joint-stock companies. In the same year, the STA issued Guoshuifa (1993) No. 139 (hereinafter Circular 139) to address the unprecedented income tax issues arising from the tide of restructuring foreign-invested enterprises into joint-stock companies.

According to Article 1(1) of Circular 139, where a foreign-invested enterprise transfers assets in the course of a merger with another joint-stock company, the tax consequences of the transfer of assets would be the same as for any ordinary asset sale. That is to say, the foreign-invested enterprise would recognize gain or loss on the transfer of assets, and the joint-stock company as the transferee would receive the transferred assets with a tax basis at the fair market value.[31] Caishui (1994) No. 83, which was promulgated by the MOF and the STA jointly in 1994, confirmed the realization rule prescribed in Article 1(1) of Circular 139 by requiring foreign-invested enterprises to recognize gain on the value appreciation of non-monetary assets that are transferred to another enterprise as a capital contribution.[32]

At first glance, it seems that the tax authorities insisted on treating mergers in the same way as other transactions and were unwilling to provide any special concessions. A closer look at Circular 139, however, tells a different story. Article 1(2) of Circular 139 provided two different tax basis rules for the transferee in a merger: on the one hand, it restated the cost basis rule stipulated in Article 1(1); while on the other hand, it provided that if the foreign-invested enterprise as the transferor did not recognize gain or loss as required by Article 1(1), the transferee would take as its tax basis in the assets received the same tax basis that the transferor previously had in those assets.[33] By providing this substituted tax basis rule, the STA in effect conceded that some foreign-invested enterprises could avoid taxes on shifting assets into joint-stock enterprises.

Unlike foreign-invested enterprises, domestically owned enterprises in this period found that their tax treatments in M&A transactions were in limbo. The lack of guidance might be explicable in part by the unsettled issue of how to tax SOEs properly. From 1982 to 1983, the Chinese government rolled out the tax-for-profit reform (*li gai shui*) with an aim to replace appropriating profits from SOEs with levying income taxes on them. Unfortunately, the reform was not very successful. In 1986, the government introduced the enterprise management responsibility system, under which SOEs remitted a fixed portion of profits and retained the rest. This arrangement spelt total defeat for the tax-for-profit reform.[34] In the early 1990s, many SOEs were still under the

31. Guoshuifa (1993) No. 139, Art. 1(1).
32. Caishui (1994) No. 83, Guanyu Waishang Touzi Qiye Congshi Touzi Yewu Ruogan Shuishou Wenti de Tongzhi [Notice Regarding the Tax Treatment of the Investment Activities of Foreign-Invested Enterprises] (promulgated by the MOF and the STA and effective 13 January 1994) (PRC), Art. 2.
33. Guoshuifa (1993) No. 139, Art. 1(2).
34. Christine P. W. Wong, *Fiscal Reform and Local Industrialization: The Problematic Sequencing of Reform in Post-Mao China*, 18 Modern China 197, 216-219 (1992).

enterprise management responsibility system. As SOEs were the main participants in the M&A wave, it is no wonder that the MOF and the STA were reluctant to spell out tax rules concerning the restructurings involving domestically owned enterprises.

Having said that, the explanation for the vacuum in law likely goes beyond that the time was not ripe for specific rules. The central tax agencies might deliberately keep silent on the tax treatments to facilitate economic restructuring. This speculation is supported by the tax administration practice back then. In theory, taxpayers should pay current taxes on transactions unless a special tax rule provides otherwise, but the fact was that tax administrators, in many cases, just neglected income taxes arising from M&A transactions.[35]

§2.04 INCEPTION OF ROLLOVER RELIEF: 1997-1999

Due to the sharp expansion of the M&A market in the late 1990s, it became a pressing need for more clarity and certainty with regard to the income taxation of M&A transactions. In April 1997, the STA offered a relatively comprehensive set of rules for M&A transactions involving foreign-invested enterprises through the issuance of Guoshuifa (1997) No. 71 (hereinafter Circular 71) and Guoshuihan (1997) No. 207 (hereinafter Circular 207).[36] These two circulars drastically changed the landscape of China's income tax regime for M&A.

In Circular 71, the STA, for the first time, explicitly provided rollover relief rules for reorganizations, allowing taxes on the transfer of assets in a merger to be postponed to a later date and the transferee to inherit the transferor's tax attributes such as net operating losses. The STA did not specify the reason for introducing the rollover relief, but considering the broader context of China's economic development, a plausible explanation is that the rollover relief was designed to foster an environment conducive to foreign direct investment (FDI).

FDI has always been praised as a powerful engine of China's economic development and valued for the employment opportunities it created as well as the advanced technology, science, and management skills it brought to China.[37] To attract FDI, China

35. Cui & Krever, *supra* note 2, at 344.
36. Guoshuifa (1997) No. 71, Guanyu Waishang Touzi Qiye Hebing, Fenli, Guquan Chongzu, Zichan Zhuanrang deng Chongzu Yewu Suodeshui Chuli de Zanxing Guiding [Interim Regulations on the Income Tax Treatment of Mergers, Divisions, Restructurings of Equity, Asset Transfers and other Restructurings of Foreign-Invested Enterprises] (promulgated by the STA and effective 28 April 1997) (PRC); Guoshuihan (1997) No. 207, Guanyu Waishang Touzi Qiye he Waiguo Qiye Zhuanrang Guquan Suodeshui Chuli Wenti de Tongzhi [Notice Regarding the Income Tax Treatment of the Transfer of Company Share by Foreign-Invested Enterprises and Foreign Enterprises] (promulgated by the STA and effective 17 April 1997) (PRC).
37. *See e.g.*, Tao Zhang, *Utilization of Foreign Capital and Economic Growth in China*, 37 The Chinese Economy 62, 71-72 (2004) Stèphane Dees, *Foreign Direct Investment in China: Determinants and Effects*, 31 Economics of Planning 175, 185-187 (1998). In fact, among the reasons for adopting the open-up policy is the expectation that FDI inflows have those positive effects. *See* Chunlai Chen, *Foreign Direct Investment in China: Location Determinants, Investor Differences and Economic Impacts* 33-36 (2011).

began to offer generous tax preferences to foreign investors soon after the implementation of the economic reform and opening-up policy. In 1980, the Chinese government introduced preferential tax treatment for the FDI into four coastal special economic zones.[38] The quick success of those 'special economic zones' led the government to designate more special regions that could apply tax incentives to FDI.[39] By the end of the 1990s, more than 100 special regions, including coastal open cities, western regions, high and new industrial development areas, and so forth, provided tax incentives to FDI.[40]

The rollover relief for mergers was part of the rising tide of FDI-specific tax incentives. The STA first allowed foreign-invested enterprises to conduct tax-deferred mergers, and one year later, it issued Guoshuifa (1998) No. 97 (hereinafter Circular 97) to grant similar treatment to domestically owned enterprises.[41] It is thus reasonable to infer that one major purpose of introducing the rollover relief into China was to serve the government's pro-FDI policy.

There are two interesting aspects of the rollover relief for mergers during this period. First, tax deferral and carry-over of the original tax basis at the corporate level were mandatory. Article 1 of Circular 71 provided that 'the target company shall not be deemed to have liquidated, regardless of whether the merger takes the form of absorption or consolidation'[42] and also strictly prohibited the increase of the tax basis in the transferred assets. As a result, a merger always did not have immediate corporate-level tax consequences.

Second, the rules were silent on the tax consequences at the shareholder level, and in particular, they did not specify the type of consideration used in the transaction and how a rollover would work in a purely or partially cash-financed deal. While it is feasible to mandate a carry-over basis taxation at the corporate level regardless of whether a merger involves a cash payment, the same logic does not apply to the shareholder level as the last opportunity to levy taxes on the shareholders of the merged company is when they cash out their investments. Without any restrictions on the type of consideration used in a merger, the shareholders of the merged company would enjoy de facto exemptions to the extent of cash consideration received.

In addition to mergers, Circular 71 covered two other types of M&A transactions, namely stock acquisitions and asset acquisitions. However, the rollover treatment only applied to mergers under Circular 71. Articles 3(1) and 4(1) of it provided that the tax consequences of transfers of stock or assets in the course of acquisitions would be the same as for an ordinary sale, with full recognition of gain or loss by the transferor and

38. Those 'special economic zones' are Shenzhen, Zhuhai, Shantou and Xiamen.
39. In 1984, fourteen coastal cities such as Tianjin and Shanghai were designated as 'Costal Open Cities'.
40. For a historical overview of China's tax incentives for FDI, *see* Jinyan Li, *The Rise and Fall of Chinese Tax Incentives an Implications for International Tax Debates*, 8 Fla. Tax Rev. 669, 675-677 (2006).
41. Guoshuifa (1998) No. 97, Qiye Gaizu Gaizhi zhong Ruogan Suodeshui Yewu Wenti de Zanxing Guiding [Interim Regulations on the Income Tax Treatment of Enterprise Restructurings] (promulgated by the STA and effective 24 June 1998) (PRC), Art. 1.
42. Guoshuifa (1997) No. 71, Art. 1(1).

cost basis for the transferee.[43] Nevertheless, Circular 207 made an unexpected exception to this full recognition rule for stock acquisitions by providing that:[44]

> 'In an intra-group reorganization with a legitimate business purpose, if a foreign enterprise transfers the stock of enterprises inside of China, or if a foreign-invested enterprise transfers the stock of enterprises inside or outside of China, to another enterprise that is directly or indirectly wholly owned by it, or that directly or indirectly wholly owns it, or that is under 100% common control with it, the transfer shall be deemed as made at cost. Since there is no gain or loss from the stock transfer, no income tax shall be levied.'

According to this provision quoted, a foreign or foreign-invested enterprise could enjoy tax deferral on stock transfers as long as the transfer was within the same company group and irrespective of where the transferee was located. This lenient rollover rule not only offered foreign investors tax deferral but also facilitated them to exit and repatriate their investments in a tax-free way. By first transferring the stock of a Chinese enterprise to an offshore group member on a tax-deferred basis and then selling that offshore enterprise, a foreign investor could completely avoid the Chinese income tax. Although Circular 207 required there to exist a 'legitimate business purpose', the requirement was never seriously enforced.[45] It was until a decade had passed that the Chinese tax authority started to combat the tax avoidance scheme through indirect stock transfers by foreigners.[46]

In 1998, the STA issued Circular 97 – the first tax ruling on M&A involving domestically owned enterprises.[47] Circular 97 was basically a duplication of Circular 71, and in this way, the STA narrowed the gap between the tax treatments for foreign-invested enterprises and those for domestically owned enterprises. However, some differences remained, and the most significant one was that domestically owned enterprises could not enjoy tax deferral on intra-group stock transfers prescribed in Circular 207.

§2.05 COMPREHENSIVE YET INCONSISTENT REGIME: 2000-2007

The Chinese government has repeatedly been highlighting the need to upgrade technologies and emphasizing the importance of refocusing economic growth from investment-driven manufacturing and export to efficiency improvement since the late 1990s.[48] The shift in economic development strategy made the government less enthusiastic about granting tax incentives to foreign investors. By the turn of the

43. Guoshuifa (1997) No. 71, Arts. 3(1), 4(1).
44. Guoshuihan (1997) No. 207.
45. Cui & Krever, *supra* note 2, at 348.
46. In 2009, the STA issued Guoshuihan (2009) No. 698 to tax indirect stock transfers. For a full account of taxing indirect transfers, *see* Wei Cui, *Taxing Indirect Transfers: Improving an Instrument for Stemming Tax and Legal Base Erosion*, 33 Virginia Tax Review 653(2014).
47. Guoshuifa (1998) No. 97.
48. Whalley & Zhou, *supra* note 21, at 38-40.

century, pro-foreign investment tax policies were under scrutiny and heatedly debated.[49]

Against this backdrop, foreign-invested enterprises still referred to Circular 71 to determine their tax liabilities in M&A transactions. Domestically owned enterprises, however, welcomed a new pair of circulars issued in 2000 that replaced the previously mentioned governing rule – Circular 97. The two circulars targeting domestically owned enterprises, Guoshuifa (2000) No. 118 (hereinafter Circular 118)[50] and Guoshuifa (2000) No. 119 (hereinafter Circular 119),[51] made a considerable step towards completing the income tax framework for M&A transactions. Through Circular 119, the STA for the first time clarified that as a general rule, gains should be recognized in the course of a merger. Article 1(1) of Circular 119 provided that:[52]

> 'Typically, the target company in a merger shall be treated as transferring all of its assets at fair market value, and it shall pay taxes on the gains from the transfer of assets. The operating losses of the target company shall not be carried over to the purchasing company. The purchasing company shall determine its basis in the transferred assets based on their fair market value. The shareholders of the target company shall be treated as receiving liquidating distributions from the target company'.

The rollover treatment thus became an exception, and it was available only if certain conditions were satisfied. The key conditions included the restriction on the type of consideration used, which was apparently borrowed from foreign experience. Article 1(2) of Circular 119 classified the consideration received by the shareholders of the target company into two categories – equity interest in the purchasing company and other non-equity consideration such as cash; and to qualify for the rollover relief, the value of non-equity consideration should not exceed 20% of the par value of the equity consideration.[53] It is worth noting that the rollover relief was made optional by Circular 119, and taxpayers might elect to discard the rollover relief even if relevant conditions were satisfied.[54]

In contrast to Circular 71, Circular 119 was no longer silent on the shareholder-level tax treatment. As mentioned above, in mergers, shareholders of the target company were normally taxed as receiving liquidating distributions, and in cases where the rollover relief was applicable, the shareholders would only recognize gain to the extent of non-equity consideration received.[55] However, the STA did not answer whether the shareholder that elected the rollover relief could increase the tax basis of the equity consideration to reflect the gain recognized on the receipt of non-equity

49. Li, *supra* note 40, at 677.
50. Guoshuifa (2000) No. 118, Guanyu Qiye Guquan Touzi Yewu Ruogan Suodeshui Wenti de Tongzhi [Notice Regarding the Income Tax Treatment of Equity Investments of Enterprises] (promulgated by the STA and effective 21 June 2000) (PRC).
51. Guoshuifa (2000) No. 119, Guanyu Qiye Hebing Fenli Yewu Youguan Suodeshui Wenti de Tongzhi [Notice Regarding the Income Tax Treatment of Mergers and Divisions of Enterprises] (promulgated by the STA on 21 June 2000, repealed) (PRC).
52. Guoshuifa (2000) No. 119, Art. 1(1).
53. Guoshuifa (2000) No. 119, Art. 1(2).
54. *Ibid.*
55. Guoshuifa (2000) No. 119, Art. 1(2)(2).

consideration. Another significant difference between Circular 119 and its predecessor is the restraint on how the purchasing company could use the loss carry forward of the target company. Circular 119 placed an annual cap on the deduction of the transferred loss carry forward, which equalled: the taxable income of the purchasing company × (the market value of the net assets transferred / the fair market value of the purchasing company's total net assets).[56]

The tax treatment for M&A transactions other than mergers was stipulated in Circular 118. This circular preserved the rule that all stock transfers should trigger full recognition of gain[57] but did not keep the similar tax treatment for asset transfers. An asset transfer could be tax-deferred provided that the purchasing company purchased either all the assets or an independent-accounting branch of the target company, and like in the case of a tax-deferred merger, the value of non-equity consideration should not be more than 20% of the par value of the equity consideration.[58] Pursuant to Article 4(2) of Circular 118, the purchasing company in a tax-deferred asset acquisition should receive the transferred assets with the historical tax basis; however, it is interesting to note that in 2003 the STA repealed this substituted tax basis rule and allowed the purchasing company to use fair market value as the tax basis in the transferred assets.[59]

Circular 118 extended the rollover relief to a new type of transaction, namely asset swaps. According to Article 5(2) of Circular 118, the exchange between two companies of their entire assets or independent-accounting branches would qualify for a tax deferral if no more than 25% of the consideration received by the transferee was cash.[60] The extension of tax deferral to asset swaps created a notable inconsistency in the income tax regime for M&A. For other types of transactions to qualify for tax deferral, a majority of the consideration should be in the form of equity interest in the purchasing company, but it was not the case for asset swaps.

By extending rollover relief to asset swaps, the STA departed from its attempted stance of preventing the abusive use of this exceptional tax treatment so as to facilitate the restructuring of SOEs. As noted, the rehabilitation of SOEs has long been a major theme in China's economic reform. Commonly used tactics for reforming SOEs include increasing the operational autonomy of SOEs, closing down loss-making enterprises, and most important among them, restructuring remaining enterprises.[61] In the late-1990s, many listed SOEs performed poorly and were on the edge of being delisted. Some of them successfully returned to profitability by replacing their non-performing assets with high-quality assets of non-listed companies.[62] The rollover relief helped loss-making listed SOEs to conduct asset swaps at low tax costs.

56. Guoshuifa (2000) No. 119, Art. 1(2)(1).
57. Guoshuifa (2000) No. 118, Art. 2(1).
58. Guoshuifa (2000) No. 118, Art. 4(1).
59. Guoshuifa (2003) 45, Guanyu Zhixing 'Qiye Kuaiji Zhidu' Xuyao Mingque de Youguan Suodeshui Wenti de Tongzhi [Notice on Enterprise Income Tax Issues Concerning the Implementation of the 'Enterprise Accounting System'] (promulgated by the STA on 24 April 2003, effective retrospectively 1 January 2003) (PRC), Art. 6(2).
60. Guoshuifa (2000) No. 118, Art. 5(2).
61. Dong Zhang & Owen Freestone, *China's Unfinished State-owned Enterprise Reforms*, Economic Round-up, no. 2, 2013, at 77, 81-83.
62. Cui & Krever, *supra* note 2, at 349.

For the same purpose, the STA issued some private rulings that exempted SOEs from tax liabilities arising in pre-listing restructurings. Since the 1990s, it has become a common practice among SOEs to put their good-quality assets into a joint-stock company and then get the joint-stock company listed on a stock exchange.[63] This process involved a large number of asset transfers that qualified for rollover relief under Circular 118. However, SOEs were not content with the rollover relief.[64] They hoped to increase the tax basis in the transferred assets to fair market value so that they could claim more depreciation deduction in the future,[65] so they applied to the tax authority for private rulings that completely exempted them from paying taxes on the taxable asset transfers.[66]

During the nine years from 2000 to 2009, the MOF and the STA granted tax exemption to thirty SOEs.[67] Although criticized as illegitimate,[68] this tax exemption for SOEs has become more entrenched in the tax system as many SOEs are still on their journey to improved business performance. In 2015, the MOF and the STA issued Caishui (2015) No. 65, under which all pre-listing structuring of SOEs automatically get the tax exemption.[69] Case-by-case approval is therefore no longer needed.

§2.06 CONCLUSION

Like post-1970s Chinese legal reform process in general, decades of evolution of M&A tax rules in developed countries such as the US were compressed into a few years in China. Before 1993, there was no guidance on the taxation of M&A transactions. From 1993 to 2007, a crude circular that only provided the tax consequences of foreign-invested enterprises' mergers evolved into relatively comprehensive rules that prescribed the tax treatment for M&A transactions in various forms and between different types of enterprises.

63. Bad assets, unprofitable business operations, excess debt, pensions, and other liabilities typically remained in the group company or other subsidiaries. *See* World Bank, *SOE Dividends: How Much and to Whom*, World Bank 10 (17 October 2005), https://documents1.worldbank.org/curated/en/961421468243568454/pdf/566510WP0SOE1E10Box353729B01PUBLIC1.pdf; *See also* Wei Cui, *'Ultra Special' Tax Treatment for Restructuring of SOEs: Legal Background and Comments*, Zhongwai Faxue [Peking University Law Journal], no. 6, 2010, at 944, 945.
64. Cui, *supra* note 63, at 956.
65. Cui & Krever, *supra* note 2, at 349.
66. For example, when the Bank of China sought to be listed on the Hong Kong Stock Exchange in 2003, the MOF and the STA issued Caishui (2003) 126 to exempt income tax on transfers of assets in the company group's pre-listing restructuring. Caishui (2003) No. 126, Guanyu Xianggang Zhongyin Jituan Chongzu Shangshi Youguan Shuishou Wenti de Tongzhi [Notice on Tax Treatment of the Pre-Listing Restructuring of the Bank of China] (promulgated by the MOF and the STA and effective 9 September 2003) (PRC).
67. Cui, *supra* note 63, at 949-952.
68. *Ibid.*, at 954-957 (arguing that the tax exemption violated the EITL and the tax authorities acted ultra vires).
69. Caishui (2015) No. 65, Guanyu Qiye Gaizhi Shangshi Zichan Pinggu Zengzhi Qiye Suodeshui Chuli Zhengce de Tongzhi [Notice on Policy Concerning the Enterprise Income Tax Treatment of Asset Appreciation of SOEs in Restructuring for Listing] (promulgated by the MOF and the STA on 23 June 2015, and effective retrospectively from 1 January 2015) (PRC).

Table 2.1 Milestones in the History of China's M&A Taxation

Type of Target Company	*Phase*	*Key Circulars*	*Transaction Eligible for Rollover Relief*
Foreign-Invested Enterprise	1993-1996	Circular 139	None
	1997-1999	Circular 71	Merger
		Circular 207	Intra-Group Stock Transfer
	2000-2007	Circular 71	Merger
		Circular 207	Intra-Group Stock Transfer
Domestically Owned Enterprise	1993-1996	N/A	N/A
	1997-1999	Circular 97	Merger
	2000-2007	Circular 119	Merger
		Circular 118	Asset Acquisition
			Asset Swap

Table 2.1 summarizes the milestones in the early history of China's M&A taxation. As shown in this table, China's path to developing its income taxation for M&A from 1993 to 2007 has two interrelated features: (1) dual-track regimes for foreign-invested and domestically owned enterprises and (2) inconsistent application of rollover relief.

First, China did not unify the income tax systems for foreign-invested and domestically owned enterprises until the promulgation of EITL in 2008, and not surprisingly, in the pre-2008 era, the income taxation of M&A evolved in a bifurcated manner. The tax rules for foreign-invested enterprises came out as early as 1993 and were significantly amended in 1997, but it was not until 1998 that the STA decided to fill up the vacuum of law for domestically owned enterprises. Before 2000, this dual-track tax regime was generally in favour of foreign-invested enterprises especially considering that only foreign-invested enterprises might apply for the rollover relief on intra-group stock transfer; however, the situation was largely reversed in 2000 when the STA updated the tax rules for domestically owned enterprises but left those for foreign-invested enterprises unchanged. The dissonance within the dual-track tax regime vividly illustrates how the goal of economic development moulded the early history of China's M&A taxation.

Second, the tax law launched rollover relief measures in an inconsistent way. Rollover relief was formally introduced into China's income tax regime for M&A by Circular 71 in 1997, and back then, there were barely any conditions for a taxpayer to apply for it. In order to prevent tax evasion, the STA learned from foreign experience and imposed the requirement that in tax-deferred mergers or asset acquisitions, the value of non-equity consideration should not exceed 20% of the par value of the equity consideration. However, due in large part to the desire to promote economic outcomes, the attempt at reining in the abusive use of rollover relief was doomed to fail. In 2000, the STA allowed rollover relief for so-called asset swaps to facilitate the restructurings of SOEs, even though a swap of assets did not require any payment of equity consideration.

Both of the above two features were obviously induced by the tension between a view that China's taxation of M&A should be consistent with a foreign benchmark model and another view that tax law should be used to facilitate economic reforms. As will be shown in the following chapters, this tension creates continuous difficulties in the improvement of China's M&A taxation regime.

CHAPTER 3

Convergence and Divergence: China's Modernization of Its M&A Taxation

§3.01 INTRODUCTION

On 1 January 2008, the EITL came into effect, marking the end of a decade-long process of unifying various enterprise income tax laws for different types of enterprises. Yet despite its profound importance as a foundational piece of tax legislation, the EITL only contains sixty abstract articles that set out the broad elements of the income tax system and provides little or no detail on the taxation of specific business arrangements including M&A transactions. The task of promulgating a single set of rules on M&A taxation naturally fell on the State Council and its two ministerial departments in charge of taxation – the MOF and the STA.

The central tax authorities had started to consider putting together the various circulars on M&A taxation even before the EITL was formally passed by the NPC on 16 March 2007. In 2006, the MOF and the STA incorporated tax provisions for M&A transactions into early drafts of the implementation regulations for the yet-to-be-passed EITL. However, the State Council removed those provisions from the final version of the regulations – the EITL Implementation Regulations (EITLIR) – on the basis that they were too detailed and complex to fit into the regulations' framework,[1] and instead announced in the EITLIR that the MOF and the STA are authorized to promulgate detailed rules on the tax treatment of M&A transactions.[2]

On 30 April 2009, the MOF and the STA jointly promulgated Caishui (2009) No. 59 (hereinafter Circular 59) – *Notice on Several Issues on the Enterprise Income Tax Treatment of Enterprise Restructurings*, which takes effect retrospectively from 1

1. Internal Report of the STA, *cited in* Wei Cui, *Qiye Chongzu Shuiwu Guize Qicao Guocheng de Fansi [Reflections on the Making of the Income Tax Rules for Enterprise Reorganizations]*, *in* 1 *Shuifa Jieshi yu Panli Pingzhu [Tax Law and Case Review]* 163, 174 (Wei Xiong ed., 2010).
2. EITLIR, Art. 75.

January 2008. All the old circulars discussed in Chapter 2 immediately ceased to be effective upon the release of Circular 59. As a piece of tax legislation governing the M&A transactions by different types of enterprises, Circular 59 provides a better structured legal framework and a more consistent approach for taxing M&A transactions.[3] In the following decade, the central tax authorities have released an array of circulars to supplement Circular 59, and those supplementary further completed China's M&A taxation puzzle.

Based on the discussion of the historical development of China's M&A taxation, this chapter will address in detail some basic elements of China's current income tax regime for M&A transactions, including how the tax law differentiates between M&A and regular asset or stock transactions, what are the default tax treatments for M&A, how the special tax treatments for M&A differ from the default tax treatments, as well as who and in what circumstances may apply the special tax treatment for M&A. More specifically, §3.02 introduces the M&A transactions recognized by China's tax law. This is followed by a critical analysis of the ordinary tax treatments for M&A in §3.03. Then, §3.04 examines the content of the special tax treatments for M&A. Based on the analysis in the previous three sections, §3.05 concludes with some observations on the features and problems of China's current income tax regime for M&A transactions.

§3.02 M&A TRANSACTIONS RECOGNIZED IN TAX LAW

Circular 59 uses the term 'restructuring' to describe transactions that significantly change the legal or economic structure of one or more companies.[4] Article 1 of Circular 59 enumerates six types of restructurings: merger, asset acquisition, stock acquisition, corporate division, bankruptcy restructuring, and change in legal form.[5] This research focuses on the first three types, i.e., merger, asset acquisition, and stock acquisition, which are usually collectively known as acquisitive reorganizations or M&A.

[A] Merger

A merger (*hebing*), as defined in Circular 59, is a transaction in which one or more transferor companies transfer all the assets and liabilities to a single transferee company, and the shareholders of the transferor receive consideration from the transferee, resulting in a statutory amalgamation of two or more enterprises.[6] Due to the 'statutory amalgamation' requirement, a merger recognized by Circular 59 shall be conducted pursuant to the Company Law. According to Article 172 of the Company Law, there are two types of mergers – merger by absorption (*xishou hebing*) and merger by consolidation (*xinshe hebing*).[7] In a merger by absorption, one or more companies are integrated into an existing company and subsequently dissolved. A

3. Caishui (2009) No. 59.
4. Caishui (2009) No. 59, Art. 1.
5. *Ibid.*
6. Caishui (2009) No. 59, Art. 1(5).
7. Company Law, Art. 172.

merger by consolidation refers to the consolidation of two or more companies into a new company, with all parties to the transaction dissolved.[8] In either of the two types of mergers, the tax law always has to address the tax consequences for three types of participants: the transferor company (the target company), the shareholders of the target company, as well as the transferee (the purchasing company).

[B] Asset Acquisition

According to Circular 59, an asset acquisition is a transfer of some or all of the 'substantive business assets' by one company to another company in exchange for any form of consideration – stock, cash or mixed payment.[9] STA Gonggao (2010) No. 4 (hereinafter Circular 4) – *Administrative Measures on the Enterprise Income Tax Treatment of Enterprise Restructurings*[10] further clarifies 'substantive business assets' as various types of tangible and intangible assets used in a company's business operation.[11]

Following an asset acquisition, the transferor company may continue to exist or may make a liquidating distribution to its shareholders. In the latter case, the tax consequences are generally akin to what happens in a merger – three types of entities get affected, while an acquisition without liquidation only incurs tax implications for two parties, i.e., the purchasing company and the target company.

Being one type of 'restructuring' that involves significant changes in the structure of at least one participating company and thus differ from a mere sale of assets, an asset acquisition governed by Circular 59 is supposed to entail the disposal of substantial assets by the transferor company. However, Circular 59 does not include any transfer ratio requirement in its definition of asset acquisition.

[C] Stock Acquisition

Circular 59 defines stock acquisition as transactions where a company purchases some or all of the stock of another company with consideration in any form, thereby gaining control of the latter.[12] It is interesting to compare the definitions of stock acquisition and asset acquisition. The definition of stock acquisition contains the requirement that the purchasing company needs to purchase control of the target company, while as mentioned above, there is no similar wording in the definition of asset acquisition.

8. *Ibid.*
9. Caishui (2009) No. 59, Art. 1(4).
10. STA Gonggao (2010) No. 4, Qiye Chongzu Yewu Qiye Suodeshui Guanli Banfa [Administrative Measures on the Enterprise Income Tax Treatment of Enterprise Restructurings] (promulgated by the STA on 26 July 2010, effective retrospectively 1 January 2010) (PRC).
11. STA Gonggao (2010) No. 4, Art. 5.
12. Caishui (2009) No. 59, Art. 1(3).

§3.03 ORDINARY TAX TREATMENT

Circular 59 classifies the tax treatments for M&A transactions into two groups: the ordinary tax treatment (*yibanxing shuiwu chuli*) and the special tax treatment (*teshuxing shuiwu chuli*).[13] Transactions under the ordinary and special tax treatments are analogous to taxable and tax-free rules for M&A transactions in other countries. The ordinary tax treatment reflects the general principle of income tax law that requires a transferor of assets to recognize gain or loss at the time of the transaction. As the default rule, the ordinary tax treatment applies where a transaction fails to meet the conditions for the special tax treatment, or taxpayers reject the special tax treatment even if the conditions are satisfied.

[A] Merger

[1] Tax Consequences to the Target Company and Its Shareholders

For the target company and its shareholders, a merger brings similar tax consequences as a liquidation of the target company.[14] That is to say, the target company needs to recognize gain or loss for transferring all of its assets, and then the sale proceeds received by the shareholders of the target company will be taxed in the same way as a liquidating distribution from the target company.

The amount of gain or loss at the corporate level, by reference to Caishui (2009) No. 60 (hereinafter Circular 60) – the governing rule for the taxation of a corporate liquidation, shall be the difference between the total consideration received in the merger and the tax basis of the target company's assets.[15] This calculation method of taxable income is different from those adopted by some other jurisdictions. For instance, in the US, the amount and character of gain or loss on the sale of assets are determined on an asset-by-asset basis, and the target company which receives a lump-sum price for all the assets sold must allocate the sale price among those assets.[16]

The calculation method prescribed in Circular 59 and Circular 60 is relatively simple but suffices for calculating the gain or loss to be recognized by the target company. Unlike the US tax law that makes a distinction between capital gain and ordinary income, the EITL and EITLIR consider all capital gains – as the term is used in some jurisdictions that distinguish them from ordinary income – derived from the transfer of fixed assets, biological assets, intangible assets, equity interests, debt claims as merely a subcategory of income, i.e., income from transfer of assets,[17] and impose

13. Caishui (2009) No. 59, Art. 3.
14. Caishui (2009) No. 59, Art. 4(4)(2).
15. Caishui (2009) No. 60, Guanyu Qiye Qingsuan Yewu Qiye Suodeshui Chuli Ruogan Wenti de Tongzhi [Notice on Several Issues on the Enterprise Income Tax Treatment of Enterprise Liquidation] (promulgated by the MOF and the STA on 30 April 2009, and effective retrospectively from 1 January 2008) (PRC), Arts. 3(1), 4.
16. *Williams v. McGowan*, 150 F.2d 570 (2d Cir. 1945) ('Congress plainly did mean to comminute the elements of a business; plainly it did not regard the whole as "capital assets".').
17. EITL, Art. 6(3); EITLIR, Art. 16.

the same tax rate on them together with other gain recognized by a company. Therefore, in the context of China's income tax system, the gain or loss recognized by the target company in a merger is the same whether it is calculated on a pooling basis or an asset-by-asset basis.

Apart from the corporate-level tax, a merger also results in a second, shareholder-level tax. The target shareholders need to report gain or loss on receiving liquidating distributions.[18] Based on Article 5 of Circular 60, liquidating distributions will be treated as dividend income to the extent that they get paid out of the retained earnings and surplus of the target company. For corporate and individual shareholders that are Chinese tax residents,[19] the standard tax rates on dividend income are 25% and 20% respectively.[20]

It is worth noting that the EITL provides for a tax exemption on dividend payments between Chinese resident companies.[21] Dividends received by individuals are also subject to a reduced tax burden in certain circumstances. Take dividends from a target company listed on the Shanghai or Shenzhen Stock Exchanges as an example. Those shareholders who hold the listed company's shares for less than one month recognize the full amount of the dividend income. If the holding period is between one month and one year, 50% of the dividend income enjoys tax exemption. As to the stock that investors have held for more than one year, only 25% of the dividend income from it is taxable.[22]

As to the portion of liquidating distribution in excess of the retained earnings and surplus of the target company, it is not treated as dividend income but as a payment in exchange for the stock of the target company, and shareholders of the target company shall recognize gain or loss on the difference between this deemed selling price and the tax basis of the stock.[23]

[2] Tax Consequences to the Purchasing Company

Consistent with the full recognition of gain or loss on the transfer of assets by the target company, the purchasing company in a merger receives the transferred assets with an aggregate cost basis equal to the purchase price. In order to allocate the aggregate tax basis among each item of the transferred assets, the asset-by-asset method, which is

18. Caishui (2009) No. 59, Art. 4(4)(2).
19. The tax treatment of a partnership as target company's shareholder will be discussed in § 3.04[C][2] below.
20. EITL, Art. 4 Zhonghua Renmin Gongheguo Geren Suodeshui Fa [Individual Income Tax Law of the People's Republic of China] (promulgated on 10 September 1980, amended in 1993, 1999, 2005, 2007, 2011 and 2018) (PRC) (hereinafter IITL), Art. 3(3).
21. EITL, Art. 26.
22. Caishui (2012) No. 85, Guanyu Shishi Shangshi Gongsi Guxi Hongli Chabiehua Geren Suodeshui Zhengce Youguan Wenti de Tongzhi [Notice on Issues Concerning the Implementation of Differentiated Individual Income Tax Policies for Dividends Distributed by Listed Companies] (promulgated by the MOF, the STA, and the CSRC on 16 November 2012, effective 1 January 2013) (PRC), Art. 1.
23. Caishui (2009) No. 60, Art. 5.

interchangeable with the pooling approach in the calculation of the taxable amount for the target company, is now indispensable.

Generally speaking, the purchasing company is inclined to minimize the tax basis assigned to the assets that are not depreciable or amortizable or not intended for resale and allocate tax basis to items with a short period of depreciation or amortization as much as possible. For the purpose of preventing the purchasing company from manipulating the allocation of tax basis, Article 4(4)(1) of Circular 59 stipulates that each item of assets transferred in a merger shall have a tax basis reflecting its fair market value.

It is not uncommon that, in some mergers, the total purchase price exceeds the aggregate fair market value of the transferred assets and the purchasing company books the discrepancy as goodwill.[24] The amortization of goodwill is generally deductible for tax purposes in tax jurisdictions like the US; however, it is not the case in China. Pursuant to Article 67 of the EITLIR, goodwill can only be deducted in a lump sum until the purchasing company sells all of its assets or goes into liquidation.[25] Taxpayers in China therefore would naturally attempt to reduce the amount of goodwill to guarantee more tax-deductible depreciation or amortization in the future.

In the wake of a taxable merger, all tax attributes of the target company vanish, and particularly as emphasized in Circular 59, the purchasing company is forbidden from carrying forward the unused net operating losses of the target company.[26] As a result, a merger by consolidation will create a new company that does not have any net operating losses, tax incentives or other tax attributes, while a merger by absorption does not impair the tax attributes of the purchasing company.[27] For instance, the surviving company in a merger by absorption may continue to enjoy the tax incentives granted to it before the merger, provided that there is no change in the nature of the company and the conditions for granting the tax incentives.[28]

[B] Asset Acquisition

Tax positions of the purchasing company and the target company in an asset acquisition are similar to those in a merger. That is to say, the target company recognizes gain or loss on the sale of assets, and the purchasing company receives the transferred assets with a cost basis.[29]

Mergers and asset acquisitions both involve the transfer of assets from one company to another, but they still differ in three aspects as follows. First, in an asset

24. Caikuai (2006) No. 3, Qiye Kuaiji Zhunze Di Ershi Hao [Enterprise Accounting Standards No. 20-Business Combinations] (promulgated by the MOF on 15 February 2006, effective 1 January 2007) (PRC), Art. 13(11).
25. EITLIR, Art. 67.
26. Caishui (2009) No. 59, Art. 4(4).
27. Caishui (2009) No. 59, Art. 9.
28. *Ibid.* An example of such changes is that a company no longer qualifies as a high-tech enterprise after absorbing another company and thus becomes ineligible for the preferential tax rate of 15%.
29. Caishui (2009) No. 59, Art. 4(3).

acquisition, the purchasing company only acquires substantive business assets of the target company, while in a merger, the purchasing company not only acquires the assets of the target company but also assumes its liabilities. Second, all the assets of the target company are transferred in a merger, but an asset acquisition may involve a transfer of only a portion of the target company's assets. Third, unlike in the case of a merger, the target company may continue to operate after transferring assets in an asset acquisition.

For the above reasons, the tax consequences of an asset acquisition are more straightforward than those of a merger. An asset acquisition typically involves just two parties, namely the purchasing company and the target company, and does not trigger a shareholder-level tax. Only in cases where the target company liquidates shortly after disposing of its assets the shareholder -level tax arises pursuant to the tax rules on liquidating distributions.

[C] Stock Acquisition

In a stock acquisition, shareholders of the target company recognize gain or loss on the sale of their stock in the target company, which is equal to the difference between the consideration received by them and the tax basis of the stock transferred. Due to the full recognition of gain or loss on the transfer of stock, the purchasing company is entitled to a cost basis in the target company's stock transferred. As a transaction only between the purchasing company and the shareholders of the target company, a stock acquisition does not incur immediate tax consequences for the target company. Following an asset acquisition, the target company owns its assets with the same tax basis that they had before the stock acquisition, and other tax attributes of the target company also remain unchanged.

Among various tax attributes of the target company, net operating losses that can offset future gains are of particular importance. A profitable company lured by the value of net operating losses may acquire an unprofitable company merely to obtain the latter's loss carry forward. Such a problem of trafficking in loss carry forward may arise in a stock acquisition, as the Chinese law does not impose any constraint on the use of the target company's pre-acquisition net operating losses. For instance, a successful company may purchase the stock of a failing company with plenty of unused net operating losses and then merge its profitable business into the acquired company to utilize the loss carry forward.

Some other tax jurisdictions have established rules to combat trafficking in company losses through stock acquisitions. To take the US tax law as an example, the ability of a US company to recover net operating loss carry forward will be subject to limitation if the percentage of its stock held by one or more 5% shareholders increases by more than 50% over the lowest percentage of stock owned by such shareholders during a three-year testing period.[30] China may consider adopting similar anti-loss

30. Internal Revenue Code (US), § 382(g). The three-year testing period ends on the day of ownership change, *see* Internal Revenue Code (US), § 382(i).

trafficking rules to impose a limitation on the recovery of loss carry forwards in stock acquisitions.

§3.04 SPECIAL TAX TREATMENT

If an M&A transaction meets certain conditions prescribed in Circular 59, the participants in the transaction may elect the special tax treatment. Generally speaking, under the special tax treatment, no gain or loss is recognized at the time of M&A transactions at either the corporate level or the shareholder-level, and any unrecognized gain or loss in such tax-deferred M&A transactions is reflected in the substituted tax basis of the equity consideration received by the target company or its shareholders and kept for recognition in subsequent taxable disposals. Many income tax systems, including the one in China, provide this kind of tax deferral treatment (also known as rollover relief or non-recognition treatment) for M&A transactions on the notion that the law should not impose a current tax on transactions that do not sever the connection between investors and their original investments.

[A] General Conditions for the Special Tax Treatment

The specific conditions for the application of the special tax treatment vary from one type of transaction to another and will be discussed in the latter part of this section. Apart from the requirements specific to each type of M&A transaction, Circular 59 prescribes several general conditions for the special tax treatment, which can be classified into three categories: (1) continuity of interest; (2) continuity of business enterprise; and (3) reasonable commercial purpose.

[1] Continuity of Interest

Continuity of interest is the core condition for the special tax treatment. It requires the transferor company or its shareholders to preserve their interests in the transferred business enterprise by holding substantial equity interests in the purchasing company. China's first attempt to introduce the continuity of interest requirement can be traced back to 2000. In Circular 119, the STA stipulated that the transfer of assets in a merger would qualify for rollover relief only if the value of non-equity consideration did not exceed 20% of the value of equity consideration.[31] With the issuance of Circular 59, this simple cap on the non-equity consideration ratio evolved into a comprehensive set of rules.

Unlike the US, where the judicially developed continuity of interest doctrine still plays a crucial role, China has thoroughly codified the continuity of interest condition. According to Circular 59, only 'equity consideration' which is the stock of the purchasing company or the purchasing company's controlling company, counts

31. Guoshuifa (2000) No. 119, Art. 1(2).

towards the continuity of interest requirement.[32] Circular 4 further clarifies that 'the purchasing company's controlling company' refers to a company in which the purchasing company owns stock.[33]

The continuity of interest requirement demands that no less than 85% of the total consideration paid in an M&A transaction be equity consideration.[34] In other words, non-equity consideration (commonly known as 'boot' in the US) that covers cash, bank deposits, receivables, tradable securities except for the stock of the purchasing company and the purchasing company's controlling company, inventories, fixed assets, other assets, and undertaking of liabilities,[35] cannot exceed 15% of the total consideration.

Another component of the continuity of interest requirement is the length of time for which the selling shareholders should keep the equity consideration received in an M&A transaction. The special tax treatment will be withdrawn if, after the consummation of an M&A transaction, any shareholder that originally holds more than 20% of the target company sells the equity consideration received within twelve consecutive months.[36] Without such restraint, the stringent ratio requirement on equity consideration would be rendered meaningless. Suppose, for instance, that in a stock acquisition the purchasing company acquires all the stock of the target company with nothing but its stock and immediately after the transaction buys back half of its stock paid. If this scheme did not affect the application of the special tax treatment, the proportion of equity consideration to total consideration required would effectively be reduced from 85% to only 50%.

Apart from the post-transaction sale of equity consideration, a multistep transaction is another likely way to circumvent the ratio requirement. To take one example, instead of purchasing all the target stock with half in cash and half in equity consideration in one go, the purchasing company may first pay for half of the target stock with pure cash and then buys the rest of the target stock with pure equity consideration. The acquisition of the second half of the target stock at least formally satisfies the ratio requirement, notwithstanding that the two steps as a whole fail the requirement.

Circular 59 restricts this leeway by importing the US judicially developed step-transaction doctrine, under which a series of sales of stock or assets will be combined and assessed against the continuity of interest criteria as a single transaction if those sales are in substance integrated. However, compared to the highly flexible US judicial step-transaction doctrine, the Chinese statutory rule on step-transaction is very rigid since it only looks at sales of assets or stock that happen before or after the reorganization within twelve months.[37] Considering the complexity and diversity of

32. Caishui (2009) No. 59, Art. 2.
33. STA Gonggao (2010) No. 4, Art. 6. For further discussion on the notions of 'equity consideration' and 'controlling company', *see* § 5.02[B][2] below.
34. Caishui (2009) No. 59, Arts. 6(2), 6(3), 6(4).
35. Caishui (2009) No. 59, Art. 2.
36. Caishui (2009) No. 59, Art. 5(5); STA Gonggao (2010) No. 4, Art. 20.
37. Caishui (2009) No. 59, Art. 10.

M&A transaction arrangements, whether such an inflexible rule is effective in preventing the circumvention of continuity of interest requirement is quite doubtful.[38]

[2] Continuity of Business Enterprise

Even if most of the consideration in an M&A transaction is paid with equity interests in the purchasing company, the transferors still may break the connection with the transferred business enterprise, in particular where the purchasing company disposes of the transferred assets or redeploy them in drastically different business activities. Therefore, in addition to the continuity of interest requirement, the tax law establishes the continuity of business enterprise requirement to ensure that the transferors whose investments are effectively discontinued cannot take advantage of the benefits of the special tax treatment.

Article 5(3) of Circular 59 stipulates that, to be eligible for the special tax treatment, within twelve consecutive months after an M&A transaction the substantive business operation of the transferred assets shall remain unchanged.[39] While the law is clear on how long the purchasing company must not change the business operation of the target company, it is less so regarding what constitutes a 'change' to its substantive business operation. Would it be sufficient for the business operation of the transferred assets to be similar before and after the transaction? In cases where the target company has more than one line of business, does the purchasing company have to continue all these lines of business? Further guidance is needed from the central tax authorities to ensure a consistent application of the continuity of business enterprise test across the whole nation.

[3] Reasonable Commercial Purpose

The third general condition prescribed in Circular 59 is an anti-avoidance test. Article 5(1) of Circular 59 provides that the special tax treatment is only applicable to M&A transactions that have a 'reasonable commercial purpose' and are not conducted mainly for reducing, avoiding, or deferring tax liabilities.[40] Frankly speaking, the reasonable commercial purpose requirement is not unique to the M&A tax regime but applies to the taxation of various business arrangements.

Under the general anti-avoidance rule (GAAR) prescribed in the EITL, for a company that conducts any business arrangement without reasonable commercial purposes and thus reduces its taxable income, the tax authorities may cancel the tax benefit or assess a different tax liability against the company.[41] Since Circular 59 does not specify what can be regarded as a 'reasonable commercial purpose', the GAAR and

38. It is worth noting that the step-transaction rule is not always to the disadvantage of taxpayers because those engaging in creeping acquisitions can revoke the rule to obtain the special tax treatment.
39. Caishui (2009) No. 59, Art. 5(3).
40. Caishui (2009) No. 59, Art. 5(1).
41. EITL, Art. 47.

the GAAR-related tax circulars have been an important reference for the interpretation of this vague notion.

In the *Interim Measures for Implementing Special Tax Adjustments*, which provides a detailed guideline for the implementation of the GAAR, the STA enumerates four typical types of business arrangements lacking a business purpose, which include the abuse of tax incentives, the abuse of tax treaties, the abuse of the corporate form as well as the avoidance of tax by using a tax haven.[42] This circular also provides that the tax authorities should examine whether a business arrangement is conducted for tax avoidance purposes from several aspects as follows: the form and the substance of the arrangement, the conclusion time and the effective period of the arrangement, the implementation method of the arrangement, the relation between different steps or components of the arrangement, the changes in financial conditions of all parties involved in the arrangement, and the tax consequences of the arrangement.[43]

Circular 4 and its supplementary – the *Announcement on Several Issues Concerning the Administration of Enterprise Income Tax in Enterprise Restructurings* (STA Gonggao (2015) No. 48, hereinafter Circular 48) – basically replicate the provisions in the *Interim Measures for Implementing Special Tax Adjustments*, listing five factors to be considered in the examination of whether an M&A transaction possesses a reasonable commercial purpose. The five factors include: (1) whether the mode of the transaction is provided in Circular 59; (2) whether the substantive outcome of the transaction contravenes Circular 59; (3) whether or how the tax status of the participating parties in the transaction changes; (4) whether or how the financial status of the participating parties in the transaction changes; and (5) whether the participation in the transaction by non-residents follow the pattern specified in Circular 59.[44]

Notwithstanding those clarifications, the reasonable commercial purpose test is still too abstract to be applied in a specific context and leads to significant uncertainties. For example, the STA highlights the changes in the tax status of the participating parties caused by M&A transactions as a key factor for determining the reasonable commercial purpose, but it does not provide any guidance on to what extent the change in tax status is acceptable.[45] More importantly, an M&A transaction fails the reasonable commercial purpose test only if its primary purpose is not to generate tax benefits according to Circular 59,[46] but clear criteria or rules for identifying the primary purpose or differentiating it from other purposes are missing from the current law.[47]

---

42. Guoshuifa (2009) No. 2, Tebie Nashui Tiaozheng Shishi Banfa (Shixing) [Provisional Measures for Implementing Special Tax Adjustments] (promulgated by the STA on 8 January 2009, effective retrospectively 1 January 2008) (PRC), Art. 92.
43. Guoshuifa (2009) No. 2, Art. 93.
44. STA Gonggao (2010) No. 4, Art. 18; STA Gonggao (2015) No. 48, Guanyu Qiye Chongzu Yewu Qiye Suodeshui Zhengshou Guanli Ruogan Wenti de Gonggao [Announcement on Several Issues Concerning the Administration of Enterprise Income Tax in Enterprise Restructurings] (promulgated by the STA on 24 June 2015) (PRC), Art. 5.
45. *See* Chang Cai, *Defects with the M&A Taxation System and Anti-Avoidance Arrangements*, Shuiwu Yanjiu [Taxation Research], no. 6, 2011, at 81, 81.
46. Caishui (2009) No. 59, Art. 5(1).
47. *See* Hui Li & Xiuyao Wu, *Application of the Special Tax Treatment to Cross-border Intra-group Reorganizations*, Shuiwu Yanjiu [Taxation Research], no. 8, 2015, at 26, 29.

Despite the importance of the reasonable commercial purpose requirement, it is not the focus of this book. As mentioned above, Circular 59 is not the place where the reasonable commercial purpose test first comes up, and as early as in 2007 when the NPC enacted the EITL, the concept of 'reasonable commercial purpose' was incorporated into the law as a component of the GAAR. To in-depth explore this issue, a thorough analysis of China's GAAR would be indispensable, which can be the topic of another book.

[4] Additional Conditions for Cross-Border M&A

In the fear that taxpayers may take advantage of the non-recognition treatment to shift the profits taxable in China to other tax jurisdictions via schemes such as indirect share transfers, Circular 59 provides several additional conditions for a cross-border M&A to qualify for the special tax treatment.

According to Article 7 of Circular 59, on top of complying with the conditions discussed in other parts of this section, a cross-border M&A transaction can apply the special tax treatment only if it falls within a narrow category. For instance, a transfer of the stock of a resident enterprise held by a non-resident enterprise to another non-resident enterprise may qualify for the special tax treatment if it is a direct 100% subsidiary of the transferor, in which the withholding tax burden on a subsequent disposal of the equity transferred shall be identical as under the present equity transfer, and the transferor will not transfer the stock of the transferee owned by it within three years afterwards.[48] Briefly speaking, only cross-border M&A transactions that constitute intra-group restructurings get the opportunity to apply the special tax treatment.

[B] Tax Implications for Corporate Taxpayers

Almost all M&A-specific tax circulars including the pivotal Circular 59 are promulgated primarily to stipulate the tax treatments of companies involved in M&A transactions. Take Circular 4 as an example. It lists 'the parties to a corporate restructuring' as including the purchasing company, the target company as well as the corporate shareholders of the target company[49] but omits the non-corporate participants in M&A transactions. In line with this division of corporate and non-corporate entities, this subsection will focus on the tax implications for companies that participate in M&A transactions, and the tax implications for non-corporate participants will be discussed in the following subsection.

48. Caishui (2009) No. 59, Art. 7(1).
49. STA Gonggao (2010) No. 4, Art. 3.

[1] Merger

[a] Tax Consequences to the Target Company and Its Shareholders

Assume that a company with only corporate shareholders gets absorbed into another company in a tax-deferred merger where all of the transaction consideration is in the form of the stock of the purchasing company. The tax positions of the target company and its shareholders in such a non-cash merger are quite straightforward: the target company transfers all the assets and liabilities without bearing any tax consequences, and the shareholders have no gain or loss to report, carrying forward their previous tax basis in the stock of the target company to the equity consideration received in the merger.[50]

Where non-equity consideration is involved in applying the special tax treatment, the tax consequences can become much more complicated; particularly, as discussed, the tax law only allows partial tax deferral in a merger funded with a mix of equity interest and other property. Pursuant to Article 6(6) of Circular 59, the selling parties to a partially tax-deferred M&A transaction shall recognize gain or loss to the extent that the transfer of assets or stock is compensated by non-equity consideration.[51] As to mergers that, from a tax perspective, involve both a transfer of assets by the target company and exchange of stock by the shareholders of the target company, the difficulty of how to treat the non-equity consideration portion is encountered not only at the corporate level but also at the shareholder level.

Generally speaking, there are two common approaches to the problem of partial tax deferral in a merger. The first approach is to adhere to the classical income tax system, which requires a two-level recognition. That is to say, the target company is taxed to the extent that the transfer of assets gets compensated for non-equity consideration, and the target shareholders are taxed to the extent that they exchange the stock in the target company for non-equity consideration.[52] An illustration of this approach is given in Example 1.

> Example 1
>
> T is a company that has net assets with a basis of zero and a fair market value of RMB 2,000. Company S is the sole shareholder of T, and S has a zero basis in the T stock that has a market value of RMB 2,000. T merges into P for RMB 1,700 of P stock and RMB 300 in cash. After paying a 25% tax on the receipt of cash, T distributes the RMB 1,700 P stock and the remaining RMB 225 cash to S, which in turn recognizes a gain of RMB 225 for the receipt of cash. The total taxable gain in this example is RMB 525.

The second approach is one that the US law has adopted. Under Section 361(b)(1)(A) of the Internal Revenue Code (IRC), the target company will not report

50. Caishui (2009) No. 59, Art. 6(4).
51. Caishui (2009) No. 59, Art. 6(6).
52. A variation of this approach is to treat the non-equity payment received by the shareholders as a dividend distribution from the target company. To keep the analysis succinct, this variation will not be covered.

any gain if it distributes all of the 'boot' in pursuance of the plan of reorganization.[53] In other words, the US law treats the target company as a mere conduit for passing the transaction consideration to its shareholders, and the law only imposes a tax on the shareholders of the target company. Apparently, this approach incurs much less compliance and administration costs compared to the first one because taxpayers and tax authorities circumvent the tricky problems of computing the firm-level tax as well as assigning new tax basis to various categories of assets.[54] The example below is an illustration of such an approach.

Example 2

Assume the facts are the same as in Example 1, but instead of having the receipt of non-equity consideration first taxed to the target company and then taxed again at the shareholder level upon distribution, the income from the merger is only subject to tax at the shareholder level. Thus, the total taxable gain will be RMB 300.

The current Chinese tax law does not prescribe which of the above two approaches to follow, but it has been a long-time practice of the STA to look through the target company. Circular 119, one of the precursors to Circular 59, stated that in a tax-deferred merger, there would be no tax burden at the corporate level[55] and emphasized that the target shareholders must recognize gain or loss with respect to non-equity payment received.[56] In the official interpretation of Circular 119, the Income Tax Department of the STA gave an illustration similar to Example 2.[57]

Another problem arising in taxing partially tax-deferred mergers is how to align the recognition of taxable gain or loss in regard to non-equity consideration with the adjustment of the tax basis in the equity consideration. As prescribed in Article 6(6) of Circular 59, the proportion of the difference between the fair market value and the aggregate tax basis of the target shares which is attributable to the non-equity consideration shall be regarded as the taxable gain or loss of the target shareholders, and the equation is as follows:[58]

'Taxable gain or loss with respect to non-equity consideration = (Fair market value of shares surrendered – Aggregate tax basis of shares surrendered) × (Fair market value of the non-equity consideration received ÷ Fair market value of shares surrendered)'

Circular 59, while providing an equation on the calculation of taxable gain or loss with respect to non-equity consideration, does not adequately address the issue of the tax basis adjustment. Instead, it simply states that the tax basis of the relevant stock

53. Internal Revenue Code (US), § 361(b)(1)(A).
54. *See* §3.03[A][2] above.
55. Guoshuifa (2000) No. 119, Art. 1(2)(1).
56. Guoshuifa (2000) No. 119, Art. 1(2)(2).
57. Shukui Dong, et al., *Shuiqian Kouchu yu Touzi Gaizu Yewu Suodeshui Wenti Jiexi [Explanations of Income Tax Issues Concerning Before-Tax Deductions and Reorganizations]* 220-221 (2001).
58. Caishui (2009) No. 59, Art. 6(6).

shall be adjusted correspondingly.[59] Due to the lack of instructions, even tax professionals often get confused on this issue. Nevertheless, by scrutinizing the calculation logic behind the Article 6(6) equation, it is possible to identify the most suitable method for effecting a 'corresponding adjustment' to the tax basis of the equity consideration.

When calculating the taxable gain or loss of a target shareholder engaging in a partially tax-deferred merger, the first step is to allocate the total consideration received by the shareholder among its shares surrendered in the merger. The choice of allocation method would be especially crucial in the case where the shareholder owns shares with different tax bases. Suppose, for example, that shareholder X exchanges two shares – share *a1* (tax basis: RMB 0) and share *a2* (tax basis: RMB 100) – in Company T for Company P's stock (fair market value: RMB 100) and RMB 100 cash in a partially tax-deferred merger. Since each T share has a fair market value of RMB 100, shareholder X realizes a gain of RMB 100 on the exchange. If shareholder X can treat all the cash as the consideration paid for share *a2*, and all the purchasing company stock as the consideration paid for share *a1*, it will defer the full amount of the realized gain and pay no current tax. Alternatively, if all the cash is allocated to share *a1*, and all the purchasing company stock is allocated to share *a2*, shareholder X will recognize RMB 100 gain and thus get no tax deferral at all.

After properly allocating the consideration, the next step is to determine the portion of each share's tax basis that can get deducted in computing the taxable gain or loss. As the deductible amount increases, more of the non-equity consideration becomes taxable. To illustrate this, imagine that another shareholder of Company T, shareholder Y, exchanges one T share (tax basis: RMB 40; fair market value: RMB 100) for RMB 50 worth of P stock and RMB 50 cash in the merger. Shareholder B has RMB 60 realized gain with respect to the share. If the law allows shareholder B to deduct all the tax basis, B will only have RMB 10 gain to report. If, however, like in the US, the tax basis is not deductible unless the non-equity consideration exceeds the realized gain,[60] shareholder B will recognize a gain of RMB 50.

By providing the equation quoted above, Circular 59 has, in effect, adopted a pro rata approach to determine both the allocation of consideration and the amount of deductible tax basis. That is, a target shareholder needs to allocate the equity as well as non-equity consideration received proportionally to all its shares in the target company, and the tax basis of each share gets apportioned between the equity and non-equity consideration. To prove this, consider the following scenario. Shareholder Z is another T shareholder, which surrenders n shares in T (tax basis: $c1, c2, ..., cn$) in exchange for E worth of P stock and $(100n - E)$ cash. Under the proportional allocation approach, the law sees shareholder Z as receiving E/n worth of P stock and $(100 - E/n)$ cash for each T share owned by it. The tax basis of each share gets split into $E/n : (100 - E/n)$, and only the portion corresponding to cash received is deductible in computing the taxable income. Therefore, the taxable gain from transferring the n T shares is:

59. *Ibid.*
60. Internal Revenue Code (US), § 356(a)(1)(B) ('the gain, if any, to the recipient shall be recognized, but in an amount not in excess of the sum of such money and the fair market value of such other property').

$$\sum_{i=1}^{n}\left(100-\frac{E}{n}-c_i\times\frac{100-\frac{E}{n}}{100}\right)$$

$$\text{or}\quad 100n-E-\frac{100-\frac{E}{n}}{100}\times\sum_{i=1}^{n}c_i$$

$$\text{or}\quad 100n\times\frac{100n-E}{100n}-\frac{100n-E}{100n}\times\sum_{i=1}^{n}c_i$$

$$\text{or}\quad \left(100n-\sum_{i=1}^{n}c_i\right)\times\frac{100n-E}{100n}$$

100n is the total value of all T shares surrendered by Z, $\sum_{i=1}^{n} c_i$ is the aggregate tax basis of all those T shares, and (100n - E) is the value of the non-equity consideration received by C. Obviously, the equation provided by Circular 59 is derived:[61]

> Taxable gain or loss concerning non-equity consideration = (Fair market value of shares surrendered – Aggregate tax basis of shares surrendered) × (Fair market value of the non-equity consideration received ÷ Fair market value of shares surrendered)

As noted in the analysis above, when computing a target shareholder's taxable gain, the law splits the tax basis of each target share held by the shareholder into two parts. While one part applies against the non-equity consideration, the other gets preserved for the equity consideration. Thus, it is reasonable to determine the shareholder's basis in each share received from the purchasing company according to the equation below:

> Tax basis of each share received = Aggregate tax basis of target shares surrendered × (Fair market value of equity consideration received – Fair market value of shares surrendered) ÷ Number of shares received

[b] *Tax Consequences to the Purchasing Company*

In conformity with the non-recognition treatment at the corporate level in a tax-deferred merger, the target company's assets retain their original tax basis despite being transferred from one company to another. Also, the target company's other tax attributes are carried over to the purchasing company.[62] In order to prevent taxpayers

61. Caishui (2009) No. 59, Art. 6(6).
62. Caishui (2009) No. 59, Art. 6(4)(2).

from trafficking in tax losses via tax-deferred mergers, the Chinese tax authorities have been increasing restrictions on the purchasing company's use of transferred loss carry forward. Circular 59 includes the strictest constraint on loss trafficking ever implemented in China.

As noted in Chapter 2, the first attempt of the Chinese tax authorities to limit the transfer of loss carry forwards from one company to another in tax-deferred mergers can be traced back to 2000. Circular 119 sets a yearly cap on the amount of the target company's loss carry forwards that could be absorbed by the purchasing company's taxable income, which is equal to multiplying the purchasing company's taxable income for a given year by the percentage that the assets of the target company represented in the total assets of the combined company.[63] In other words, Circular 119 earmarked on the target company's loss carry forwards for offsetting the portion of the purchasing company's income that the tax law deemed as generated from the target company's assets.

The idea behind the Circular 119 annual limitation was to imagine that after the merger, the target company would operate as an independent entity and could deduct previous losses to the extent of its deemed income. In calculating that deemed income, Circular 119 presumed that the return rate of the target company's assets was the same as the return rate of the total assets of the combined company. As a result, the more profitable the purchasing company is, the faster it can use the target company's loss carry forwards, and accordingly, the more present value it can obtain from the acquired loss carry forwards. Since Circular 119 imposed a quite weak limitation on the use of acquired loss carry forwards by profitable companies, it was not very helpful in combating the trade of loss carry forwards.

Like Circular 119, Circular 59 also places a quantitative limitation on the use of loss carry forwards transferred in tax-deferred mergers. According to Article 6 (4) of Circular 59, the annual limitation on the deduction of the target company's loss carry forwards is equal to multiplying the fair market value of the target's net assets by the interest rate of the longest-term China government bond issued as of the end of the year when the merger occurs.[64] The logic here is similar to that behind the Circular 119 limitation. Circular 59 limits the value of loss carry forwards to the purchasing company to an amount deemed recoverable by the target company should it continue to operate. However, unlike Circular 119, Circular 59 treats the target company as if it invested in assets that generate a return equivalent to the longest-term China government bond. It is interesting to note that Article 6(4) of Circular 59 is similar to Section 382(b)(1) of the IRC, which provides that the annual limitation on transferred loss carry forwards is an amount equal to 'the value of the old loss corporation, multiplied by the long-term tax-exempt rate'.[65]

63. Guoshuifa (2000) No. 119, Art. 1(2).
64. Caishui (2009) No. 59, Art. 6(4).
65. Internal Revenue Code (US), § 382(b)(1)

[2] Asset Acquisition

If in an asset acquisition, all of the general conditions for the special tax treatment discussed above are satisfied and at the same time, the purchasing company acquires more than a particular portion of the total assets of the target company, then the parties to the transaction can elect the special tax treatment. In Circular 59, the MOF and the STA required that in a tax-deferred asset acquisition, the purchasing company should acquire at least 75% of the target company's assets.[66] In 2014, five years after the issuance of Circular 59, the central tax authorities issued Caishui (2014) No. 109 (hereinafter Circular 109), reducing the minimum acquisition percentage to 50%. Furthermore, Circular 109 specifies that the transfer of assets between a parent company and its wholly owned subsidiary or between two companies under the same 100% control will be eligible for the special tax treatment even if it does not meet the 50% acquisition percentage requirement.[67]

In a tax-deferred asset acquisition, the target company's shareholders are not exchanging anything directly with the purchasing company and are therefore not a party to the transaction.[68] As for the target company, it will not recognize gain or loss on the exchange of its assets for equity consideration, and its tax basis in the equity consideration received will be the same basis it had in the transferred assets.[69] Similarly, the tax basis of the purchasing company in the acquired assets will also be identical to the tax basis of those assets in the hands of the target company.[70] If a tax-deferred asset acquisition involves non-equity consideration, the target company will recognize gain or loss to the extent of the non-equity consideration received, and the purchasing and target companies will make corresponding adjustments to the tax bases of the assets acquired and the equity consideration received.[71]

The previous analysis of the proper methods for calculating taxable income and making tax basis adjustments in partially tax-deferred mergers can be extended to the case of partially tax-deferred asset acquisitions. That is to say, in a partially tax-deferred asset acquisition, the target company will divide the tax basis into two parts in the ratio of the value of equity consideration to the value of non-equity consideration. The part corresponding to the non-equity consideration can be deducted when calculating taxable gain or loss, and the other part shall be regarded as the tax basis of the equity consideration received. As to the purchasing company in a partially

66. Caishui (2009) No. 59, Art. 6(3).
67. Caishui (2014) No. 109, Guanyu Cujin Qiye Chongzu Youguan Qiye Suodeshui Chuli Wenti de Tongzhi [Notice on Issues Concerning the Enterprise Income Tax Treatment for the Promotion of Enterprise Restructurings] (promulgated by the MOF and the STA on 25 December 2014, effective retrospectively 1 January 2014) (PRC), Art. 3.
68. The MOF and the STA define 'parties to an asset acquisition' as including the purchasing and target companies. STA Gonggao (2010) No. 4, Art. 3(3); STA Gonggao (2015) No. 48, Art. 1(3).
69. Caishui (2009) No. 59, Art. 6(3)(1).
70. Caishui (2009) No. 59, Art. 6(3)(2).
71. Caishui (2009) No. 59, Art. 6(6).

tax-deferred asset acquisition, it will either increase the tax basis in the assets acquired by the amount of gain recognized by the target company or reduce that tax basis by the amount of loss recognized by the target company.

[3] Stock Acquisition

Before 2008, the Chinese tax law only granted non-recognition treatment to participants in particular mergers and asset acquisitions, and stock acquisitions were always taxable. When drafting Circular 59, the central tax authorities highlighted the need to extend non-recognition treatment to participants in certain stock acquisitions. In an internal report, the STA explained the reason for allowing tax-deferred stock acquisitions as follows:

> 'Stock acquisitions and asset acquisitions are the same in terms of economic substance. Their only difference is that in an asset acquisition, the purchasing company acquires assets directly from the target company, while in a stock acquisition, the purchasing company acquires indirect control over the target company's assets. Disallowing tax-deferred stock acquisition violates the principle of neutrality. Moreover, in the current circumstances, the purchasing company to a potential stock acquisition would prefer first to merge the target company and then spin it off to obtain tax deferral. Such a practice results in unnecessary transaction costs'.

According to Article 6(2) of Circular 59, the parties to a stock acquisition may elect to treat the transaction as a tax-deferred reorganization if all of the general conditions for the special tax treatment are satisfied and the purchasing company acquires at least 75% of the stock of the target company.[72] In 2014, the MOF and the STA reduced the minimum acquisition percentage to 50%.[73]

It is worth noting that in determining whether a stock acquisition meets the ratio requirement, the focus is on the percentage of the target company's stock transferred in the acquisition rather than the percentage of stock held by the purchasing company after the acquisition. Thus, if a 95% shareholder of a company wants to buy out minority shareholders, it has no choice but to conduct a taxable stock acquisition. This acquisition percentage requirement under the Chinese tax law contrasts sharply with its US counterpart, which looks at all the stock of the target company owned by the purchasing company. Under Section 368(a)(1)(B) of the IRC, one significant element of a tax-deferred stock acquisition is that the purchasing company has 'control' of the target company immediately after the acquisition;[74]'control' pursuant to Section 368(c) requires ownership by the purchasing company of 'at least 80% of the total combined voting power of all classes of stock entitled to vote' and 'at least 80% of the total

72. Caishui (2009) No. 59, Art. 6(2).
73. Caishui (2014) No. 109, Art. 1.
74. Internal Revenue Code (US), §368(a)(1)(B)

number of shares of all other classes of stock' in the target company.[75] The US Treasury Regulations further clarify that the purchasing company does not have to acquire more than 80% of the stock of the target company during a stock reorganization.[76]

The simplest tax-deferred stock acquisition is one in which the target company's shareholders transfer all of the stock of the target company to the purchasing company entirely in exchange for the purchasing company's stock. In such a transaction, the target company's shareholders will not recognize gain or loss. Under Article 6(2) of Circular 59, the target company's shareholders will have a tax basis in the stock received equal to the tax basis that they previously had in the target company's shares, and the purchasing company's tax basis in the shares acquired will be the same as the original tax basis of those shares.[77] In a stock acquisition that involves non-equity consideration, the target company's shareholders will recognize gain or loss to the extent of the non-equity consideration received, and the selling shareholders and the purchasing company will make corresponding adjustments to the tax bases of their new shares.[78] The methods for calculating taxable income and adjusting tax basis in such a transaction are similar to those in the case of partially tax-deferred asset acquisition and will not be repeated here.

Like a taxable stock acquisition, a tax-deferred stock acquisition does not lead to any tax liability at the corporate level. The target company will retain its historical tax basis in its assets as well as its various tax attributes.[79]

[C] Tax Implications for Non-corporate Taxpayers

As noted in the preceding subsection, the tax treatments of non-corporate participants in M&A transactions, that is, the non-corporate shareholders of the target company, are by and large not covered in the M&A-specific tax circulars. Therefore, it is unclear how non-corporate taxpayers would pay taxes on their gains from an M&A transaction, and many uncertainties affecting the operation of the special tax treatment arise. In particular, are non-corporate shareholders eligible for the rollover relief? If the answer is no, then another question follows: would the transaction consideration received by non-corporate taxpayers be considered for the continuity of interest test?

In general, the non-corporate shareholders of the target company fall into two common types, i.e., individuals and partnerships. Their tax implications in tax-deferred M&A transactions are analysed as follows.

75. Internal Revenue Code (US), § 368(c).
76. Treasury Regulations (US), § 1.368-2(c)
77. Caishui (2009) No. 59, Arts. 6(2)(1), 6(2)(2).
78. Caishui (2009) No. 59, Art. 6(6).
79. Caishui (2009) No. 59, Art. 6(2)(3).

[1] Individuals

In 2015, the STA for the first time broke its silence on the above issue of how to tax non-corporate taxpayers involved in tax-deferred M&A transactions. Circular 48 explicitly provides that individuals involved in reorganizations shall refer to the *Individual Income Tax Law of the PRC* (IITL) and its supplementary rules to determine their tax liabilities.[80] As the special tax treatment is not available under the individual income tax system, individuals always need to pay current tax on income associated with reorganizations. Moreover, Circular 48 expands the definition of 'parties to a restructuring' to cover individual shareholders of the target company,[81] and consequently, when deciding whether a transaction fulfils the criteria for the special tax treatment, the consideration received by individual shareholders should also be taken into account.

[2] Partnerships

The tax treatment of partnerships (generally referred to as 'partnership enterprises' under the Chinese tax law) in the context of M&A transactions is even more ambiguous than that of individuals because of the very primitiveness of existing tax law applicable to partnerships. The two income tax statutes, namely the IITL and the EITL, are both silent on the taxation of partnerships: the word 'partnership' does not appear even once in the entire IITL, and Article 1 of the EITL explicitly provides that 'partnership enterprises are not subject to this law'.[82] Circular 59 and its supplementary, which are enacted based on the EITL, not surprisingly keep away from the problem of taxing partnerships. Despite the lack of explicit and clear rules, by analogy with the treatment of individuals provided in Circular 48, it is reasonable to infer that the transaction consideration received by partnerships counts against the continuity of interest test. The real difficulty is whether a partnership – as a shareholder of the target company – can enjoy the rollover relief.

The Chinese tax law used to consider partnerships as entities separate from the partners. Prior to 2000, partnerships were subject to the enterprise income tax just like companies; if a partnership made distributions, its partners would pay a second layer of income tax. But since 2000, the Chinese tax law has started to view a partnership as more of an aggregation of partners than an independent entity. In Caishui (2000) No. 91, the MOF and the STA announced that partnerships formed by individuals are no longer subject to the enterprise income tax, and each partner would be directly taxable on a portion of the income accruing to partnerships.[83] The 2006 amendment to the

80. STA Gonggao (2015) No. 48, Art. 1.
81. *Ibid.*
82. EITL, Art. 1.
83. Caishui (2000) No. 91, Guanyu Geren Duzi Qiye he Hehuo Qiye Touzizhe Zhengshou Geren Suodeshui de Guiding [Rules on the Application of the Individual Income Tax to Sole Proprietorships and Investors in Partnerships] (promulgated by the MOF and the STA on 19 September 2000, effective retrospectively 1 January 2000) (PRC), Art. 3.

Partnership Enterprise Law of the PRC reiterates this transition by stating that 'the income of a partnership should be taxed separately to its partners',[84] and Caishui (2008) No. 159 further clarifies that the income of a partnership is taxed only at the partner level – individual and corporate partners paying the individual income tax and the enterprise income tax respectively.[85]

Consistent with the aggregate view of partnerships, the tax position of a partnership in an M&A transaction seems to be as follows: individual partners on the one hand always need to pay a 20% tax on capital gains at the time of the transaction, and corporate partners, on the other hand, may enjoy tax deferral on their share of the equity consideration. However, a closer look reveals a different story.

Under Caishui (2000) No. 91, when calculating an individual partner's liabilities, different types of income received by a partnership are all categorized into a single type of income – 'income from trade and business',[86] which is a distinct category of income under the IITL and subject to a separate progressive rate schedule ranging from 5% to 35%.[87] The STA subsequently made a minor exception to Caishui (2000) No. 91, allowing interest and dividend income received by a partnership to be taxed as interest and dividends to individual partners. Thus, all types of income except for interest and dividend income,[88] although treated differently under the schedular tax system adopted by the IITL, incur taxes at the progressive tax rates of up to 35% to individual partners. In other words, individual partners have to pay tax on their capital gains derived through partnerships at a marginal tax rate of 35% as opposed to the standard capital gain tax rate of 20%.[89]

The fact that partnerships in China have limited tax transparency also holds for corporate partners. Tax authorities appear to take the stance that companies cannot enjoy any enterprise income tax preference for income derived through partnerships unless the law explicitly stipulates otherwise. Two examples from the last decade can illustrate this observation. One example is Article 26 of the EITL, which exempts dividends paid by one Chinese resident enterprise to another from income tax. Can a company claim tax exemption on corporate dividends paid to a partnership owned by it? Most local tax authorities give a negative answer to this question. For instance, in responding to an inquiry on this issue, the Ningbo Local Taxation Bureau stated that the EITL only provides an exemption for dividend payments between two companies,

84. Zhonghua Renmin Gongheguo Hehuo Qiye Fa [Partnership Enterprise Law of the People's Republic of China] (promulgated 23 Febuary 1997, effective 1 August 1997, amended 2006) (PRC), Art. 6.
85. Caishui (2008) No. 159, Guanyu Hehuo Qiye Hehuoren Suodeshui Wenti de Tongzhi [Notice on Income Tax Issues Concerning Partners of Partnership Enterprises] (promulgated by the MOF and the STA on 23 December 2008, effective retrospectively 1 January 2008) (PRC), Art. 2.
86. Caishui (2000) No. 91, Art. 4.
87. IITL, Art. 3(2).
88. Guoshuihan (2001) No. 84, Guanyu Geren Duzi Qiye he Hehuo Qiye Touzizhe Zhengshou Geren Suodeshui de Guiding Zhixing Koujing de Tongzhi [Notice Regarding How to Implement the Rules on the Application of the Individual Income Tax to Sole Proprietorships and Investors in Partnerships] (promulgated by the STA on 17 January 2001) (PRC), Art. 2.
89. IITL, Art. 3(3).

and therefore, corporate partners should pay tax on dividends received through partnerships.[90]

The second example is Article 31 of the EITL, which stipulates that where a venture capital company engages in key venture capital investments supported and encouraged by the state, the amount of its taxable income may get reduced by a certain percentage of the investment amount.[91] Based on this provision, the EITLIR provides that if a venture capital company invests in unlisted small and medium-sized high-tech enterprises by way of equity investment for two years or more, it may deduct 70% of the investment amount against the taxable income of the year when it has held the equity for two years, and the unused deductible amount may be carried forward to subsequent tax years.[92]

What if a company invests through a partnership? Is it still eligible for the tax deduction? In 2013, the MOF and the STA announced that where a registered venture capital limited partnership registered in Zhongguancun National Innovation Demonstration Zone makes an equity investment in unlisted small and medium-sized high-tech enterprises for two years or more, its corporate partners may claim deductions up to 70% of their portions in the investment amount once the two-year period is complete.[93] This rule was subsequently extended to venture capital limited partnerships registered in other national innovation demonstration zones.[94] In 2015, the MOF and the STA eventually decided to implement this tax policy nationwide.[95] The gradual expansion of the tax incentive for venture capital clearly shows that enterprise income tax preferences, by default, are not applicable in the partnership tax area.

Provided that the Chinese tax authorities consistently use the above-described approach to the taxation of partners and partnerships, the rollover relief for M&A, as an enterprise income tax preference, cannot apply to companies that indirectly participate

90. Ningbo Local Taxation Bureau, *Qiye Suodeshui Redian Zhengce Wen Da (2014 Nian Di Yi Qi) [Answers to Frequently Asked Questions Concerning the Enterprise Income Tax (Issue 1 of 2014)]* (2014).
91. EITL, Art. 31.
92. EITLIR, Art. 97.
93. Caishui (2013) No. 71, Guanyu Zhongguancun Guojia Zizhu Chuangxin Shifanqu Youxian Hehuo Zhi Chuangye Touzi Qiye Faren Hehuoren Qiye Suodeshui Shidian Zhengce de Tongzhi [Notice on the Pilot Enterprise Income Tax Policy for Corporate Partners in Venture Capital Limited Partnerships in Zhongguancun National Innovation Demonstration Zone] (promulgated by the MOF and the STA on 29 September 2013, effective retrospectively 1 January 2013, repealed) (PRC), Art. 1. The State Council sets up the national innovation demonstration zones (NIDZs) to spur innovation and growth of high-tech industry. The first national innovation demonstration zone, Zhongguancun NIDZ, was established in 2009. As of February 2018, there are 17 NIDZs in China.
94. Caishui (2015) No. 62, Guanyu Tuiguang Zhongguancun Guojia Zizhu Chuangxin Shifanqu Shuishou Shidian Zhengce Youguan Wenti de Tongzhi [Notice on Expanding the Pilot Tax Policies for Zhongguancun National Innovation Demonstration Zone] (issued 9 June 2015, effective retrospectively 1 January 2015) (promulgated by the MOF and the STA on 9 June 2015, effective retrospectively 1 January 2015, repealed) (PRC), Art. 2(1).
95. Caishui (2015) No. 116, Guanyu Jiang Guojia Zizhu Chuangxin Shifanqu Youguan Shuishou Shidian Zhengce Tuiguang Dao Quanguo Fanwei Shishi de Tongzhi [Notice on Expanding the Pilot Tax Policies for National Innovation Demonstration Zones to Nationwide] (promulgated by the MOF and the STA on 23 October 2015) (PRC), Art. 1(1).

in transactions through partnerships unless there is a rule specifying otherwise. Unfortunately, such a rule does not exist so far.

[D] Tax Administration Issues

Under Article 11 of Circular 59, if the parties to an M&A transaction elect the special tax treatment, they must file required documents with the competent tax authority to prove that the transaction satisfies all the conditions for the special tax treatment. Failure to properly file the required information will render the transaction ineligible for the special tax treatment.[96] In situations where taxpayers engage in a tax-deferred M&A transaction but do not comply with the filing obligations, the tax authority may deny the taxpayers' election for the special tax treatment and regard the transaction as taxable. In practice, there exist cases in which the tax authority in charge decided to deprive the parties of a stock acquisition of the special tax treatment after discovering that the parties had not performed their record-filing obligations.[97]

Circular 59 and Circular 4 do not expressly require M&A participants to get approval from the tax authorities before carrying out transactions on a tax-deferred basis. Nevertheless, during the first five years after the issuance of Circular 59, ex ante approval was a prerequisite for carrying out tax-deferred M&A transactions. On 13 February 2014, the STA published a circular which explicitly listed the 'approval for the special tax treatment' as a 'non-administrative licensing approval item'.[98] Tax authorities exercised such approval power through the record-filing administration mechanism, and it happened that the competent tax authority refused to accept filing documents without specifying reasons.[99]

The situation changed after 2015. In May 2015, the STA proclaimed that the 'approval for the special tax treatment' was no longer an administrative approval item, and in June 2015, the STA issued Circular 48, which establishes comprehensive record-filing-based management of the special tax treatment. The transformation of the administration of the special tax treatment was mainly attributable to two factors.

The first factor is the Chinese government's systematic efforts to reduce red tape. On 27 August 2003, the SCNPC enacted the Administrative Licensing Law (ALL) to limit the power of administrative agencies to set administrative licences that enterprises and citizens must obtain before engaging in certain activities.[100] According to Article 14 of the ALL, statutes enacted by the NPC and the SCNPC can establish

96. Caishui (2009) No. 59, Art. 11.
97. *See e.g.*, Tianyong Liu, *Jianxi Qiye Chongzu Shiyong Teshuxing Shuiwu Chuli Wei Jishi Bei'an de Falv Houguo [A Brief Analysis on the Consequence of Failure to Filing Documentation for the Special Tax Treatment on Time]* (24 October 2021), http://www.xingtao.cn/news/1325.html).
98. STA Gonggao (2014) No. 10, Guanyu Gongkai Xingzheng Shenpi Shixiang deng Xiangguan Gongzuo de Gonggao [Announcement on Issues Relating to Disclosing Administrative Approval Items] (promulgated by the STA on 13 February 2014) (PRC).
99. Liu, *supra* note 97.
100. Zhonghua Renmin Gongheguo Xingzheng Xuke Fa [Administrative Licensing Law of the People's Republic of China] (promulgated 27 August 2003, effective 1 July 2004, amended 2019) (PRC) (hereinafter ALL).

administrative licences; in the absence of a specific statute, administrative regulations promulgated by the State Council may set administrative licences;[101] and if there is neither a statute nor an administrative regulation, local government regulations may create administrative licences.[102] The ALL only recognizes these three types of ways for establishing administrative licences, so the State Council's constituent departments, such as the MOF and the STA, do not have any power to set administrative licences.

Nevertheless, for many years, the constraint imposed by the ALL was ineffective as the constituent departments of the State Council introduced a lot of so-called non-administrative licensing approvals which operated outside of the parameters of the ALL. Like administrative licences, non-administrative licensing approvals also stipulate conditions for enterprises and citizens to conduct certain activities, but they are not subject to any regulation.[103] The 'approval for the special tax treatment' required by the STA before 2015 was a typical non-administrative licensing approval.

As the reform of streamlining administration and scaling back administrative power deepens, the State Council decided to cut down the number of administrative approvals, in particular, the number of non-administrative licensing approvals. At his inaugural press conference in March 2013, Premier Li Keqiang vowed to slash the existing administrative approvals by a third in five years.[104] In order to achieve the objective, the State Council took seven rounds of clearing administrative approvals in 2013 and 2014. In May 2015, the State Council eliminated another forty-nine approval items and decided to phase out non-administrative licensing approvals completely.[105] Following the State Council's mandate, the STA abolished eighty non-administrative licensing approval items, which included the 'approval for the special tax treatment',[106] and one month later, the STA issued Circular 48.

Another factor leading to the reform of the administration of the special tax treatment is China's long-term plan to establish a self-assessment system and implement risk-based tax administration. Since as early as the 1990s, the Chinese government has accepted the mainstream view on tax administration that self-assessment and

101. ALL, Art. 14.
102. ALL, Art. 15.
103. Vivienne Bath, *Reducing the Role of Government – The Chinese Experiment*, 3 Asian Journal of Comparative Law 1, 16 (2008) ('non-administrative approval items may not be clearly regulated, lists of the items and their content may be difficult to locate since the disclosure requirements of the ALL do not specifically apply to non-administrative licences and approvals, standardization of fees, and forms is not subject to the ALL and those rights of action that are granted by the ALL may not apply to applicants or holders of non-administrative licences').
104. Xinhua News Agency, *Li Keqiang Zongli deng Huijian Caifang Lianghui de Zhongwai Jizhe bing Huida Tiwen [Premier Li Keqiang's Press Conference and Q&A Session]* (17 March 2013), http://www.xinhuanet.com//2013lh/2013-03/17/c_124469054_2.htm.
105. Guofa (2015) No. 27, Guanyu Quxiao Fei Xingzheng Xuke Shenpi Shixiang de Jueding [Decision on Eliminating Non-Administrative Licensing Approval Items] (promulgated by the State Council on 10 May 2015) (PRC).
106. Shuizongfa (2015) No. 74, Guanyu Guanche Luoshi Guowuyuan Guanyu Quxiao Fei Xingzheng Xuke Shenpi Shixiang de Jueding de Tongzhi [Notice on Implementing the Decision of the State Council on Eliminating Non-Administrative Licensing Approval Items] (promulgated by the STA on 25 May 2015) (PRC).

risk-based tax management are central to a modern system of revenue administration.[107] The *Implementation Plan for Reforming the Industrial and Commercial Tax System*, which was the guiding document for the 1994 tax reform, highlighted the necessity of building a tax return filing system and transforming the tax agencies' administrative patterns.[108]

In the *Plan for Deepening the Reform of Tax Administration*, the State Council took one step further and specified five main elements of the tax administration reform. The first element is to establish a self-assessment and self-reporting system. The second element is to improve services for taxpayers, including the publication of laws, the establishment of taxpayer service centres, and the development of tax agent services. The third element is to develop computerized systems that enable tax authorities to efficiently monitor taxpayer compliance. The fourth element is to set up a tax audit system that covers not only regular tax compliance but also industries and taxpayers with comparatively high tax risks. The last element is to establish a streamlined and efficient tax administration system. The State Council regarded establishing the taxpayer's self-assessment system as the cornerstone and setting up a risk-based tax audit system as the focus of the reform.[109]

Despite more than twenty years of reform, China is still on the way to building a risk-based tax administration system. In 2015, the CPC and the State Council jointly published a reform blueprint,[110] which aims at establishing a modern tax administration system that meets the requirements of a modernized public governance system.[111] A primary task of the reform is to strengthen ongoing and post-filing administration. Accordingly, the tax authorities are required to shift their focus from *ex ante* administrative approvals to post-filing inspections.[112] The issuance of Circular 48 perfectly signifies that the tax administration is moving away from the traditional ex ante approval towards *ex post* tax audit.

However, the change in the regulatory approach does not necessarily reduce compliance costs for taxpayers. First and foremost, the strengthening of record-filing requirements follows the cancellation of administrative approvals. Under Circular 48, if the special tax treatment is elected, the M&A participants must submit a form ('Declaration Form for Special Tax Treatment on Corporate Reorganization') and

107. International organizations such as the World Bank and the OECD have promoted the benefits of a risk-based tax management mechanism. *See e.g.*, OECD, *Compliance Risk Management: Managing and Improving Tax Compliance*, 8 (October 2004), https://www.oecd.org/tax/administration/33818656.pdf; Munawer Sultan Khwaja, *Overview, in Risk-Based Tax Audits: Approaches and Country Experiences* 1, 2 (Munawer Sultan Khwaja, et al. eds., 2011).

108. Guofa (1993) No. 90, Gongshang Shuizhi Gaige Shishi Fang'an [Implementation Plan for Reforming the Industrial and Commercial Tax System] (approved by the State Council on 25 December 1993, effective 1 January 1994) (PRC), Art. 6.

109. Guobanfa (1997) No. 1, Shenhua Shuishou Zhengguan Gaige Fang'an [Plan for Deepening the Reform of Tax Administration] (approved by the State Council on 23 January 1997) (PRC).

110. General Office of the CPC Central Committee and General Office of the State Council, *Shenhua Guoshui Dishui Zhengguan Tizhi Gaige Fang'an [Blueprint for Deepening the Reform of Tax Collection and Administrative Systems of State and Local Tax Administrations]* (24 December 2015).

111. *Ibid.*, at para. 1(2).

112. *Ibid.*, at para. 2(8).

relevant supporting documents to the competent tax authority at the time of filing the income tax return for the year in which the transaction is done.[113] The documentation requirements prescribed by Circular 48 are much more comprehensive than those prescribed by Circular 4. A rough comparison of the numbers of supporting documents to be filed under the two circulars will illustrate the point. Circular 4 and Circular 48 require the parties to a stock acquisition to submit five and nine types of supporting documents respectively. Under Circular 4, the parties to a merger only need to file six types of documents, and Circular 48 has doubled the number to twelve.

By elevating documentation requirements, the tax authorities can better monitor whether a transaction satisfies the conditions for the special tax treatment. For instance, Circular 59 adopts a step-transaction rule that integrates related sales of assets or stock occurring within twelve months into a single transaction;[114] however, under Circular 4, taxpayers do not have any obligation to report related transactions. Circular 48 plugs the loophole by mandating the parties to an M&A transaction to disclose whether there are related sales of assets or stock during the twelve months and explain whether such transactions (if any) constitute step transactions.[115]

Last but not least, Circular 48 emphasizes that the tax authorities in charge should strengthen the post-filing monitoring of subsequent transfers of assets or stock exchanged in tax-deferred M&A transactions. Article 10 of Circular 48 expressly provides that the tax authorities should compare the tax basis of the assets or stock at the time when they were transferred in a tax-deferred M&A transaction and at the time when they are disposed of subsequently. If the tax authorities discover that the tax basis reported by taxpayers is inaccurate, they will make adjustments to the tax basis.[116]

§3.05 ANALYSIS AND CONCLUSION

[A] Features of China's M&A Taxation System

There are many distinctive features of China's M&A taxation system due to the transitional nature of the country's legal system. Although these features are fading somewhat as reform proceeds, they are expected to persist in the foreseeable future. As an exhaustive account of all the features is neither possible nor necessary, here some features of particular relevance to this research will be further explored.

[1] Segregated Systems for Enterprises and Individuals

The first feature of China's M&A taxation system is that it has a dual system for individuals and enterprises including companies and other taxable entities. Of course,

113. STA Gonggao (2015) No. 48, Art. 4.
114. Caishui (2009) No. 59, Art. 10.
115. STA Gonggao (2015) No. 48, Art. 6.
116. STA Gonggao (2015) No. 48, Art. 10.

because of the inherent differences between natural persons and legal persons, even in countries that have a unified income tax code, it is impossible to have identical provisions for these two groups of taxpayers. However, the uniqueness of China's case is the strict segregation between the tax rules for individuals and enterprises.

In China, the administration of the enterprise and the individual income tax have been separate for much of history until recently. Before 2018, China had two parallel systems of tax administration: national tax bureaus and local tax bureaus. While both national and local tax bureaus were responsible for collecting the enterprise income tax, the individual income tax was administered solely by local tax bureaus. In 2018, national tax bureaus merged with local tax bureaus, putting an end to the separate tax administration. Nevertheless, the legislation for individual and enterprise income taxes is still separate, and the government has been supplementing each primary income tax statute with an array of administrative regulations, ministerial regulations, and circulars. There is minimal overlap between these two sets of law, and almost all pieces of income tax legislation – formal or informal – specify in the title that they deal exclusively with one type of income tax but not the other.

Even where the tax treatments for individuals and enterprises are similar, the tax authorities prefer to issue two separate circulars rather than an integrated one. An example from recent years illustrates the point. On 31 December 2014, the MOF and the STA jointly issued Caishui (2014) No. 116 – the *Notice on the Enterprise Income Tax Treatment of Non-Monetary Assets Investments* – to grant tax incentives for a company making non-monetary capital contributions to another company. Only three months later, the central tax agencies issued Caishui (2015) No. 41 – the *Notice on the Individual Income Tax Treatment of Non-Monetary Assets Investments*, providing similar preferential treatment for non-monetary contributions from an individual to a company. The two circulars have similar titles and provisions, and in fact, Caishui (2015) No. 41 is basically a simplified version of Caishui (2014) No. 116 in the area of individual income tax.

The segregation between the two income tax systems is deeply rooted in the history of China's modern income tax. On 10 September 1980, the NPCSC enacted the *Income Tax Law on Chinese-Foreign Equity Joint Ventures* and the IITL, signifying the start of China's modern income tax legislation and indicating that the income tax for enterprises and individuals would evolve along parallel trajectories and at different paces.

The enterprise income tax system has undergone several rounds of reforms since 1980. Shortly after establishing income tax laws for Chinese-foreign joint ventures and foreign enterprises, China started to build the income tax system for SOEs and other types of domestically owned enterprises in a gradual but quick manner. Before 1983, SOEs repatriated to the government the profits after paying turnover taxes. With the 'profit-for-tax' reform starting in 1983, China transformed the delivery of profits (*li*) into the payment of income taxes (*shui*). In 1984, the State Council enacted the *Provisional Regulations on Income Tax of SOEs*, building up the SOE income tax system. In 1985 and 1988, the State Council promulgated the *Provisional Regulations on Income Tax of Collectively-Owned Enterprises* and the *Provisional Regulations on Income Tax of*

Private Enterprises respectively. As such, all types of enterprises were subject to the enterprise income tax.

Entering the 1990s, China began to consolidate and reform the existing taxes. In 1991, the income tax laws for Chinese-foreign joint ventures and foreign enterprises were merged to become the *Income Tax Law on Foreign-Invested Enterprises and Foreign Enterprises*. Moreover, the State Council abolished the three domestically owned enterprise income taxes in 1993 and enacted the *Provisional Regulations on Enterprise Income Tax*, which uniformly applied to all domestically owned enterprises, regardless of ownership. With the reforms in 1991 and 1993, China streamlined the multiple enterprise income tax systems into a dual-track system for domestically owned and foreign-invested enterprises. The entry into force of the EITL in 2008 put an end to the dual-track system and signalled the emergence of unified corporate income taxation.

While the enterprise income tax system developed in step with the economic reform, the individual income tax reform stalled for a long time. As mentioned above, the SCNPC enacted the IITL and the first piece of legislation on enterprise income tax on the same day. The IITL levied taxes on very few types of income, including salaries, other compensation for personal services, royalties, dividends, and rentals. To tax the income of proliferating individual businesses, in January 1986, the State Council promulgated the *Provisional Regulations on Income Tax for Urban and Rural Individual Businesses*. In September of the same year, the State Council promulgated the *Provisional Regulations on Individual Income Adjustment Tax* to impose a surtax on the rich. In 1993, the SCNPC incorporated those interim regulations into the IITL and improved the IITL's provisions regarding the definition of a tax resident, the scope of taxable income and tax-exempted items, tax rates, as well as deductions. In the 2000s, the IITL changed only slightly. It was not until 2018 that the SCNPC substantially amended the law.

The segregation between individual and enterprise income taxes has profoundly affected the landscape of China's M&A taxation system. The taxation of M&A transactions has developed as a part of the enterprise income tax, and the rules in this area focus on tax consequences to enterprises. As noted, among the numerous M&A-specific circulars issued in the past quarter of a century, Circular 48 is the only one that mentions tax consequences to individuals; however, it merely provides that 'individuals pay taxes according to the IITL and relevant individual income tax regulations'. Because of the disparity between the two sets of rules, an individual in an M&A transaction and a similarly situated company are likely to face very different tax consequences.

[2] Orientation Towards Encouraging M&A Activities

From the discussion in earlier parts of this chapter, it is evident that the development of China's M&A taxation system closely tracks the path of China's economic reform. In recent years, the Chinese government has been putting more and more stress on the importance of M&A activities in further developing the economy. In the *Opinions on*

Promoting Corporate Mergers and Restructurings, the State Council enthusiastically trumpets its pro-M&A policy:[117]

> 'Major Objectives
>
> We should, through promoting corporate mergers and reorganizations, deepen the reform of economic systems and mechanisms, and improve the basic economic system with public ownership as the mainstay and the joint development of diverse forms of ownership. We should accelerate the strategic adjustments of the state-owned economy, ensuring the state capital can reasonably enter and exit the market, encouraging private enterprises to participate in the restructuring of state-owned enterprises in competitive industries, and promoting the development of the non-public sector economy as well as small and medium-sized enterprises. Through mergers and restructurings, enterprises can transform their operational mechanisms, improve their corporate governance structure, establish the modern enterprise mechanism, strengthen internal management, promote technological upgrade and innovation, eliminate outdated industrial capacity, reduce excessive production, promote energy saving and emission reduction, and enhance their competitiveness.
>
> We should further adjust and revitalize major industries, including automobile, steel, cement, machinery manufacturing, electrolytic aluminium, as well as rare earth, and support competitive enterprises to grow stronger and larger. We should promote trans-regional mergers and reorganizations, outbound M&A and cooperation among enterprises in order to improve industrial concentration ratios, promote large-scale enterprises, support the growth of critical enterprises with independent intellectual property rights and famous brands, cultivate a number of large corporate groups with international competitiveness, and promote the optimization and upgrading of industrial structure.'

To summarize, the Chinese government is determined to promote M&A activities to achieve three main objectives. The first one is to accelerate the restructuring of SOEs and to provide a channel for state capital to enter into and exit from specific industries. The second objective is to modernize enterprises' operational mechanisms, which cover the corporate governance structure, internal management, and so on. Moreover, the government hopes to promote the revitalization of major industries such as automobiles and steel. As China has suffered from widespread overcapacity in heavy industries such as steel, cement, and aluminium during the past decade, the government has been emphasizing the benefits of M&A transactions in solving the overcapacity problem.[118]

Consistent with the positive attitude towards M&A, the Chinese government is very willing to use tax policies to achieve the goal of encouraging M&A activities. Under Guofa (2010) No. 27, the MOF and the STA are mandated to implement tax incentives for M&A activities.[119] Table 3.1 gives an unexhausted summary of recent government documents that mention preferential tax policies for M&A transactions.

117. Guofa (2010) No. 27, Art. 2(1).
118. Guofa (2014) No. 14 *See also* Shusong Ba & Yafang Yu, *Coordination of Market-Oriented M&A and Government Policy to Address Overcapacity*, Shuiwu Yanjiu [Taxation Research], no. 11, 2013, at 3, 3-4.
119. Guofa (2010) No. 27, Art. 4(1).

Table 3.1 Government Documents on Using Tax Law to Promote M&A Activities

Time of Issuance	*Rule-making Organ*	*Title*
September 2010	State Council	*Opinions on Promoting Corporate Mergers and Restructurings* (Guofa (2010) No. 27)
January 2013	Twelve ministries including the MOF and the STA	*Guiding Opinions on Stimulating Corporate Mergers and Restructurings in Key Industries* (Gongxinbu Lianchanye (2013) No. 16)
March 2014	State Council	*Opinions on Further Optimizing the Market Environment for Corporate Mergers and Restructurings* (Guofa (2014) No. 14)
May 2014	State Council	*Several Opinions on Further Promoting the Healthy Development of the Capital Market* (Guofa (2014) No. 17)
December 2014	MOF and STA	*Notice on Issues Concerning the Enterprise Income Tax Treatment for the Promotion of Corporate Restructurings* (Caishui (2014) No. 109)
December 2014	MOF and STA	*Notice on Policy Issues Concerning the Enterprise Income Tax Treatment of Non-Monetary Assets Investments* (Caishui (2014(No. 116)
March 2015	MOF and STA	*Notice on Policies Concerning the Individual Income Tax Treatment of Non-Monetary Assets Investments* (Caishui (2015) No. 41)

[3] Importation of Foreign Experience

The other feature of China's M&A taxation system is its utilization of overseas experience. China's M&A taxation system has significantly benefited from valuable foreign experience, particularly from the US. Indeed, the modern evolution of Chinese income tax law is mostly a process of legal transplants.[120] The advanced foreign experience provided China with a good starting point to establish its income taxation system, and learning from overseas experience has enabled China to significantly reduce legislative costs and thus facilitates the enactment of rules for taxing M&A transactions. With the benefits of overseas experience, China's M&A taxation system

120. Jinyan Li, *Tax Transplants and the Critical Role of Processes: A Case Study of China*, 3 Journal of Chinese Tax and Policy 85, 91 (2013).

has become increasingly comprehensive since the STA enacted the first M&A-specific regulation in 1993.

To better understand China's active use of foreign experience in developing its M&A taxation system, we should take into consideration the global convergence in tax policies for M&A, which is most evident concerning the rules on rollover relief. Influenced by the US, which is one of the first countries that allow taxpayers to defer the recognition of gain or loss on certain M&A transactions, it has become a global trend to grant rollover relief to corporate reorganizations. According to a report of the OECD, as of 1 July 2004, almost all the members of the OECD have enacted certain rollover relief provisions for M&A transactions.[121]

During the past three decades, the EU has been a significant force behind this trend. In July 1990, in order to remove tax barriers to transnational corporate restructurings, the Council of the European Communities adopted the Merger Directive to harmonize its Member States' taxation system applicable to cross-border mergers, divisions, transfers of assets as well as exchanges of shares.[122] One salient feature of the Merger Directive is that it grants deferral of taxes on the transfer of assets or stock in the four types of corporate restructurings.[123] As an EU directive, the Merger Directive sets out a goal – removing taxation obstacles to transnational reorganizations – which all EU countries must achieve. Although the directive only applies to cross-border transactions, it affects how the EU Member States treat corporate reorganizations between domestic companies. For instance, Spain has extended the tax relief provided in the Merger Directive to its domestic cases.[124] Thus, through the enactment of the Merger Directive, the EU has powerfully promoted the spread of the practice of providing rollover relief for M&A transactions.

Around the same time when China started its journey to establish the income tax regime for M&A transactions, Australia was also considering revamping its tax system. In 1998, the federal government of Australia established the Review of Business Taxation to make recommendations on reforms to the Australian tax system.[125] In the following one-year period, the Review of Business Taxation released four reports (generally named 'Ralph Report' after the Chairman of the Review, John Ralph): two discussion papers, one information paper, and a final report. Those reports provided a comprehensive analysis of the existing Australian business tax laws, the motivations and objectives for reform, as well as over 280 reform recommendations.[126]

121. OECD, *supra* note 9, at 112-118.
122. Council Directive 90/434/EEC of 23 July 1990 on the common system of taxation applicable to mergers, divisions, transfers of assets, and exchanges of shares concerning companies of different Member States (EU) (hereinafter EU Merger Directive), Arts. 1, 2.
123. EU Merger Directive, Art. 4.
124. Timothy A. Kearney, *An Overview of the EC Merger Directive and Its Implementation by Member States*, 21 Int'l Tax J. 26, 27 (1995).
125. On the background of the establishment of the Review of Business Taxation, *see* Paul Kenny, *The 1999 Review of Business Taxation: Should We Fast Track Small Business Tax Reform?*, Revenue L.J. 138, 141-142 (2008).
126. For an overview of the reports, *see* Paul Kenny, *Business Tax Reform Down Under: The 1999 Ralph Report* 6-8 (18 October 2013), https://ssrn.com/abstract=2340891.

One of the recommendations that have been accepted by the Australian government is to provide rollover relief for investors who exchange interests in one company for similar interests in another.[127] Such equity interest exchanges are known as 'scrip-for-scrip transactions', and the rollover relief for them is accordingly termed as 'scrip-for-scrip rollover'.[128] According to the Review of Business Taxation, a reason for introducing the scrip-for-scrip rollover was to remove tax barriers to mergers and takeovers and to facilitate the development of a more efficiently functioning capital market in Australia.[129]

A more significant driving force behind the enactment of the scrip-for-scrip rollover was the desire to bring the Australian tax treatment for stock acquisitions into line with other countries.[130] The Review of Business Taxation stressed the importance of international competitiveness in tax design and devoted one of its four reports to providing information on other countries' taxation systems and international trends in tax reform. In the foreword of the report titled 'An International Perspective', the Review of Business Taxation highlighted the necessity to consider international competitiveness in setting tax policies:[131]

> 'In taxation, as in virtually all areas of economic policy, a small open economy like Australia cannot ignore globalization pressures and their impact on trade and finance. Taxation will often not be the primary factor that drives international investment decisions in a particular direction, but it nevertheless carries considerable weight. If factors relating to international competitiveness are ignored in the redesign of our tax system, we risk a situation where the key aims of the Review, including improving the efficiency of the economy and providing a stable source of revenue, will not be met'.

The strong trend towards allowing tax-deferred corporate restructurings imposes great pressure upon Australia to adopt similar practices. The Review of Business Taxation was worried that the lack of rollover relief rules for scrip-for-scrip transactions hampered the international competitiveness of the Australian taxation system. When illustrating how the enactment of scrip-for-scrip rollover would enhance the international competitiveness of the Australian taxation system, the Review of Business Taxation highlighted a specific benefit: encouraging start-ups and innovative enterprises that consider going public to remain in Australia. In the final report titled 'A Tax System Redesigned', the Review of Business Taxation discussed the risk of start-ups leaving Australia to avoid capital gains tax liabilities arising in connection with IPOs. If in an IPO process, entrepreneurs need to exchange equity interest in the pre-IPO company for interest in the post-IPO company, under the general tax rule, they would be subject to capital gains tax on the scrip-for-scrip transaction. To avoid the potential tax burden, the entrepreneurs would tend to relocate their business to other countries, which could harm Australia's economy. With the scrip-for-scrip rollover, the entrepreneurs could defer paying taxes on the capital gains until they dispose of the

127. Review of Business Taxation, *A Tax System Redesigned* 615 (1999).
128. *Ibid.*
129. Review of Business Taxation, *A Platform for Consultation* 294-295 (1999).
130. *Ibid.*, at 295; *see also* Review of Business Taxation, *A Strong Foundation* 2 (1998).
131. Review of Business Taxation, *An International Perspective* (1998).

interests in the post-IPO company, and thus fewer enterprises would relocate for tax reasons.

Like Australia, China also aspires to build an internationally competitive corporate taxation system. This aspiration is perfectly demonstrated by the design and drafting process of the EITL. For instance, the Chinese lawmakers, after carefully comparing prevailing corporate tax rates in other countries, set the standard corporate income tax rate at 25%, which was internationally competitive. When explaining the draft of the EITL to the NPC in 2007, the then Minister of Finance noted:

> 'The average enterprise income tax rate is 28.6% in 159 countries (regions) around the world, while that in China's 18 neighbouring countries (regions) is 26.7%. The rate of 25% set in the Draft is relatively low in the world and will be conducive to enhancing enterprise competitiveness and attracting foreign investment'.

Apart from the reasons such as path dependence and cost reduction, the strong desire to enhance the competitiveness of the taxation system may also help explain why China has not hesitated to follow suit of other countries in introducing the special tax treatment for M&A transactions.

[B] Problems with China's M&A Taxation System

Although China has made remarkable progress in setting up its M&A taxation system, there are many problems with the tax rules for M&A transactions. Generally speaking, it appears that China has been too willing to import foreign experience, and the lawmakers have simply grafted some foreign experience onto the existing income tax system without thorough digestion. This practice of learning from foreign experiences with little criticism has led to many problems. Indeed, the Chinese policymakers have come to firmly believe that a successful M&A taxation system would be similar to that in developed countries, most notably the US. This belief has adversely affected the rule-making process because it precludes a careful examination of the necessity and effects of transplanting foreign tax rules for M&A transactions.

For this reason, in practice, China's M&A taxation system is far from perfect. The following is a brief description of this aspect, and more detailed discussions will be carried out in the following chapters.

First, the M&A taxation system is still incomplete and has many serious flaws. The issues concerning the essential elements of the taxation of M&A transactions, such as the tax basis adjustment rules and the treatment of tax losses of the target company, are unsettled, and some of them are even left entirely unaddressed. More profoundly, the policymakers seem to be unclear about the rationale and effects of the special tax treatment, which significantly decreases the efficacy of the special tax treatment.

Second, the totality of all the rules related to taxing M&A transactions is mutually conflicting. There are two major reasons behind this. The first one lies in China's uncritical transplantation of foreign laws. The other reason is that some tax provisions for M&A transactions are hasty responses of the central tax authorities to the State Council's order to reform the tax system to promote M&A activities.

CHAPTER 4
Overarching Principle for M&A Taxation

§4.01 INTRODUCTION

Key objectives of this research include assessing China's tax laws for M&A transactions and appraising legal reform proposals for the tax regime. But what are the guiding principles against which the tax rules for M&A transactions - either in effect or under consideration - are measured? Without clearly established principles, a convincing examination of such an incredibly complex system would be impossible.

In the policymaking process and in the scholarly discourse about the taxation of corporate restructurings, Chinese legislators, tax authorities, as well as academics invariably refer to taxation principles, but there lacks a systematic account of them. In many cases, taxation principles are misinterpreted and misapplied. Therefore, this research finds it wise first to examine taxation principles before applying them to appraise any particular M&A tax rules.

This chapter proceeds as follows. Section §4.02 introduces some influential formulations of taxation principles. Section §4.03 scrutinizes the principles picked out in §4.02 to decide whether they are appropriate for guiding policymaking in the context of M&A taxation and highlights tax neutrality as the overarching principle in this regard. Section §4.03 looks at how tax law affects the business and investment decisions of taxpayers, which is the focus of tax neutrality. Section §4.04 provides the concluding remarks.

§4.02 TAXATION PRINCIPLES

The term 'legal principle' is often used in two different senses, one broader and one narrower. In its broader meaning, 'legal principle' refers to the values, normative criteria or even moral standards that underlie an ideal legal system. Professor Lon Fuller's 'principles of legality' are a case in point. In the second chapter of his book, The Morality of Law, Fuller sets out eight principles of what he called the 'inner morality of law'.[1] Those principles, which require that laws be general, public, prospective, clear, coherent, practicable, stable, and congruent with official action, are in essence a list of features of the rule of law.[2] In its narrower meaning, 'legal principle' is more specific. For example, Professor Cass Sunstein uses the term 'principle' to refer to the moral or political justifications behind rules. He mentions one principle – it is wrong to kill a human without sufficient cause.[3] This principle is concretized into a range of rules prohibiting homicide. Overarching principles of tax policy belong to the former group, as they only describe some essential characteristics of a good tax system and do not mandate a specific array of rules as to how to levy taxes.[4]

Principles, even in the narrowest sense, are more general than rules. They have to be general to gain the necessary flexibility for dealing with the points not expressly covered by rules, but the flip side of flexibility is uncertainty. As noted by Professor H.L.A. Hart, 'uncertainty at the borderline is the price to be paid for the use of general classifying terms in any form of communication concerning matters of fact'.[5]

[A] Adam Smith's Four Canons

The study of the policy considerations of modern tax law-making can be traced back to Professor Adam Smith. In his monumental work, An Inquiry into the Nature and Causes of the Wealth of Nations, Smith lays down four taxation principles which he called canons of taxation. They are:[6]

> 'I. The subjects of every state ought to contribute to the support of the government, as nearly as possible, in proportion to their respective abilities; that is, in proportion to the revenue which they respectively enjoy under the protection of the state ... In the observation or neglect of this maxim consists what is called the equality or inequality of taxation ...
>
> 'II. The tax which each individual is bound to pay ought to be certain, and not arbitrary. The time of payment, the manner of payment, the quantity to be paid, ought all to be clear and plain to the contributor and to every other person ...
>
> 'III. Every tax ought to be levied at the time, or in the manner in which it is most likely to be convenient for the contributor to pay it. A tax upon the rent

1. Lon L. Fuller, *The Morality of Law* 42 (rev. ed., 1969).
2. According to Fuller, laws must be general, providing rules applying to all; laws must be publicized to ensure citizens know what are allowed and what are prohibited; laws should be prospective, clarifying how individuals should behave in the future rather than prohibiting behaviours in the part; laws should be promulgated in a clear and non-contradictory manner, so that individuals can be certain that they behave in conformity with the law; laws must neither ask the impossible, nor should they change frequently; and finally there should be congruence between law on books and law in action. *See ibid.*, at 46-90.
3. Cass R. Sunstein, *Problems with Rules*, 83 Cal. L. Rev. 953, 966 (1995).
4. Unless specified, 'taxation principles' in this thesis refers to general principles of tax policy. There are also many specific taxation principles, such as source principle and residence principle in the context of income tax law. However, the line between rules and such kind of principles is blurred. For example, source principle and residence principle are also known as source rule and residence rule.
5. H. L. A. Hart, *The Concept of Law* 128 (3d ed., 2012).
6. 4 Adam Smith, *An Inquiry into the Nature and Causes of the Wealth of Nations* 164-166 (1791).

> of land or of houses, payable at the same term at which such rents are usually paid, is levied at the time when it is most likely to be convenient for the contributor to pay; or, when he is most likely to have wherewithal to pay ...
>
> 'IV. Every tax ought to be so contrived as both to take out and to keep out of the pockets of the people as little as possible over and above what it brings into the public treasury of the state ...'

The four canons or maxims can be summed up as the principle of equity, the principle of certainty, the convenience of payment, and the economy in tax collection. The principle of equity entails that the allocation of tax burdens should reflect the economic ability of taxpayers. The principle of certainty, which excludes arbitrariness in tax rule-making and collection, is an indispensable component of the rule of law.[7] The convenience of payment principle requires the tax authority to adjust itself to facilitate taxpayers' fulfilment of tax obligations. The principle of economy in tax collection means that the government should keep tax administration costs lower than the revenue collected.

[B] OECD Principles

Modern economists have proposed new formulations of taxation principles.[8] This section highlights the one proposed by the Organization for Economic Cooperation and Development (OECD). In October 2015, the OECD published the Addressing the Tax Challenges of the Digital Economy, Action 1 - 2015 Final Report, providing a comprehensive account of Base Erosion and Profit Shifting (BEPS) issues in the digital economy and broader tax challenges raised by the digital economy.[9] Chapter 2 of the report is about the fundamental principles of taxation. Although the principles are provided in the report about tax challenges of the digital economy, the OECD articulates them without specifically referring to the digital economy or electronic commerce; instead, they are treated as the principles guiding the development of taxation systems in general. The OECD principles include equity, neutrality, efficiency, certainty and simplicity, effectiveness and fairness, and flexibility.

The OECD's formulation of taxation principles is highlighted in this research for OECD's great influence. As a club of the most developed economies in the world, the OECD has long been a significant force in harmonizing tax policies across countries, and the latest example is the BEPS project which has changed the global landscape in the fight against tax evasion. The influence of the OECD is also magnified due to its impact on other prominent international organizations such as the WTO, the World Bank and the International Monetary Fund (IMF). Table 4.1 summarizes the OECD's explanation of these principles.

7. The canon of certainty overlaps with Fuller's eight principles that require laws be clear and stable. *See supra* note 2.
8. Clinton Alley and Duncan Bentley enumerated 11 contemporary formulations of tax principles. *See* Clinton Alley & Duncan Bentley, *A Remodelling of Adam Smith's Tax Design Principles*, 20 Australian Tax Forum, 586-588 (2005).
9. OECD, *Addressing the Tax Challenges of the Digital Economy, Action 1 – 2015 Final Report* (2015).

Table 4.1 OECD Principles

	OECD (2015)[10]
Equity	- Equity has two main elements: horizontal equity and vertical equity. - Inter-nation equity is also important.
Certainty and Simplicity	- Tax rules should be clear and simple to understand so that taxpayers know where they stand.
Efficiency	- Compliance costs to business and administration costs for governments should be minimized as far as possible.
Neutrality	- Taxation should seek to be neutral and equitable between forms of business activities. - A neutral tax will contribute to efficiency by ensuring that the optimal allocation of the means of production is achieved. - Same principles of taxation should apply to all forms of business
Effectiveness and Fairness	- Taxation should produce the right amount of tax at the right time while avoiding both double taxation and unintentional non-taxation. - The potential for evasion and avoidance should be minimized
Flexibility	- Taxation systems should be flexible and dynamic enough to ensure they keep pace with technological and commercial developments.

[C] Summary

Some observations can be made on the aforementioned two formulations of taxation principles. First, Adam Smith's canons not only prevailed in the nineteenth century but also hold their ground to contemporary conditions. All of the four canons have been incorporated into the OECD's formulation of principles. However, it is equally true that Adam Smith's canons cannot adequately reflect the social and economic goals of present societies. Adam Smith only emphasized the importance of certainty but neglected the necessity of flexibility – a tax system has to be flexible to keep pace with technological and commercial developments and combat tax evasions and avoidances. Also, Adam Smith did not answer the question of to what extent taxation shall affect the economy.

Second, although the OECD's list of principles is longer than Adam Smith's, their differences are not as profound as it seems. Most noticeably, the OECD's principles contain some redundancy. The principle of effectiveness and fairness requires that laws be designed in such a way that both double taxation and unintentional non-taxation are avoided, and the potential for evasion and avoidance is minimized; the

10. *Ibid.*, at 30-31.

principle of neutrality imposes similar requirements. Moreover, the effectiveness and fairness principle emphasizes that tax rules should be practically enforceable, which overlaps with the convenience of payment principle as well as the economy in tax collection principle. Therefore, it is feasible to combine and refine Smith's and OECD's taxation principles, and the merged formulation of taxation principles is as follows.

Equity

- Equity has two dimensions – horizontal and vertical.
- In the context of international taxation, inter-nation equity needs special attention.

Neutrality

- Tax systems should minimize their impact on a taxpayer's decisions as to whether to engage in a transaction and how to carry out a particular transaction.

Administrability

- Compliance costs to business and administration costs for governments should be minimized as far as possible.

Certainty and Simplicity

- Tax rules should not be arbitrary.
- Tax rules should be clear and simple to understand so that taxpayers know the tax consequences of a transaction.
- Tax rules and their making process should be transparent and visible.

Flexibility

- Tax systems should be flexible and dynamic enough to ensure they keep pace with technological and commercial developments.

Some commentators criticize traditional formulations of tax principles like those discussed above for containing ideas that conflict with each other and assert that the social and economic considerations such as equity should be excluded from tax policy criteria so as to make the efficient collection of revenue the central tenet of taxation. Although the critics correctly point out the inherent contradictions within those formulations, the existence of contradictions is not a compelling reason to abandon the 'traditional tax policy theory'. The function of tax law has been extended far beyond revenue collection, and the art is to strike a balance between differential policy goals.

§4.03 TAXATION PRINCIPLES IN THE CONTEXT OF M&A

Through a formal comparison of existing well-recognized formulations, the previous section has identified several taxation principles that may be pertinent to this research but has not yet inspected their contents. These highlighted taxation principles serve as a starting point for our inquiry into the guiding principles for M&A taxation, and in this section, they will be systematically scrutinized by taking into consideration the special context of the taxation of M&A.

[A] Neutrality and Equity: Two Normative Principles

[1] First and Second Order Principles

In explaining the features of the principles of the rule of law, Professor Robert Summers makes a distinction between what he calls 'first order' and 'second order' principles. First order principles, according to him, are the principles of ordinary first order law. Those principles are identified as 'first' because they apply directly to determine legal relations between subjects of the relevant law.[11] One example of first order principles given by Summers is the well-known maxim of equity law – 'no one should benefit from his own wrong', which can be directly applied to deny a murderer the inheritance from the deceased.[12]

Second order principles, on the contrary, do not directly address specific legal relations. They provide instructions on how first order law, including its rules and relevant first order principles, should be created and implemented.[13] Compared to the first order principles, the second order principles have two key features. First, they have a much broader application scope that covers all the components of a legal system.[14] Second, they are formal rather than substantive. While first order principles provide substantive values, second order principles serve those values indirectly through first order principles.[15]

Inspired by the classification method of Summers, this research divides the taxation principles highlighted by the previous section into two groups: (1) first order taxation principles; and (2) second order taxation principles.

The first group includes principles of equity, neutrality, and administrability. These principles contain substantive criteria that tax design should follow. For instance, the principle of equity mandates a progressive tax schedule,[16] the principle of neutrality requires taxing income from various sources in the same manner, and the principle of administrability refrains the law from taxing a mere accretion in the value of assets. These principles can, at least in academic discussion, be applied directly to address specific tax issues.

The second group includes the principles of certainty and simplicity, as well as the principle of flexibility. Those principles enjoy a vast application scope. Take the principle of certainty as an example. All tax provisions are expected to abide by the principle of certainty and must not be arbitrary. The principles in the second group

---

11. Robert S. Summers, *The Principles of the Rule of Law*, 74 Notre Dame L. Rev. 1691, 1692 (1999).
12. *Ibid.*
13. *Ibid.*
14. *Ibid.*, at 1697-1701.
15. *Ibid.*, at 1701-1703.
16. This statement is based on the popular perception of vertical equity. For detailed discussion of the principle of vertical equity, see § 4.03[C][2] below.

provide minimal instructions as to the substantive matters in tax design, such as who is liable for taxes and how much the taxpayer should pay. In other words, those principles are formal and only address the manner in which tax law should be promulgated and how the tax law should be shaped. Because those principles are formal, whether they are compatible with a particular tax provision does not depend on the substantive content of that provision. They can even be satisfied by two tax provisions with contrasting substantive contents yet addressing the same issue. The choice between source-based and residence-based taxation is a case in point. An income tax system that is premised on the source rule and its counterpart that adopts the residence rule may both satisfy the principle of simplicity.

In fact, the second group principles are not specific to tax law. Most members of the legal community would agree that rules in all areas of law should be certain, simple, and flexible.[17] Those values are the components of the rule of law.[18] As this research is investigating a particular topic of taxation and is concerned more about substantive issues in designing tax provisions, the principles in the second group seem to be too general and formal, and the first group of principles, i.e., equity, neutrality, and administrability, are more pertinent.[19]

[2] Normative Principles and Pragmatic Concern

The first order taxation principles can be further divided into two subcategories, one containing the principles that constitute the normative foundation of tax rules and the other containing the principles that are in essence pragmatic concerns. The former subcategory includes the principles of equity and neutrality that describe the attributes of an ideal tax. Administrability, which reflects the compromise between ideal and practical measures, falls into the latter subcategory. Equity and neutrality in many cases have to give way to administrability to reach a practically workable tax system; however, administrability as merely a pragmatic concern should never be the starting point in tax design.

Another factor disqualifying administrability as an essential normative principle is that it does not impose a static requirement. The weight of administrability concern hinges on the government's administrative capacity. Where the government's administrative capacity develops over time with ever-increasing technological assistance, the need to make compromises to the principles of equity and neutrality is diminishing. The development of China's tax system perfectly illustrates this point.

China used to have weak tax administration, and as a result, it relied heavily on easy-administered taxes such as VAT. In 2012, 26.2% of China's total tax revenue came

17. Legal principles always compete with each other and the key is to strike a balance between them. This observation is best exemplified by the case of certainty and flexibility. Each of the two may prevail over the other, depending on the circumstances.
18. For example, that laws should be certain and simple is provided in Fuller's 'principles of legality', *see* Fuller, *supra* note 1, at 46-90. Roscoe Pound emphasizes that the legal order must be flexible as well as stable, *see* Roscoe Pound, *Interpretations of Legal History* 1-2 (1923).
19. This assertion coincides with some scholars' views on the goals of taxation. *See e.g.*, Reuven S. Avi-Yonah, *The Three Goals of Taxation*, 60 Tax L. Rev. 1, 1-4 (2006).

from the VAT, while only 5.8% came from individual income tax. By comparison, the OECD average of the VAT as a percentage of total taxation was 20% in 2012, compared with 25% for the individual income tax.[20] The concern over administrability held China back from replacing its schedular individual income tax system with a global system that better reflects people's ability to pay.[21] As the tax administration capacity improves, the administrability concern is decreasing in importance, and China has started modernizing its individual income tax system. In 2013, the Third Plenary Session of the eighteenth Central Committee of the CPC announced a plan to establish an individual income tax system that combines elements of both global and schedular systems.[22] On 31 August 2018, the SCNPC approved an amendment to the IITL, which features the combination of four income categories that are subject to different tax rates under previous law into a unified category of comprehensive income,[23] marking a significant step towards the global tax system.

To summarize, it is fair to say that equity and neutrality are more relevant to the design of substantive rules for taxing M&A transactions. The following subsections will provide a thorough examination of these two taxation principles.

[B] Principle of Neutrality

Neutrality means that taxation should refrain from interfering with the market mechanism and hence treat different forms of business activities in a non-partial way. This principle relies on the classic assumption of an efficient market; that is, the actors in the market are rational and can deploy resources to meet their ordered preferences most efficiently. A neutral tax that does not alter the decisions of economic actors preserves the efficient functioning of the market, while a non-neutral tax prevents the market from functioning efficiently. Influenced by a non-neutral tax, relative prices change, which then alters market players' economic behaviour. With market players substituting more efficient choices for less-efficient ones, total social wealth reduces and creates deadweight loss.[24]

As pointed out by the OECD, neutrality requires not only an unbiased implementation of tax rules but also an equal application of taxation principles to all forms of business in the same manner.[25] In this sense, neutrality is a fundamental meta-principle – a principle about the implementation of other principles. Due to the tax

20. OECD, *Revenue Statistics 1965-2013* (2014).
21. For a discussion of schedular and global systems and China's latest individual income tax reform, *see* notes 112-117 below and accompanying texts.
22. CPC Central Committee, *Zhonggong Zhongyang Guanyu Quanmian Shenhua Gaige Ruogan Zhongda Wenti de Jueding [Decision of the CPC Central Committee on Some Major Issues Concerning Comprehensively Deepening the Reform]* (12 November 2013), para. 18.
23. IITL, Art. 2.
24. *See* Harvey S. Rosen & Ted Gayer, *Public Finance* 329-336 (9th ed., 2010).
25. OECD, *supra* note 9, at 30.

challenges brought about by electronic commerce, in recent years, neutrality has been more and more cherished by countries and international organizations.[26]

[1] Two Faces of Neutrality

For an income tax system to be entirely neutral, it should equalize the tax treatment of income from different sources. The only way to achieve this is to broaden the tax base to ensure that all gains and benefits are subject to tax. Therefore, neutrality calls for a comprehensive definition of income. The Haig-Simons income concept[27], which postulates that income is the sum of consumption expenditure and an increase in wealth over a period, is widely recognized as the most comprehensive model to determine one's income and the model that best conforms to the principle of neutrality.[28]

Despite the fact that the Haig-Simons model can eliminate distortions between different income-generating activities, Professor Douglas Kahn treats the Haig-Simons standard and the no distortion requirement as two faces of income tax neutrality.[29] In his opinion, the most common usage or the first face of income tax neutrality refers to tax provisions that conform to the Haig-Simons model,[30] and the second face of income tax neutrality describes tax provisions that do not induce a taxpayer to choose one investment over another.[31]

Kahn's differentiation is of limited help in the context of tax design from scratch because an income tax system free from distortions is certainly the one that adopts the Haig-Simons concept. However, from a tax reform perspective, Kahn's differentiation is crucial.[32] In line with the two faces of neutrality, there are two possible ways to address biases already caused by a tax system: one is to improve the conformity between the existing tax system and the Haig-Simons model, and the other is to adopt adjustments that neutralize biases. There could be a conflict between the two approaches of seeking neutrality since an adjustment for removing a bias can either move the tax system towards or away from the Haig-Simons model.

Kahn's differentiation provides an analytical framework for further study. We can assess the tax rules for M&A transactions against two different benchmarks, each of which corresponds to one face of the income tax neutrality. Where the assessments

---

26. For a detailed account of how neutrality is cherished by countries and international organizations, *see* Alley & Bentley, *supra* note 8, at 592-596.
27. In recent decades, some English-writing scholars have recognized Georg von Schanz, a German legal scholar, as the first one defining income in terms of wealth accrual. Therefore, the Haig-Simons model is also known as the Schanz-Haig-Simons Model. See *e.g.*, Kevin Holmes, *The Concept of Income: A Multi-Disciplinary Analysis* 57 (2001).
28. *Ibid.*, at 82.
29. Douglas A. Kahn, *The Two Faces of Tax Neutrality: Do They Interact or Are They Mutually Exclusive* 18 N. Ky. L. Rev. 1, 1, 11 (1990).
30. *Ibid.*, at 1.
31. *Ibid.*, at 11.
32. Tax design measures and tax reform measures are different. *See* Martin Feldstein, *Compensation in Tax Reform*, 29 National Tax Journal 123, 123-124 (1976). ('the optimal reform of an existing tax system differs from the optimal design of a new tax structure')

against these two benchmarks lead to divergent results, we will have to decide between different options for reforming the law.

[2] Neutrality and Efficiency

In the school of law and economics, it has been the prevailing view that legal rules should be designed to achieve economic efficiency, i.e., the situation where the allocation of resources in society has reached the highest possible level of utility.[33] Influenced by this thought, some tax theorists enshrine efficiency as the fundamental standard applied to the structural details of the income tax law.[34] Although many others do not share this extreme opinion, one can hardly deny efficiency as an essential consideration in tax policy.[35] For some commentators, efficiency, along with equity and administrability, constitute the three grounds for evaluating tax policy.[36]

Efficiency, as used in the literature of law and economics, is to a large extent interchangeable with neutrality. The OECD explains the benefits of a neutral tax by reference to efficiency: 'a neutral tax will contribute to efficiency by ensuring that optimal allocation of the means of production is achieved'.[37] When examining a tax law from the perspective of efficiency, scholars usually ask whether the law causes distortions that affect the efficient allocation of resources[38] but seldom differentiate the objectives of efficiency and neutrality.

Nevertheless, this book prefers to use neutrality rather than efficiency in the discourse of M&A taxation. Efficiency is a complex, multifaceted concept with many other meanings and interpretations that might be confused with 'economic efficiency'.[39] For instance, in everyday language, efficiency refers to the quality of 'achieving maximum productivity with minimum wasted effort or expense',[40] and this common usage of 'efficiency' has been adopted by the OECD in articulating its formulation of tax principles.[41] Even if one restricts the usage of 'efficiency' to the context of economics, confusion over its nuanced interpretations is still unresolved as

33. In this sense, economic efficiency is also termed as allocative efficiency. *See* David W. Pearce (ed.), *Economic efficiency, The MIT Dictionary of Modern Economics* (4th ed., 1992).
34. Boris Bittker pointed out a paradigm shift in tax discourse – efficiency was replacing equity as the standard for assessing the income tax. *See* Boris Bittker, *Equity, Efficiency, and Income Tax Theory: Do Misallocations Drive Out Inequities?*, 16 San Diego L. Rev. 735, 735-738 (1979).
35. *See e.g.*, Alex Raskolnikov, *Accepting the Limits of Tax Law and Economics*, 98 Cornell L. Rev. 523, 524-529 (2012).
36. *See e.g.*, Avi-Yonah, *supra* note 19, at 1-4.
37. OECD, *supra* note 9, at 30.
38. For example, Joseph Bankman and David Weisbach compared the relative distortions of an income tax and those of a consumption tax and concluded that the consumption tax better serves the objective of efficiency. *See* Joseph Bankman & David A. Weisbach, *The Superiority of an Ideal Consumption Tax Over an Ideal Income Tax*, 58 Stan. L. Rev. 1413, 1420-1421 (2005).
39. *See* Holley H. Ulbrich, *Public Finance in Theory and Practice* 163-164 (2nd ed., 2011).
40. John Adrew Simpson and Eva S. Weiner, *Efficiency, Oxford English Dictionary* (2nd ed., 1989).
41. OECD, *supra* note 9, at 30.

economists have defined economic efficiency in various ways.[42] In contrast, there is a consensus on the meaning of neutrality.

[3] Neutrality and Economic Growth

Economic growth is a primary policy objective of most governments, which is more proactive than neutrality in the sense that it dictates a tax system to take an active role in promoting economic development. In the pursuit of this objective, governments often use tax as an instrument to guide business activities or implement their industrial policies. For instance, many countries rolled out tax incentives such as the increased deduction for R&D costs and accelerated depreciation for high-tech equipment investment to encourage technological innovation.[43]

It is apparent that the notion of using tax policy as a tool of economic progress runs squarely against the principle of tax neutrality. Take China's preferential tax rate for the high-tech industry as an example. In order to encourage technological innovation, China has slashed the corporate income tax rate for high-tech enterprises from the standard rate of 25% to 15%.[44] This preferential tax treatment violates the principle of neutrality as it influences the investment choice of market players. With the tax rate reduction, the after-tax yield rate of investment in the high-tech industry is likely to be higher than that of investment in other industries, and thus more capital would flow into the high-tech industry.

In this particular case, the violation of tax neutrality is justifiable on the ground of economic efficiency. The normative force behind tax neutrality stems from the idea that a non-distortive tax does not restrict the market from efficiently allocating resources. Where the market mechanism is defective, corrective tax policies become desirable. Pigouvian subsidies to technological innovation are a case in point. Innovators produce knowledge spillovers to the rest of the economy, but they cannot get fully compensated through the market mechanism,[45] which leads to a positive externality –

---

42. Pareto efficiency and Kaldor-Hicks efficiency are the two most frequently used criteria for economic efficiency. Pareto efficiency is also called Pareto optimality, and it refers to a social state where it is no longer possible to improve the situation for one person without making anyone else worse off. The action that changes the resources allocation to benefit at least one person while harming no one else is called Pareto improvement. Unlike Pareto efficiency, which objects the deterioration in the welfare of every individual, Kaldor-Hicks efficiency is less stringent as it only requires the increase of the aggregate interests of all the persons in a society. All Kaldor-Hicks efficient scenarios are Pareto optimal since Pareto improvement is impossible in these situations, but the reverse does not hold. *See* Uwe E. Reinhardt, *Reflections on the Meaning of Efficiency: Can Efficiency Be Separated from Equity?*, 10 Yale L. & Pol'y Rev. 302, 306-314 (1992).
43. For an international comparison of tax incentives for R&D, *see* Silvia Appelt, et al., *R&D Tax Incentives: Evidence on Design, Incidence and Impacts*, OECD Science, Technology and Industry Policy Papers, No. 32, 22-23, 39-44 (2016).
44. EITL, Art. 28.
45. *See* Michael J. Graetz & Rachael Doud, *Technological Innovation, International Competition, and the Challenges of International Income Taxation*, 113 Colum. L. Rev. 347, 349-350 (2013).

a typical example of market failure. By providing Pigouvian subsidies to innovators, the economic inefficiency caused by the positive externality would be reduced.[46]

However, if there is no market failure, violating tax neutrality to pursue economic goals is hardly justifiable. One example is tax-exempt government bonds. Under the Chinese tax law, interest income from the bonds issued by the central and local governments is exempted from tax, while interest income from corporate bonds is taxable.[47] One rationale behind this is to let the government, especially local government, finance projects that are believed to be of benefit to the economy at a lower cost. Despite the good intention, this tax policy is likely to be counterproductive. Because of the tax exemption, a government bond that has a relatively low interest rate can produce the same after-tax return as a corporate bond that has a higher interest rate. Provided that the two bonds have the same risk, they will be equally attractive to an investor, and as a result, the tax exemption will divert funds that should have flowed to the taxable bond-financed projects with higher economic productivity to those financed by the tax-exempt bond, resulting in an economic efficiency loss.[48]

Economic growth is unsuitable as a taxation principle, especially in a country like China. Although China's transition to a market economy has been quite successful during the last four decades, the legacy of the planned economy is still influential. When skimming through the EITL and tax circulars regarding the enterprise income tax or taking a look back at the history of the Chinese corporate income tax system, one can easily sense the Chinese government's constant emphasis on the regulatory function of taxation – there have been numerous tax incentives for various types of economic activities. This excessive use of tax incentives has received criticisms from both academia and from inside the government,[49] and it has been observed that in very few cases, the government successfully uses tax incentives to achieve its desired economic goals.[50]

The principle of tax neutrality, on the contrary, helps prevent the government from arbitrarily exercising its power to intervene in the market by mandating that the tax law must minimize its effects on a taxpayer's decisions regarding whether to

46. Although tax incentives for R&D are justifiable, it does not mean that such tax incentives can be granted without limitation. The optimal tax incentive should just compensate the innovator for the marginal positive externality produced by its activities. *See* Noam Noked, *Integrated Tax Policy Approach to Designing Research & Development Tax Benefits*, 34 Va. Tax Rev. 109, 141 (2014).
47. EITL, Art. 26(21); (exempting corporate income taxes on interest income from central government bonds) IITL, Art. 4(2); (exempting individual income taxes on interest income from central government bonds); Caishui (2011) No. 76, Guanyu Difang Zhengfu Zhaiquan Lixi Suode Mianzheng Suodeshui Wenti de Tongzhi [Notice Concerning the Exemption of Tax on Interest Income from Local Government Bonds] (promulgated by the MOF and the STA and effective 26 August 2011) (PRC) (exempting individual and corporate income taxes on interest income from local government bonds).
48. Boris Bittker has provided an in-depth analysis on how tax-free government bonds hamper economic efficiency. *See* Bittker, *supra* note 34, at 739-740.
49. *See e.g.*, Zongtao Wang, *The Regulation of Tax Incentives in China*, 23 Henan Shehui Kexue [Henan Social Sciences] 52, 54-55 (2015).
50. *See e.g.*, Dahong Liu & Jianhui Zhang, *Neutrality and the Regulatory Function of Taxation*, Zhongnan Caijing Zhengfa Daxue Xuebao [Journal of Zhongnan University of Finance and Economics], no. 4, 2002, at 94, 99.

engage in a particular behaviour or how to behave. In this respect, tax neutrality is of some constitutional significance as it implies minimum interference with individual decisions.

Even if government intervention in the market is necessary, tax law may not be the best approach to implement it. During the past several decades, there has been heated debate over the effectiveness of using tax policy to achieve economic objectives. The school of tax expenditure analysis[51] argues that compared to direct spending, providing tax incentives is a poor means of achieving public policy.[52] In spite of the challenges faced with the theory of tax expenditure,[53] it is now a consensus that the government should prudently use tax incentives.

Although every real-world income tax system violates the principle of tax neutrality for various economic, social and political reasons, tax policy should be as neutral as possible unless there exists a strong reason for a departure from tax neutrality. This observation is especially important in the context of M&A taxation, which centres on the issue of how to properly tax various forms of M&A transactions. The principle of tax neutrality, no doubt, should be regarded as an overarching principle in this area of tax law.

[C] Principle of Equity

The idea of equity or fairness is hard to define. What is or is not considered fair depends on the status of those being affected by a decision, and it is common that a rule is fair in the eyes of some people but unfair in the eyes of others. The OECD uses the term 'fairness' in the sense that a tax system should prevent tax evasion to avoid being perceived as unfair by the public.[54] As observed by James Wetzler, 'fairness is a question largely of perception: a tax system is fair when taxpayers believe that their tax burdens are not out of line with their situations and to burdens imposed on other taxpayers'.[55]

However, in spite of the difficulty in defining equity, scholars generally accept that there are two dimensions to the notion – horizontal and vertical. Horizontal equity

---

51. Stanley S. Surrey creates the term 'tax expenditure' to describe those government expenditures made through the tax system by providing tax deductions, tax credits, etc. Under the tax expenditure analysis, those various tax incentives are treated as substitutes for direct spending of the government. *See* Stanley S. Surrey, *Tax Incentives as a Device for Implementing Government Policy: A Comparison with Direct Government Expenditures*, 83 Harv. L. Rev. 705, 706 (1969).
52. *Ibid.*, at 727-34 (noting that tax expenditures complicate the consideration of government programmes and the tax system).
53. For example, Edward Zelinsky points out that one advantage of tax expenditure over direct expenditure is that it permits the dissemination of government policies at a lower transactions cost. *See* Edward A. Zelinsky, *Efficiency and Income Taxes: The Rehabilitation of Tax Incentives*, 64 Tex. L. Rev. 973, 1010-1012 (1986).
54. OECD, *supra* note 9, at 31.
55. James W. Wetzler, *The Role of Fairness in State Tax Policy*, 47 Rec. Ass'n B. City N.Y. 38, 39 (1992).

means that people in the same positions pay the same amount of tax, and vertical equity refers to people in different positions paying different amounts of tax.

[1] Horizontal Equity

Horizontal equity has multiple definitions. The simplest one is that equals should be taxed equally.[56] Another common definition of the term is that the law should treat taxpayers with the same income equally.[57] These two definitions are interpretations of horizontal equity at different levels. Apart from them, there exist two other levels of interpretations of the principle. This subsection examines horizontal equity by looking at the four different levels of interpretations of it.

[a] First Level Interpretation: Equals Treated Equally

The strongest criticism of horizontal equity is that it is a hollow concept. Professor Richard Musgrave is probably the first one to criticize the notion of horizontal equity as having no independent content. In his monograph published in 1959, he argues that horizontal equity and vertical equity are different sides of the same coin, and both of them have no independent content as they are dependent upon an objective index for distinguishing equals from unequals.[58] Without identifying such an objective index, discussion about equity leads nowhere.

Professor Peter Westen has fully explored the issue of whether horizontal equity has independent content. In a richly referenced article, Westen adopts a logical analysis of equality and argues that equality is an 'empty idea' and 'should be banished from moral and legal discourse as an explanatory norm'.[59] His argument focuses on Aristotle's classical formula of equality – things that are alike should be treated alike, which is in essence the first level interpretation of horizontal equity (as defined in this subsection).

Westen divides Aristotle's formula into two components, with the first component being the determination of who are alike, the second component being exploring how to treat similar people alike. Since no two people are alike in every aspect and all people are alike in some respects, Westen posits that the concept of equality is meaningful only if its first component deals with 'people who are morally alike in a certain respect'. As a result, the concept of equality will be rendered tautological – 'people who by a rule should be treated alike should by the rule be treated alike',[60] and as a logical truth, the idea of equality is empty and meaningless.

56. *See* Louis Kaplow, *Horizontal Equity: Measures in Search of a Principle*, 42 National Tax Journal 139, 139 (1989); Richard A. Musgrave, *Horizontal Equity, Once More*, 43 National Tax Journal 113, 113 (1990).
57. *See* Holmes, *supra* note 27, at 19.
58. Richard A. Musgrave, *The Theory of Public Finance: A Study in Public Economy* 160-161 (1959).
59. Peter Westen, *The Empty Idea of Equality*, 95 Harv. L. Rev. 537, 542 (1982).
60. *Ibid.*, at 543-48.

The argument on the emptiness of equality is so strong that many critics have to get around it and challenge the analysis approach taken by Westen.[61] The sharpest critique comes from Professor Steven Burton. He argues that if one follows Westen's logical positivist approach of analysis to scrutinize legal principles and norms, all of them will inevitably be hollow.[62] However, Westen does not push his argument that far. After declaring equality as an empty idea, he tries to find a concrete logical basis for the notion. Westen argues that equality is a derivation from substantive rights, which have independent content and 'can be described without reference to a person's relationship to other right holders',[63] and accordingly, equality is a requirement that people who satisfy the criteria for a governing rule of treatment should be deemed as equals and be treated equally.[64]

Burton further points out that if Westen consistently applied his logical positivist approach, he would conclude that substantive rights, like equality, depend on unspecified values outside themselves and lack independent content.[65] Burton is right in that legal reasoning is analogical and substantive rights need to be determined by comparison,[66] but he exaggerates the danger of Westen's approach of analysis. Burton's belief that one can replicate Westen's analysis to assert the emptiness of all legal norms is to a large extent fallacious. He neglects a critical difference between equality and legal rules: legal rules do have content, even though the content is not independent; equality, on the other hand, has no content at all.

Despite the emptiness of equality, academics generally refuse to extirpate equality from the moral and legal discourse. Burton claims that equality may be meaningless under philosophical investigations but is valuable as a thought instrument. In his words, equality has been 'central, even essential, to much that we consider progress over the centuries. We may on that ground alone treat both ideas as pragmatically valuable instruments of thought and argument. At least for non-philosophers, this is a fact of life'.[67] Some other scholars see equality as a meaningful deterrence against arbitrary government decisions. Professor Kent Greenawalt claims that equality possesses the moral power which 'exerts a significant pull against unequal benefits or burdens',[68] and according to Professor Erwin Chemerinsky, equality requires the government to communicate the rationale for treating people differently and is helpful in ensuring even-handed law enforcement.[69]

61. *See e.g.*, Kent Greenawalt, *How Empty Is the Idea of Equality?*, 83 Colum. L. Rev. 1167(1983); (arguing that Westen improperly constrict the range of the principle of equality) Erwin Chemerinsky, *In Defense of Equality: A Reply to Professor Westen*, 81 Mich. L. Rev. 575(1983) (claiming that Westen's approach of trashing legal and philosophical principles is dangerous).
62. Steven J. Burton, *Comment on 'Empty Ideas': Logical Positivist Analyses of Equality and Rules*, 91 Yale L.J. 1136, 1147-1150 (1982).
63. Westen, *supra* note 59, at 551.
64. *Ibid.*, at 548-49.
65. Burton, *supra* note 62, at 1140-1147.
66. *Ibid.*, at 1143.
67. *Ibid.*, at 1152.
68. Greenawalt, *supra* note 61, at 1170-1173.
69. Chemerinsky, *supra* note 61, at 581, 588.

Those assertions in support of equality, although they reveal some positive effects accrued in the practical usage of the notion of 'equality', do not stand rigorous scrutiny. Burton has in effect negated equality as a normative principle, and other scholars make a paradoxical argument that equality lacks normative content but can operate as a deterrence regardless. To function as deterrence against arbitrariness, equality shall at least provide basic criteria for determining who equals are, but unfortunately, such criteria do not exist. Therefore, equality or the first interpretation of horizontal equity is of limited help not only for guiding the taxation of M&A transactions but also for evaluating other tax rules.

[b] Second Level Interpretation: Equal Income, Equal Tax

Influenced by Westen, some later scholars stress that the normative problem of horizontal equity lies in the selection of a set of 'normatively appropriate variables' to define individuals as equals.[70] An example of the variable is the health condition of a person. Shall we consider people's health when determining if they are equals? The answer depends on the redistributive policy adopted.[71] Under prevailing tax theories, taxpayers with the same ability to pay, i.e., the same capacity to bear the tax burden, are deemed equals.[72]

Many countries such as Spain, Germany, and Italy have accepted the ability to pay a constitutional principle.[73] In China, although the ability to pay principle is not explicitly included in the Constitution, it is arguably inherent in the constitutional requirements that 'all citizens are equal before the law'[74] and that the 'state respects and preserves human rights'.[75] Lots of Chinese scholars contend that the ability to pay should be regarded as a fundamental principle of China's tax system.[76]

The ability to pay is expected to infuse horizontal equity with normative contents, but the principle itself suffers the problem of emptiness.[77] The principle involves the assumption that there is a standard according to which one can choose the tax base that properly reflects people's abilities. However, there has never been a

70. Roberto Galbiati & Pietro Vertova, *Horizontal Equity*, 75 Economica 384, 388 (2008).
71. *Ibid.*, at 386.
72. Stephen Utz, *Ability to Pay*, 23 Whittier L. Rev. 867, 867-868 (2001). Unlike the benefit principle, which treats tax as a return for the service rendered by government, the ability to pay requires the allocation of tax burdens in accordance with one's ability to bear the sacrifice of well-being. *See* Joel Slemrod & Jon Bakija, *Taxing Ourselves: A Citizen's Guide to the Debate over Taxes* 64-65 (4th ed., 2008). For an account of the origin and development of the ability to pay, *see* Alfred G. Buehler, *Ability to Pay*, 1 Tax L. Rev. 243(1945).
73. Frans Vanistendael, *Legal Framework for Taxation*, *in* 1 *Tax Law Design and Drafting* 15, 22-23 (Victor Thuronyi ed., 1996).
74. Zhonghua Renmin Gongheguo Xian Fa [Constitution of the People's Republic of China] (promulgated and effective on 4 December 1982, amended in 1988, 1993, 1999, 2004 and 2018) (PRC) (hereinafter China's Constitution), Art. 33(32).
75. China's Constitution, Art. 33(33).
76. *See e.g.* Duoqi Xu, *On the Ability to Pay Principle of Taxation*, Zhongguo Faxue [China Legal Science], no. 5, 2013, at 65, 70; Zhengwen Shi, *Distributive Justice and Individual Income Tax Law Reform*, Zhongguo Faxue [China Legal Science], no. 5, 2011, at 32, 32.
77. Slemrod & Bakija, *supra* note 72, at 65-66.

consensus on such a standard. Well-being appears to be optimal for measuring the ability to pay because it comprehensively covers various characteristics of a person.[78] However, well-being is not measurable in most cases, as it is essentially a subjective notion that closely relates to the degree of one's psychological satisfaction – a depressed millionaire is arguably in a worse situation than a happy middle-class in well-being terms.[79]

To tackle the problem of subjectivity, some scholars try to ascertain some objective indicators of the ability to pay. For instance, Victor Thuronyi argues for a monetized tax base because 'taxes are paid in money and tax equity is, therefore, appropriately based on monetary factors or on observable factors that can be translated into money'.[80]

In the context of income tax, the notion of 'income' serves as a surrogate of well-being. Thus, the second interpretation of horizontal equity can be derived – taxpayers with the same income should pay equal taxes. In contrast to the first interpretation, the second one gains normative contents by referring to 'income', but this interpretation is also unworkable since 'income' is a vague term to be defined.

[c] Third Level Interpretation: Equal Haig-Simons Income, Equal Tax

Scholars have advanced many definitions of income, some of which limit income to consumption expenditure and exclude capital gains. There has been a wealth of literature debating the choice between consumption and other definitions of income as the tax base, and both of them have been argued as better reflecting one's ability to pay. The most well-known consumption tax model is the one proposed by Professor Irving Fisher. Fisher defines one's income as 'the total flow of services yielded to him from his property' and thus excludes savings from the scope of income.[81] According to him, savings are 'merely a present expression or reflection of future income.'[82]

Unlike Fisher's model, the Haig-Simons concept of income tries to bring all items representing one's economic power under the umbrella of income. According to Haig, 'income is the money value of the net accretion to one's economic power between two points of time.'[83] Simons further defined personal income as 'the algebraic sum of (1) the market value of rights exercised in consumption and (2) the change in the value of the store of property rights between the beginning and end of the period in question'.[84]

78. Holmes, *supra* note 27, at 9-10.
79. *Ibid.*, at 8.
80. Victor Thuronyi, *The Concept of Income*, 46 Tax L. Rev. 45, 56 (1990).
81. Irving Fisher, *The Nature of Capital and Income* 101 (1906).
82. Irving Fisher, *Are Savings Income?*, 9 American Economic Association Quarterly 21, 34 (1908).
83. Robert Murray Haig, *The Concept of Income-Economic and Legal Aspects*, *in The Federal Income Tax* 1, 7 (Robert Murray Haig ed., 1921) (emphasis omitted).
84. Henry C. Simons, *Personal Income Taxation: The Definition of Income as a Problem of Fiscal Policy* 50 (1938).

In other words, under the Haig-Simons formula, income is 'the sum of consumption and the change in value of property'.[85]

The Haig-Simons definition of income is generally considered by most tax scholars to be the ideal definition of income.[86] Compared to other theories of income, the Haig-Simons income definition, to the highest possible extent, encompasses all economic gains that we can measure with objectivity. If one chooses the Haig-Simons concept as the tax base, there emerges the third level interpretation of horizontal equity, that is, two people with equal Haig-Simons income should pay the same tax.

It is evident that the third interpretation of horizontal equity has a close link to the first face of tax neutrality, which also calls for a tax system based on the Haig-Simons model. A tax provision that defies either the third interpretation of horizontal equity or the first face of tax neutrality would deviate from the Haig-Simons model and thus violates the other. That is to say, the third interpretation of horizontal equity can be subsumed under the first face of tax neutrality.

[d] Fourth Level Interpretation: Equal Income under Current Law, Equal Tax

An income tax system in the real world usually deviates from the theoretically optimal Haig-Simons model by a large margin. If horizontal equity is to be applied in a real-world setting, the current law has to be relied on for identifying equals. According to the literature on tax expenditure analysis, tax provisions generally fall into two categories: the first category consists of tax provisions that are structurally necessary for the implementation of a 'normal income tax';[87] and tax provisions in the second category are departures from the normal income tax structure.[88] Based on this classification, the fourth level interpretation of horizontal equity is that people with the same income, according to the first category provisions, should pay equal tax. Although scholars usually adopt this interpretation to examine the second category provisions that favour a particular activity or class of taxpayers,[89] it is questionable to what extent this interpretation of horizontal equity is useful for such purposes.

Considering the influence of the market mechanism on the allocation of resources, the fact that people with equal before-tax income pay different taxes may

85. David J. Shakow, *Taxation without Realization: A Proposal for Accrual Taxation*, 134 U. Pa. L. Rev. 1111, 1114 (1986).
86. Christopher H. Hanna, *Tax Theories and Tax Reform*, 59 SMU L. Rev. 435, 436 (2006).
87. *See* Stanley S. Surrey & Paul R. McDaniel, *The Tax Expenditure Concept: Current Developments and Emerging Issues*, 20 B.C. L. Rev. 225, 227-228 (1978). According to Surrey and McDaniel, these structural provisions include 'the definition of net income; the specification of accounting periods; the determination of the entities subject to tax; and the specification of the rate schedule and exemption levels'.
88. *Ibid.*, at 228. ('The second element consists of the special preferences found in every income tax system.')
89. For example, according to Surrey and McDaniel, 'not only are the tax expenditure provisions the primary cause of tax inequity, but it seems safe to say that the provisions do not even achieve what most Americans would perceive to be a fair distribution of funds, measured by criteria applied to direct spending programmes'. *Ibid.*, at 255.

misleadingly reflect inequity.[90] Due to the impact of taxes on profits, an investor should generally be willing to pay a higher price for a tax-favoured activity than for its economically similar tax-disfavoured alternative, and therefore the before-tax yield of the tax-favoured activity would usually be lower than that of its disfavoured alternative.[91] The difference depends on the relative elasticity of demand and supply.

If the supply is very inelastic, that is, the supply of activities available for purchase increases slightly due to the relatively high price that the purchaser enjoying the tax preference can afford, the aforementioned difference will be equal to the amount of the tax preference, and thus the tax-favoured activity will produce the same after-tax yield as its disfavoured alternative. In such a case, it looks like the purchasers of tax-favoured activities enjoy extra tax benefits than similarly situated taxpayers who do not purchase them, but the former purchasers are not better off than the latter because the expected tax benefit has been wholly capitalized into the price of the tax-favoured activity.[92] Put differently, the purchasers of tax-favoured activities pay the entire tax benefit as an 'implicit tax' to the suppliers.[93]

Tax benefits may be capitalized fully, partially, or not at all, and it is difficult to accurately determine whether or to what extent a tax preference affects the income of taxpayers.[94] Hence, the fourth interpretation of horizontal equity is unworkable because its criteria for identifying equals are unreliable. This observation is crucial for the discussion of the taxation of M&A transactions. For instance, in a tax-deferred stock acquisition, the target shareholders can enjoy a tax deferral on the exchange of their stock in the target company for the stock of the purchasing company.[95] This special tax treatment is no doubt a departure from the 'normal income tax' that demands one to pay current tax on gains from a stock transfer,[96] and on the surface, it violates horizontal equity as in the same transaction, a seller receiving equity consideration obtains extra tax benefits than a similarly situated seller who receives cash. However, this assertion does not bear scrutiny. The tax deferral benefits are likely to be capitalized into the price of the stock of the purchasing company. In such circumstances, a seller receiving equity consideration from the purchasing company pays an implicit tax, and the difference between the after-tax income of this seller and that of a seller receiving cash is not as significant as expected or even non-existent.

90. Slemrod & Bakija, *supra* note 72, at 90-91.
91. Scholars provide various examples to illustrate the effect of a tax allowance on the price of the tax-preferred activity. A businessman who can deduct the cost of buying a piece of equipment may bid a higher price for the equipment than his competitors who cannot claim deductions, *see* Charlotte Crane, *Some Explicit Thinking about Implicit Taxes*, 52 SMU L. Rev. 339, 340-345 (1999). An investor the bond market is willing to pay more for a tax-exempt bond than for a taxable bond or accept a lower interest rate on the tax-exempt bond, *see* David A. Weisbach, *Implications of Implicit Taxes*, 52 SMU Law Review 373, 374 (1999). People may accept lower wages if they are paid in the form of tax-exempt fringe benefits, *see* Slemrod & Bakija, *supra* note 72, at 91.
92. The phenomenon is known as 'tax capitalization'. David Weisbach defines 'tax capitalization' as 'assets change price in response to taxes', *see* Weisbach, *supra* note 91, at 374.
93. *See* Crane, *supra* note 91, at 345-356; Weisbach, *supra* note 91, at 376.
94. *See* Crane, *supra* note 91, at 350-351.
95. Caishui (2009) No. 59, Art. 6(2).
96. EITLIR, Art. 75.

By way of illustration, consider the following hypothetical example. Suppose two corporate shareholders, X and Y, both realize capital gains of RMB 100 and are subject to the standard corporate income tax rate of 25%[97]. X receives equity consideration and can defer its tax liability. Y, meanwhile, receives cash and must pay current tax. Assume in this scenario that the present value of deferred tax liability is always 80% of its nominal value, so the special tax treatment in effect reduces the tax rate for a seller to 20% (i.e., 25% × 80%). Therefore, X can be viewed as paying a current tax of RMB 20 and has an after-tax income of RMB 80, while Y pays a tax of RMB 25 and has an after-tax income of RMB 75.

At first glance, the special tax treatment is horizontally inequitable because X and Y have the same before-tax income but pay different taxes. However, this assertion is untenable considering the impact of tax capitalization. X will refuse to accept equity consideration if the present value of the equity consideration is lower than 75%/80% (i.e., (1-25%) ÷ (1-20%)) of the market value of its stock in the target company.[98] In other words, X is willing to bear an implicit tax only to the extent of the potential tax deferral benefit. Assume a full tax capitalization for convenience. If, in this hypothetical case, X eventually decided to accept cash consideration instead of equity consideration, it would have received RMB 320/3 (i.e., 100 × 80% ÷ 75%). By the same logic, Y would have received only RMB 375/4 (i.e., 100 × 75% ÷ 80%) if it chose equity consideration. Again, before-tax income is proved to be an inadequate basis for measuring horizontal equity.

One should compare X with X', which has got RMB 320/3 of cash consideration in the acquisition. Similarly, instead of being compared with X, which receives RMB100 in the form of equity consideration, Y should be compared with Y', which receives equity consideration worth RMB 375/4. When receiving the stock, Y', in fact, pays a current tax of RMB 75/4 and has an after-tax income of RMB 75 – the same amount that Y gets from its sale of stock for cash. This hypothetical scenario involves no inequity: X and X', as well as Y and Y', have the same after-tax income for selling the target shares at the same fair market value. Table 4.2 summarizes the above analysis.

Table 4.2 Misleading Inequity in M&A Taxation

	Consideration		*Fair Market Value of Stock Sold*	*Present Value of Tax*	*Present Value of After-Tax Income*
	Type	*Value*			
X	Equity	RMB 100	RMB 320/3	RMB 20	RMB 80
Y	Cash	RMB 100	RMB 100	RMB 25	RMB 75
X'	Cash	RMB 320/3	RMB 320/3	RMB 80/3	RMB 80
Y'	Equity	RMB 375/4	RMB 100	RMB 75/4	RMB 75

97. EITL, Art. 4(1).
98. In this hypothetical, selling shareholders' tax bases in the target company's stock are zero.

Repealing the special tax treatment can make the law better conform to the fourth level interpretation of horizontal equity; however, it may impair rather than necessarily promote equal treatment among taxpayers. X and Y' in the above hypothetical have already paid the entire tax benefit as an implicit tax, so the repeal will put an extra tax burden on them.

[e] An Impediment to Tax Reform

This research has explored several possible levels of interpretations of horizontal equity and found that some interpretations are not useful while others can be subsumed under the principle of tax neutrality. In addition to that, Professor Louis Kaplow also offers a compelling argument against using horizontal equity in the discourse of tax reform.

According to Kaplow, horizontal equity has two facets. First, like vertical equity, horizontal equity condemns moving people further apart in the income distribution. In this respect, horizontal equity can be subsumed under vertical equity and will not survive as an independent criterion.[99] Second, horizontal equity is against moving people closer together, which distinguishes it from vertical equity. Condemning 'moving individuals closer together in the income distribution' differentiates horizontal equity from other principles and therefore is the 'central defining characteristic' of horizontal equity.[100]

Thus, from a tax reform perspective of view, horizontal equity mandates maintaining the status quo, and 'any disruption in the pre-reform distribution of income' constitutes a violation of horizontal equity.[101] Kaplow posits that horizontal equity has no normative underpinning and refuses to use horizontal equity as a tax policy tool because those who use it fail to specify why the status quo is of normative significance.[102] A reform proposal may be rejected for not meeting horizontal equity, even if it moves the tax system towards some chosen distributive criteria or enhances efficiency. Kaplow urges proponents of horizontal equity to reflect on the question of 'whether one should object to prima facie reasonable tax reforms, motivated by concerns of efficiency or distribution, because of the incidental, inevitable, and often unavoidable effects of such reforms on the pre-reform distribution of income'.[103]

The following example illustrates Kaplow's criticism of horizontal equity. Assume a tax system where a taxpayer pays taxes at a 40% rate for the first RMB 5,000 of income and pays zero tax for the income exceeding RMB 5,000. A and B have the same income of RMB 5,000. C and D have the same income of RMB 10,000. According to that regressive tax schedule, all of the four taxpayers pay the same tax of RMB 2,000. Suppose now that a reform imposes a 40% tax on C's income above RMB5,000 and keeps the treatment of the remaining taxpayers unchanged. This reform narrows the

99. Kaplow, *supra* note 56, at 143.
100. *Ibid.*
101. *Ibid.*
102. *Ibid.*, at 146-47.
103. *Ibid.*, at 139.

income gap between the rich (i.e., C) and the poor (i.e., A and B) and therefore accords well with the chosen distributive principle of equal wealth distribution. Nevertheless, the reform may be attacked for having C and D taxed in a way opposed to the standard of horizontal equity.

[2] Vertical Equity

Vertical equity attends to equity among unequals, requiring treating people who are not alike differently.[104] Like horizontal equity, it suffers from the same sorts of criticisms surrounding how to identify equals and unequals. This issue has been extensively discussed above and will not be repeated here. This subsection assumes that the law can satisfactorily deal with the identification problem. Then, the challenge for vertical equity is: how different the tax treatments for unequals should be.

Kaplow suggests that vertical equity favours moving individuals closer together in income distribution.[105] A corollary of Kaplow's idea is that vertical equity requires the adoption of a progressive income tax system to differentiate tax treatments of unequals.[106] However, vertical equity does not necessarily require a progressive system. As noted by the OECD, '[vertical equity's] definition can differ from one user to another. According to some, it suggests that taxpayers in better circumstances should bear a larger part of the tax burden as a proportion of their income. In practice, the interpretation of vertical equity depends on the extent to which countries want to diminish income variation ...'.[107] The design of progressivity or regressivity depends on the choice of distributive justice theory as well as the determination of economic assumptions.[108]

Musgrave surveys various formulations of distributive justice and concludes that under different theories, the requirement of vertical equity changes drastically.[109] Even under the same formulation of distributive justice, there is no definite answer regarding how to choose the degree of progressivity. For instance, from the perspective of a utilitarian who cares about the marginal utility of income, the tax system should be progressive, proportional, or regressive if the elasticity of the marginal utility of income is higher than, equal to, or lower than one.[110]

Here, we set aside those debates and adopt the mainstream thought that vertical equity requires a progressive income tax system.[111] Then the focus turns to whether vertical equity is pertinent in the discourse of China's M&A taxation or, put differently, whether it is meaningful to scrutinize China's tax rules for M&A transactions through

---

104. *Ibid.*, at 140-41.
105. *Ibid.*, at 143.
106. Paul R. McDaniel & James R. Repetti, *Horizontal and Vertical Equity: The Musgrave/Kaplow Exchange*, 1 Fla. Tax Rev. 607, 611 (1993).
107. OECD, *supra* note 9, at 31.
108. McDaniel & Repetti, *supra* note 106, at 610.
109. Musgrave, *supra* note 56, at 114-117.
110. Jon R. Neill, *The Benefit and Sacrifice Principles of Taxation: A Synthesis*, 17 Soc Choice Welfare 117, 120 (2000).
111. James Repetti & Diane Ring, *Horizontal Equity Revisited*, 13 Fla. Tax Rev. 135, 136 (2012).

the lens of progressivity. To answer the question, we need to look at the overall progressivity of China's individual income tax system.

In terms of implementing progressive taxation of individuals, a global income tax system that involves tax applied to a person's total income is much better than a schedular tax system that imposes separate taxes on different sources of income.[112] Under a schedular tax system, a taxpayer who has plenty of income in one schedule and lots of losses in another schedule may be subject to significant taxation, even though the taxpayer has no total income. The IITL adopts a 'composite',[113] which is much closer to a schedular tax system than to a global one. It combines some types of income to apply a progressive rate while imposing a flat rate on many secularized categories of income. Salaries, income from providing independent personal services, income from author's remuneration and income from royalties fall into the scope of 'comprehensive income', subject to a progressive tax with a top marginal rate of 45%;[114] income from conducting trade or business is taxed at a different progressive rate schedule with a top marginal rate of 35%;[115] and the remaining categories of income (including interest, dividends, profits from selling properties, and so on) are only subject to a flat rate of 20%.[116]

Although the system incorporates progressive rate schedules, it is of very limited progressivity. In particular, the working class has suffered a higher tax burden compared to their income level. Most Chinese people belong to the working class living off their salaries, to which the 3-45% progressive tax rates apply. In contrast, the principal income sources of the wealthy are not salaries but other various earnings taxed at a rate of 20%.

Vertical equity, in general, has a subordinated ranking in the value system of the Chinese government. When there is a conflict of values, vertical equity is usually traded off against other values such as efficiency. Since the market-oriented economic reform started in 1978, the dominant ideology in China has shifted away from equalitarianism. In 1993, the Third Plenary Session of the fourteenth CPC Central Committee issued the *Decision on the Reform of Economic System*, further putting forward the approach of 'giving priority to efficiency with due consideration to fairness'.[117] The fifteenth CPC National Congress reaffirmed this approach.[118] Over the

112. *See* Hugh J. Ault & Brian J. Arnold, *Comparative Income Taxation: A Structural Analysis* 256 (3rd ed., 2010).
113. Scholars use 'composite' to denote systems between pure schedular and pure global taxation. *See* Lee Burns & Richard Krever, *Individual Income Tax, in 2 Tax Law Design and Drafting* 495, 496 (Victor Thuronyi ed., 1998).
114. IITL, Art. 3(1).
115. IITL, Art. 3(2).
116. IITL, Art. 3(3).
117. CPC Central Committee, *Zhonggong Zhongyang Guanyu Jianli Shehui Zhuyi Shichang Jingji Tizhi Ruogan Wenti de Jueding [Decision of the CPC Central Committee on Some Issues Concerning the Establishment of a Socialist Market Economic Structure]* (14 November 1993), para. 2.
118. Zemin Jiang, Jiang Zemin Zai Zhongguo Gongchandang Di Shiwu Ci Quanguo Daibiao Dahui Shang de Baogao [Jiang Zemin's Report to the 15th National Congress of the CPC] (12 September 1997), (transcript available at http://www.gov.cn/test/2008-07/11/content_1042080.htm). ('we should adhere to giving priority to efficiency with due consideration to fairness.')

past several decades, the reforms in China have laid stress mainly on increasing economic growth and relatively ignored the fairness of social wealth distribution.

It is worth noting that in China, there is a trend to give equity considerations greater weight. Along with the rapid development of the economy, the wealth gap between the rich and the poor in China is expanding. Since 2003, China's Gini coefficient[119] has never dropped below 0.4[120] – a threshold defined by the UN-Habitat as an 'international alert line'. Under the background of the alarming rich-poor gap, the appeal of vertical equity becomes increasingly strong. Because of this, the sixteenth CPC National Congress gave a new interpretation of 'giving priority to efficiency with due consideration to fairness': 'in primary distribution, we should pay more attention to efficiency, ... in redistribution, we should pay more attention to fairness'.[121] The eighteenth CPC National Congress further specified that 'a proper balance should be struck between efficiency and fairness in both primary and secondary distribution, with particular emphasis on fairness in secondary distribution'.[122]

This gradual ideological transition coincides with Simons' observation that 'so long as poverty and insecurity compel the sovereign to employ every available fiscal device in order to maintain sovereignty, questions of justice are naturally subordinate. Once stable government and a measure of economic freedom appear, however, considerations of equity are forced to the front'.[123] Nevertheless, despite the recent amendment to the IITL that introduces the aforementioned composite system to replace a purely schedular system, the individual income tax system as a whole is still regressive. As mentioned above, the latest version of the IITL still levies a preferential flat rate on many secularized categories of income, but the Chinese lawmakers do not show any intention to remove this primary cause of regressivity. When the tax system is no longer fundamentally regressive, vertical equity can have more weight in guiding the taxation of M&A transactions. However, for the time being, it is not a useful gauge.

119. The Gini Coefficient is a measure of inequality of a distribution. It is a number between 0 and 1, where 0 corresponds to perfect equality and 1 corresponds to perfect inequality.

120. According to the National Statistics Bureau of China (NSB), the figures for each year between 2003 and 2016 are 0.479, 0.473, 0.485, 0.487, 0.484, 0.491, 0.490, 0.481, 0.477, 0.474, 0.473, 0.469, 0.462 and 0.465 respectively. Department of Household Surveys of the National Bureau of Statistics of China, *Zhongguo Zhuhu Diaocha Nianjian 2017 [China Yearbook of Household Survey 2017]* (2017). The figure announced by the NSB is moderate compared to the estimate provided by some scholars. For example, Xie and Zhou find that China's Gini coefficient is above 0.50 around 2010, Yu Xie & Xiang Zhou, *Income Inequality in Today's China*, 111 Proceedings of the National Academy of Sciences of the United States of America 6928, 6932 (2014).

121. Zemin Jiang, Jiang Zemin Zai Zhongguo Gongchandang Di Shiliu Ci Quanguo Daibiao Dahui Shang de Baogao [Jiang Zemin's Report to the 16th National Congress of the CPC] (8 November 2002), (transcript available at http://www.gov.cn/test/2008-08/01/content_1061490.htm).

122. Jintao Hu, Hu Jintao Zai Zhongguo Gongchandang Di Shiba Ci Quanguo Daibiao Dahui Shang de Baogao [Hu Jintao's Report to the 18th National Congress of the CPC] (8 November 2012), (transcript available at http://www.gov.cn/ldhd/2012-11/17/content_2268826.htm).

123. Simons, *supra* note 84, at 3.

§4.04 TAX NEUTRALITY AND M&A TAXATION

The former part of this chapter highlights tax neutrality, which basically requires tax law to treat different forms of business activities in a non-partial way so that interference with the market mechanism would not occur, as the overarching principle for China's M&A taxation. In order to examine the taxation of M&A in China against the standards of tax neutrality, it is necessary to have a clear understanding of to what extent the current regime influences investors' decisions concerning M&A activities and thus may have a distortive effect. Under the searchlight of the principle of tax neutrality, the impact of M&A taxation on the choice between alternative transaction options is worthy of attention.

Generally speaking, there are two basic approaches for one company to obtain control over another, covering the three types of acquisitive reorganizations acknowledged by Circular 59.[124] First, the purchasing company may acquire direct control over all or a significant portion of the target company's assets through a statuary merger or an asset acquisition. Second, the purchasing company may acquire the target company's stock from its shareholders and gain indirect control over the assets of the target company. By combining the two approaches with the ordinary or the special tax treatment provided by Circular 59,[125] we derive four alternative options for conducting an M&A transaction, each of which has different tax implications.

Table 4.3 Alternative M&A Options

	Merger/Asset Acquisition	*Stock Acquisition*
Ordinary Tax Treatment	Taxable Merger/Asset Acquisition	Taxable Stock Acquisition
Special Tax Treatment	Tax-deferred Merger/Asset Acquisition	Tax-deferred Stock Acquisition

The difference in tax implications between these alternative options impacts not only how to structure an M&A transaction but on whether to initiate a transaction in the first place. For instance, tax benefits may lure a company to acquire another, even though the acquisition does not make much sense from a commercial perspective. In order to avoid an unnecessarily complicated discussion, this research will not directly compare the tax consequences of the four alternative options. Instead, it will examine the impact of M&A taxation along two lines: one focuses on the selection between the ordinary and the special tax treatments; the other is about how tax law affects the choice between stock acquisition and merger/asset acquisition.

124. Caishui (2009) No. 59, Arts. 1(3), 1(4), 1(5).
125. *Ibid.*, at Arts. 4(3), 4(4), 4(5), 6(2), 6(3), 6(4).

[A] Ordinary Tax Treatment Versus Special Tax Treatment

The sharp distinction in tax consequences resulting from the choice between the ordinary and special tax treatments is most apparent in the case of a merger, where tax implications will occur at both the corporate and shareholder levels. If the ordinary tax treatment applies, the target company will recognize gain or loss on the disposal of its assets, and the liquidating distribution by the target company will trigger a shareholder-level recognition. However, if the special tax treatment is elected, the target company will transfer all of its assets and liabilities to the purchasing company without incurring tax liabilities, and the target company's shareholders will be entitled to non-recognition upon the exchange of their stock in the target for qualified equity consideration paid by the purchasing company.

This subsection will explore to what extent the corporate-level tax consequences in mergers differs under the ordinary and special tax treatments, as well as how taxpayers would possibly choose between taxable and tax-deferred mergers in response to the distinct tax consequences. The corporate-level tax implications of mergers are discussed as an example here because mergers lead to the most complex tax consequences – in particular at the corporate level – compared to stock or asset acquisitions, and the analysis of which is analogous to the situation of stock or asset acquisitions.

In order to better address this complicated issue, this research divides the assets of a company into two groups – the assets with build-in gains and the assets with built-in losses – and considers the tax consequences of transferring them separately. Also, as a side note, given the effect of tax capitalization, the purchasing and target companies in most circumstances will share the tax liabilities or benefits arising from a merger, regardless of which the tax authority directly collects taxes from or grants benefits to. For instance, the target company in a taxable merger may shift a portion of the tax burden to the purchasing company by requesting a higher purchase price than it would accept in a non-tax world. Therefore, it is more sensible to look at the overall tax effects rather than focusing on one particular party.

[1] Transfer of Built-In Gain Assets

In a taxable merger, the target company needs to recognize the built-in gain inherent in its appreciated assets, and the purchasing company will receive those assets with a stepped-up tax basis. Where the special tax treatment applies, the target company is not subject to taxation on the built-in gain in its assets and disappears once the merger gets completed; however, it does not mean that the law exempts the built-in gain from taxes permanently: as the purchasing company takes the original tax basis of those built-in gain assets, it will claim less depreciation or amortization deduction and thus incur more taxes in the future.

With the tax consequences of taxable mergers as a benchmark, we can easily see the differences between the ordinary and the special tax treatments: when choosing the special tax treatment instead of the ordinary one, the participants in a merger get a current tax exemption at the expense of losing additional future depreciation deductions. Normally, such a trade-off is beneficial for the taxpayers because the value of current tax (*A r*, where *A* stands for the amount of appreciation in the value of the target company's assets, and *r* represents the tax rate) is always greater than the value of a future benefit of the same amount (symbolized as *PV (A r)*, where *PV* is a symbol for present value). Expressed symbolically, most of the time, the special tax treatment will be elected because of $PV\ (A\ r) < A\ r$ (hereinafter *Inequality I*).[126]

Inequality I assumes that both the purchasing and target company are subject to the same tax rate, which, however, is not always the case. While the EITL gives a standard tax rate of 25% on most companies,[127] it also provides preferential tax rates for small-sized low-profit companies and companies in certain localities or industries. An example is the 15% tax rate for high-tech companies.[128] *Inequality I* is apparently inapplicable for situations where the purchasing and target companies have different tax rates, and therefore, instead of assigning the same rate of *r* to both companies, we designate r_a as the tax rate for the purchasing company and r_a as the rate for the target company. Accordingly, the special tax treatment election will be made, if $PV\ (A\ r_a) < A\ r_t$ (hereinafter *Inequality II*).

Since $PV\ (A\ r_a)$ is smaller than $A\ r_a$, *Inequality II* will always hold true, provided that $A\ r_a \leq A\ r_t$. In other words, if the tax rate for the purchasing company does not exceed that for the target company, the merger participants will choose the special tax treatment for sure. Where the purchasing company bears a heavier tax burden than the target does (e.g., the target company is recognized by the EITL as a small-sized low-profit company or a hi-tech company), the current tax imposed on the target might be less than the present value of additional depreciation deduction benefits brought about by the step-up in tax basis. Expressed symbolically, if $r_a > r_t$, the following inequality might hold true: $PV\ (A\ r_a) > A$ (hereinafter *Inequality III*). Therefore, it is unsurprising that some merger participants prefer the ordinary tax treatment.

Apart from the tax rates, how fast the purchasing company can claim depreciation or amortization deductions on the transferred assets also determines the truth-value of *Inequality III*. $PV\ (A\ r_a)$ is the net present value of a stream of yearly depreciation deductions. Provided that the method of depreciation does not change, the value of $PV\ (A\ r_a)$ decreases as the purchasing company takes more years to use the depreciation tax shields. The EITLIR prescribes different minimum depreciation or amortization periods, ranging from three to twenty years, for various types of assets.[129] If the target company's assets consist mainly of those with the longest minimum depreciation period, there will be a low possibility that *Inequality III* holds true. However, if a large proportion of the transferred assets can be fully depreciated over three years, *Inequality III* will be likely to hold.

126. As mentioned in the beginning of this subsection, the tax position of the target company's shareholders is omitted.
127. EITL, Art. 4.
128. EITL, Art. 28.
129. EITLIR, Art. 60.

The default method of depreciation prescribed by the tax law is the straight-line method, but in certain situations, companies may opt for a reduced depreciation period or adopt an accelerated depreciation method, which leads to a higher value of *PV* ($A\ r_a$). Under the EITLIR, companies may accelerate the depreciation of fixed assets that need to be updated frequently and that suffer from strong vibrations or are in high corrosion environments. Moreover, the Chinese government has kept expanding the application of accelerated depreciation methods to serve its industrial policies. As instructed by the State Council, the MOF and the STA issued two circulars in 2014, allowing equipment purchased for R&D purposes and fixed assets owned by companies in certain industries to be depreciated at an accelerated rate.[130]

According to these two circulars, the R&D equipment with a value of less than RMB 1 million can be fully depreciated in the year it was purchased, and some other accelerated depreciation methods apply to the R&D equipment worth more than RMB 1 million.[131] For companies in the six specified industries of biopharmaceutical manufacturing, special equipment manufacturing, transportation equipment manufacturing, electronic equipment manufacturing, instruments and meters manufacturing, as well as IT services, they can depreciate fixed assets purchased on or after 1 January 2014 using accelerated methods.[132] In 2015 and 2019 respectively, the central tax authorities extended the preferential depreciation treatment twice so that it is now available to all manufacturing companies.[133] Thus, if most of the target company's assets qualify for accelerated depreciation methods or the purchasing company is in the manufacturing sector, the possibility that the merger participants choose the ordinary tax treatment will increase.

[2] Transfer of Loss Carry Forwards and Built-In Loss Assets

Under the ordinary tax treatment, the target company may deduct loss carry forwards and recognize built-in loss against its income from selling built-in gain assets, and any

130. Caishui (2014) No. 75, Guanyu Wanshan Guding Zichan Jiasu Zhejiu Qiye Suodeshui Zhengce de Tongzhi [Notice on Improving the Enterprise Income Tax Policies Concerning the Accelerated Depreciation of Fixed Assets] (promulgated by the MOF and the STA on 20 October 2014, effective retrospectively 1 January 2014) (PRC); STA Gonggao (2014) No. 64, Guanyu Guding Zichan Jiasu Zhejiu Shuishou Zhengce Youguan Wenti de Gonggao [Announcement on Issues Relatign to Tax Policies Concerning the Accelerated Depreciation of Fixed Assets] (promulgated by the STA and effective 14 November 2014) (PRC).
131. STA Gonggao (2014) No. 64, Art. 2.
132. STA Gonggao (2014) No. 64, Art. 1.
133. Caishui (2015) No. 106, Guanyu Jinyibu Wanshan Guding Zichan Jiasu Zhejiu Qiye Suodeshui Zhengce de Tongzhi [Notice on Further Improving the Enterprise Income Tax Policies Concerning the Accelerated Depreciation of Fixed Assets] (promulgated by the MOF and the STA on 17 September 2015, effective retrospectively 1 January 2015) (PRC), Art. 1; STA Gonggao (2015) No. 68, Guanyu Jinyibu Wanshan Guding Zichan Jiasu Zhejiu Qiye Suodeshui Zhengce Youguan Wenti de Gonggao [Announcement on Issues Relating to Further Improving Tax Policies Concerning the Accelerated Depreciation of Fixed Assets] (promulgated by the STA and effective 25 September 2015) (PRC), Art. 1; MOF and STA Gonggao (2019) No. 66, Guanyu Kuoda Guding Zichan Jiasu Zhejiu Zhengce Shiyong Fanwei de Gonggao [Notice on Expanding the Applicable Scope of Tax Policies Concerning the Accelerated Depreciation of Fixed Assets] (promulgated by the MOF and STA and effective 23 April 2019), Art. 1.

unused loss cannot be carried forward to the purchasing company. In contrast, if the special tax treatment is elected, the target company will transfer its loss carry forwards and built-in losses to the purchasing company. In order to maximize the tax benefits flowing from those losses, the merger participants will elect the tax treatment that allocates the losses to the party that can better exploit them. That is to say, if the losses can produce more tax benefits in the hands of the purchasing company, the merger participants are like to opt for the special tax treatment. Otherwise, they may tend to choose the ordinary tax treatment.

Suppose that the target and purchasing companies can respectively deduct L_t and L_a out of the total amount of L of the target company's tax losses. Moreover, as in the previous subsection, we use r_t and r_a to denote the tax rates for the target company and the purchasing company. In a taxable merger, the target company can immediately deduct the tax losses and obtain a tax reduction of $L_t r_t$. While in a tax-deferred merger, the loss will be transferred to the purchasing company and produce future tax benefits with the present value of $PV'(L_a r_a)$. Accordingly, the merger participants prefer the ordinary tax treatment if $L_t r_t > PV'(L_a r_a)$ (hereinafter *Inequality IV*). Whether *Inequality IV* is true depends on three elements. The first one is about the tax rates for the two companies. If $r_t > r_a$, *Inequality IV* will be more likely to hold. The second element is how fast the purchasing company can deduct the loss – $PV'(L_a r_a)$ represents the present value of a stream of tax benefits flowing from loss deductions, which decreases when the purchasing corporation needs more time to use the transferred tax losses. The third element is the comparison between L_t and L_a.

The relative profitability of the purchasing and target companies significantly affects the second and third elements. The tax losses of a company do not produce any benefit unless the company has taxable income to absorb it. In a taxable merger, the target company faces its last opportunity to use tax losses. If it does not have any built-in gain assets, its tax losses will go wasted. Once again, let A represent the amount of built-in gain in the target company's assets. If A is less than L, L_t will be equal to A. Otherwise, L_t equals L. As to the purchasing company, the more profitable it is, the faster it can use the transferred tax losses, and thus it will reap more benefits. Suppose, for example, that company X and company Y both have acquired loss carry forwards of RMB 100 in tax-deferred mergers and that X and Y respectively make profits of RMB 100 and RMB 20 each year. X can fully deduct the RMB 100 loss carry forwards against its profits of the same amount in year 1, while Y needs four more years to use up the purchased loss carry forwards. Assume a yearly discount rate of 5%. The present value of Y's loss deductions at the end of year 1 is RMB 90.92, RMB 9.08 less than the present value of X's loss deductions.

Besides, the tax law's limitation on loss deduction has a significant impact on the value of L_a and $PV'(L_a r_a)$. Under the EITL, the maximum loss carryforward period is five years.[134] If the purchasing company is not profitable enough within a short period after the merger, it will dissipate a portion of the transferred loss carry forwards, that is, L_a will be less than L. More importantly, Circular 59 and Circular 4 impose a strict

134. EITL, Art. 18.

restriction on the use of the transferred loss carry forwards: the purchasing company can at most deduct an amount equal to the fair market value of the target company's net assets multiplying the interest rate of the longest-term government bond.[135] Due to the restriction, the purchasing company suffers a great risk of failing to fully deduct the transferred loss carry forwards before the expiration date arrives.

Taking into account both the transfer of built-in gain assets and the transfer of loss carry forwards and built-in loss assets, taxpayers will prefer a tax-deferred merger to a taxable one if $(A-L_t)\ r_t > PV\ PV'\ (L_a\ r_a)$, or, $(A-L_t)\ r_t > (PV\ (A) - PV'\ (L_a))\ r_a$ (*Inequality V*). Under such circumstances, how to structure the merger to qualify for the special tax treatment becomes a major concern. The special tax treatment only applies if the transaction consideration consists mainly of the stock of the purchasing company or the stock of the purchasing company's controlling company,[136] so the merger participants will adjust the payment method or payment composition to pursue the special tax treatment.

Based on *Inequality V*, it is evident that many tax characteristics of the purchasing and target companies determine whether, how and to what extent a tax-deferred merger is preferable to a taxable one. Therefore, the difference between the ordinary and special tax treatments has a considerable impact on a company's decisions regarding whether to engage in a merger and which company it will buy assets from or sell assets to. To illustrate this, consider the following example. T is a company ready to be merged. T has nothing other than a machine (tax basis: RMB 1,000; fair market value: RMB 1,000) and a loss carryforward of RMB 25. P1, P2, and P3 are three potential buyers of T. P1 and P2 both earn an annual profit of RMB 25. P3 is less profitable than them and makes a profit of RMB 12.5 per year. P1 and P3 are subject to the standard tax rate of 25%, while P2 is a high-tech company that pays tax at the preferential rate of 15%.

Since the machine has a tax basis equal to its fair market value, T recognizes no gain or loss in either a taxable or a tax-deferred merger. The two types of transactions only differ in the treatment of the RMB 25 loss carryforward. If a taxable merger is the only option, the loss carryforward is destined to dissipate. As a result, T is indifferent about which one of P1, P2, and P3 acquires it because they all bid the same purchase price of RMB 1,000. However, the situation will be different if a tax-deferred merger is also an available choice. In a tax-deferred merger, P1, P2, and P3 will be willing to pay an additional price for the loss carryforward of RMB 25.

For P1, the loss carryforward will produce a tax saving of RMB 6.25 by completely offsetting its current-year taxable income. Therefore, P1 will pay as much as RMB 6.25 for the loss carryforward. Compared to P1, P2 values the loss carryforward less because it is subject to a lower tax rate. If transferred to P2, the RMB 25 loss carryforward can produce a tax saving of RMB 3.75 in the current year. Therefore, P2 will only purchase the loss carryforward at a price lower than RMB 3.75. Similarly, the loss carryforward is not as appealing to P3 as to P1. Since P3 only makes an annual taxable income of

135. Caishui (2009) No. 59, Art. 6(4)(3); STA Gonggao (2010) No. 4, Art. 26.
136. Caishui (2009) No. 59, Art. 6(4).

RMB 12.5, it needs two years to absorb the loss carryforward fully. In the hands of P3, the RMB 25 loss carryforward will produce a tax saving of RMB 3.125 in both the current year and the year ahead. Assuming a 5% discount rate, the present value of the two-year tax savings is approximately RMB 6.10 (3.125 + 3.125 ÷ (1 + 0.05)). If the loss carryforward is priced higher than RMB 6.10, P3 will quit the deal. Suppose T is the only seller in the market, P1, P2, and P3 will compete to acquire T, which is expected to bid up the price of the loss carryforward to RMB 6.10. As a result, P1 will squeeze P2 and P3 out of the market and become the purchaser of T.

It has been clear up to this point how the distinction between the ordinary and special tax treatments significantly impacts merger decisions. Given the requirement of tax neutrality, an appropriate question to ask is whether it is justifiable to have two different types of tax treatments for M&A transactions, or more precisely, is it legitimate to provide the special tax treatment? If the answer is yes, then the next question is, what needs to be done to reduce unwanted distortions resulting from the special tax treatment. These issues will be dealt with in greater detail in Chapter 5 and Chapter 6.

[B] Stock Acquisition Versus Asset Acquisition

A fundamental decision required of the parties to an M&A transaction is whether the seller will sell stock or assets. Both tax and non-tax factors influence the decision. As to the non-tax aspect, an asset acquisition allows the purchaser to 'cherry pick' the desirable assets and avoid undesirable assets and liabilities. Hence, for a purchasing company that is averse to any exposure to the target company's outstanding and potential liabilities, an asset acquisition could be preferable. In cases where the target has valuable non-assignable contracts and licences, a stock acquisition may be a better choice for the purchaser. The list of such non-tax factors goes on and on.

The non-tax factors that affect the decision between stock acquisition and asset acquisition constitute part of the market mechanism, which guarantees the efficient allocation of resources. Tax factors, on the contrary, risk undermining the proper function of the market mechanism by luring market players away from the most economically efficient method of carrying out an acquisition. For example, if stock acquisitions are always taxed favourably than asset acquisitions, the M&A participants are likely to prefer a stock transaction to an asset transaction even though the latter is more economically efficient.

Under the current Chinese tax law, there are several differences in tax consequences between taxable stock acquisitions and asset acquisitions. The first and most obvious difference is that the target company typically recognizes gain or loss in an asset acquisition but does not incur any tax consequence in a stock acquisition. In a taxable asset acquisition, the corporate income can be taxed twice - first at the corporate level and then again at the shareholder level when the target shareholders receive liquidating distributions. In contrast, a stock sale by the target shareholders generally only leads to recognition at the shareholder level.

The second key difference in tax consequences between taxable stock acquisitions and asset acquisitions is corollary tax basis adjustments. The purchasing company in an asset acquisition has a cost basis in assets acquired from the target company. In contrast, the purchasing company in a stock acquisition is entitled to a cost basis only in the target company's stock acquired, while the target company's assets still retain the same basis that they had before the acquisition, and therefore the built-in gain or loss inherent in those assets will be subject to taxes in the future. Table 4.4 presents a simplified comparison between the tax consequences of taxable stock and asset acquisitions.

Table 4.4 Tax Consequences of Taxable Stock and Asset Acquisitions

	Shareholder-Level Tax	*Corporate-Level Tax*	*Tax Basis of Target's Assets*	*Tax Basis of Target's Stock*
Stock Acquisition	Yes	No	Carry-over Basis	Cost Basis
Asset Acquisition & Liquidation	Yes	Yes	Cost Basis	N/A

Parties to M&A transactions will consider those differences in tax consequences in deciding between a taxable stock acquisition and an asset acquisition. As the principle of neutrality requires minimizing tax-induced distortions, it is necessary to think of measures countering the distortive effects that are caused by the distinction in tax consequences between stock and asset acquisitions. This issue will be the focus of Chapter 7.

§4.05 CONCLUSION

In the foregoing chapter, it was suggested that China should reform the income tax regime for M&A because of its flaws and inconsistency. This chapter then began to clear up the confusion around the overarching principle for China's M&A taxation, with a view to building a solid foundation for an in-depth examination of such an incredibly complex regime and for further research on how to effectively improve the regime.

After a comparison of two well-recognized sets of taxation principles, equity, neutrality, administrability, certainty and simplicity, and flexibility stand out as the potential guiding principles for M&A taxation. Certainty and simplicity, as well as the principle of flexibility, constitute the second order taxation principles, which are too general and formal to provide guidance on the substantive issues in designing tax rules for M&A. Administrability, although containing substantive criteria that tax design should follow, is in essence a pragmatic concern that should be subordinate to the normative principles of equity and neutrality.

There are two dimensions to the notion of equity – horizontal and vertical. All the possible levels of interpretations of horizontal equity are either not useful because of emptiness or misleading due to the neglect of tax capitalization or replaceable by the principle of tax neutrality. Considering the broader context of China's income tax system, vertical equity – at least for the time being – has very limited weight in guiding how to better tax M&A transactions in China.

Thus, this chapter highlights tax neutrality, which basically requires tax law to treat different forms of business activities in a non-partial way so that interference with the market mechanism would not occur, as the overarching principle for China's M&A taxation. Tax neutrality – as pointed out by Professor Douglas Kahn – has two faces, i.e., the expectation that tax provisions should conform to the Haig-Simons model and the requirement that tax provisions should not induce a taxpayer to choose one economic activity over another. There could be a conflict between the mandates of the two faces of tax neutrality since an adjustment for removing a bias can either move the tax system towards or away from the Haig-Simons model. This potential conflict signifies the possibility that different or even diametrically opposed approaches may exist to address biases already caused by a tax system – China's income tax regime for M&A in the current case.

In order to facilitate our examination of the taxation of M&A in China against the standards of tax neutrality, this chapter also analysed to what extent the current regime influences investors' decisions concerning M&A activities and thus has a distortive effect, and two salient issues the contrasting ordinary and special tax treatments and the distinction in tax consequences between stock and asset acquisitions – thus stand out. These two issues will be fully examined in the following chapters of the book.

CHAPTER 5

Special Tax Treatment for M&A: A Theoretical and Empirical Assessment

§5.01 INTRODUCTION

This chapter aims to give an in-depth analysis of the special tax treatment for M&A transactions – the most important component of China's M&A taxation. Since 2009 when Circular 59 was enacted to establish the tax regulatory framework for M&A transactions, the special tax treatment that offers rollover relief to certain M&A transactions has taken centre stage in the discourse of M&A taxation.

Despite the significant progress that China has made in introducing the special tax treatment, there are many defects with the tax rules in this regard. Those defects cause the special tax treatment to generate inconsistencies and violations of tax neutrality. While some side issues, such as how to transplant the US law on tax-deferred triangular reorganizations into China,[1] have elicited considerable commentary, the underlying mechanism of the special tax treatment and the tensions in China's tax policies for M&A transactions are rarely examined. Logically speaking, those fundamental topics should be addressed before we can meaningfully deal with other side issues.

1. Triangular M&A are common in the US. In a triangular transaction, the purchasing company uses its subsidiary – the formal acquirer – to acquire the target company: the subsidiary exchanges the purchasing company's stock for the target company's stock or assets. If properly structured, it will qualify as a § 368 reorganization and receives non-recognition treatment. *See* generally Cheryl D. Block, *Corporate Taxation: Examples & Explanations* 455-470 (4th ed., 2010). Many Chinese scholars contend that China should follow the US and extend the special tax treatment to triangular M&A. *See e.g.*, Lanxiang Zhou, *Continuity of Interest and Equity Consideration*, Caikuai Yuekan [Finance and Accounting Monthly], no. 5, 2015, at 90, 91-92; Feng Li & Deyin Yang, *M&A Tax Policies and Continuity of Shareholder Interest*, Shuiwu Yanjiu [Taxation Research], no. 8, 2015, at 37, 39-40; Hui Li & Yudong Zhou, *The Special Tax Treatment and Neutral Principle of Taxation: Questions and Solutions of Taxation for China Enterprise Reorganizations by Way of Stock Payment*, Zhongyang Caijing Daxue Xuebao [Journal of Central University of Finance & Economics], no. 4, 2014, at 18, 24-25.

This chapter will, therefore, look at some fundamental problems plaguing the special tax treatment for M&A in China. In §5.02, adhering to the continuity of interest doctrine and expanding the eligibility for rollover relief are identified as two fundamental tax policies underlying the special tax treatment. Through a careful study, this section will investigate the theoretical background and rationale of the enshrined continuity of interest doctrine, as well as how it, together with the eagerness to expand the eligibility for rollover relief, has shaped the landscape of China's M&A taxation.

Section §5.03 will turn to examine the conflicts between the two policies and the inconsistencies within the tax regime induced by the conflicts. This section contains not only theoretical inquiries but also empirical findings on whether and to what extent the reform to the special tax treatment in 2014 makes a difference so as to reveal and assess the fundamental obstacles faced by the Chinese lawmakers in the process of attempts to improve the effectiveness of the special tax treatment. Section §5.04 concludes with some embryonic possibilities to address the fundamental obstacles.

§5.02 TWO TAX POLICIES UNDERLYING THE SPECIAL TAX TREATMENT

[A] Following the Continuity of Interest Doctrine

As noted in Chapter 2, when transplanting the rules for tax-deferred reorganizations from the US, China's lawmakers did not miss out on the continuity of interest doctrine. Although in China, the phrase 'continuity of interest' (*liyi chixu*) does not appear in the tax law, the doctrine of continuity of interest has been central to the special tax treatment regime. According to Circular 59, in a tax-deferred M&A transaction, at least 85% of the total consideration shall be paid in the form of equity consideration. This requirement is an imitation of the US continuity of interest doctrine's qualitative and quantitative components.

Many Chinese scholars have spoken favourably about the tax authorities' recognition of the continuity of interest doctrine.[2] Also, there is a consensus among them that the tax authorities should take further steps to promote better adherence to the doctrine.[3] Therefore, this subsection will investigate the theoretical background and rationale of this policy by tracing the historical development of the continuity of interest doctrine in the US due to the US creating and developing a comprehensive body of continuity of interest theories.

2. *See e.g.*, Chunyan Zhang, *Binggou Jiaoyi Suodeshui Falv Zhidu Yanjiu-Jiyu dui Liyi Chixu Yuanze de Kaoliang [Research on the Mergers and Acquisitions Income Tax Law-Based on the Continuity Doctrine]* 130 (2015); Zhou, *supra* note 1, at 91; Li & Yang, *supra* note 1, at 38-39.
3. *See e.g.*, Zhang, *supra* note 2, at 139-141; Zhou, *supra* note 1, at 92; Li & Yang, *supra* note 1, at 39-40.

[1] Origin and Development of the Continuity of Interest Doctrine

Instead of giving an exhaustive account of how the doctrine of continuity of interest emerged and developed in the US, this research only selects some early landmark cases and legislation to highlight the rationale and essential elements of the doctrine.[4]

In 1918, the US, for the first time, allowed the gain or loss from exchanging stock or securities of equal par value in 'a reorganization, merger or consolidation of a corporation' to be deferred until the recipient finally disposed of the new stock or securities.[5] In 1921, the US Congress revised the provision to eliminate the ambiguity around the undefined term 'reorganization.'[6] Under Section 202(c)(2) of the Revenue Act of 1921, the term 'reorganization' included 'a merger or consolidation (including the acquisition by one corporation of at least a majority of the voting stock and at least a majority of the total number of shares of all other classes of stock of another corporation, or substantially all the properties of another corporation)'.[7] This provision survived the modifications to the Revenue Act in 1924 and 1926.[8] A major defect of this provision was that it failed to specify the type of consideration required for a transaction to be qualified as a 'reorganization'. Asset sales for cash fit within the reorganization definition as long as a company transferred substantially all of its assets. To address this 'blunder of draftsmanship',[9] the courts created the doctrine of continuity of interest.

Cortland Specialty Co. v. Commissioner[10] marked the beginning of the evolvement of the continuity of interest doctrine.[11] The case involved an asset sale for non-equity consideration, including cash and promissory notes (payable in less than fourteen months). The target company, Cortland, after the transaction, distributed the cash and notes to Mr and Mrs Sargent – its sole shareholders. The Commissioner contended that the transaction was nothing but an ordinary sale and levied a tax on Cortland. Cortland claimed that according to the parenthetical phrase of Section

4. There has been an extensive volume of literature reviewing the development of the continuity of interest doctrine. *See e.g.* Peter L. Faber, *Continuity of Interest and Business Enterprise: Is It Time to Bury Some Sacred Cows*, 34 Tax Law. 239(1980); David S. Miller, *The Devolution and Inevitable Extinction of the Continuity of Interest Doctrine*, 3 Fla. Tax Rev. 187(1996); David F. Shores, *Reexamining Continuity of Shareholder Interest in Corporate Reorganizations*, 17 Va. Tax Rev. 419(1997).
5. Revenue Act of 1918 (US), § 202(b).
6. For a detail account of the historical development of the reorganization concept, *see* Steven A. Bank, *Mergers, Taxes, and Historical Realism*, 75 Tul. L. Rev. 1, 8-12 (2000).
7. US, Revenue Act of 1921, § 202(c)(2).
8. Section 203(h)(1) of the Revenue Act of 1926 was identical to Section 202(c)(2) of the Revenue Act of 1921. *See* Revenue Act of 1926 (US), § 203(h)(1).
9. Valentine Brookes, *The Continuity of Interest Test in Reorganizations – A Blessing or a Curse*, 34 Cal. L. Rev. 1, 5 (1946) *See also* Miller, *supra* note 4, at 195. ('The continuity doctrine developed as a sensible judicial interpretation of a poorly-drafted statute....'). David Shores argued that the continuity of interest concept's origin can be traced back to several pre-1918 cases related to the taxability of stock dividends, *see* Shores, *supra* note 4, at 420-423.
10. *Cortland Specialty Co. v. Commissioner*, 60 F.2d 937 (2d Cir. 1932).
11. *See e.g.* Shores, *supra* note 4, at 446. ('...[Cortland] is often regarded as the original source of the continuity of shareholder interest doctrine'.)

203(h)(1), the transaction where it transferred substantially all of its assets fitted the definition of reorganization and thus should be tax-free.

In determining whether the transaction qualified as a reorganization, the court rejected to apply the parenthetical language literally. It held that it 'must be interpreted in this setting [of merger and consolidation statutes]'[12] and that 'a sale of the assets of one corporation to another for cash without the retention of any interest by the seller in the purchaser is quite outside the objects of merger and consolidation statutes'.[13] Therefore, the court concluded that '[in a reorganization] there must be some continuity of interest on the part of the transferor corporation or its stockholders in order to secure exemption. Reorganization presupposes continuance of business under modified corporate forms'.[14]

Pinellas Ice & Cold Storage Co. v. Commissioner was the first case concerning the continuity of interest determined by the US Supreme Court.[15] This case involved nearly the same facts as *Cortland*. In this case, the target company, Pinellas, transferred all of the assets in exchange for cash and promissory notes from the purchasing company, the National Company. The US Supreme Court, like the Second Circuit in *Cortland*, held that the transaction failed to qualify as a reorganization because 'the mere purchase for money of the assets of one company by another is beyond the evident purpose of the provision, and has no real semblance to a merger or consolidation'.[16]

While the Second Circuit in *Cortland* negated the argument that a tax-deferred reorganization could be financed solely with cash and short-term, it did not specify the type of consideration that the purchasing company should use in tax-deferred reorganizations. The US Supreme Court took a step further, holding that to get the reorganization exemption, the transferor must 'acquire an interest in the affairs of the purchasing company more definite than that incident to ownership of its short-term purchase-money notes'.[17] Therefore, the interest in the purchasing company should have the attribute of 'definite'. However, the US Supreme Court did not clarify the meaning of 'definite' in *Pinellas Ice*.

In 1935, the US Supreme Court decided two cases that significantly enriched the continuity of interest doctrine. The first one is *Helvering v. Minnesota Tea Co.*,[18] which involved an asset transfer from Minnesota Tea to Grand Union Company. The transferor sold all of its assets to the transferee for voting trust certificates that represented the latter's common stock and cash. The US Supreme Court held that the transaction was a reorganization. In addition to the need for the transferor to acquire an interest in the transferee's affairs provided in Pinellas, the Court added that: 'this interest [in the transferee's affairs] must be definite and material; it must represent a substantial part of the value of the thing transferred. This much is necessary in order that the result accomplished may genuinely partake of the nature of merger or

12. *Cortland Specialty Co.*, 60 F.2d at 940.
13. *Cortland Specialty Co.*, 60 F.2d at 939.
14. *Cortland Specialty Co.*, 60 F.2d at 940. (emphasis added)
15. *Pinellas Ice & Cold Storage Co. v. Commissioner*, 287 U.S. 462 (1933).
16. *Pinellas Ice*, 287 U.S. at 470.
17. *Ibid.*
18. *Helvering v. Minnesota Tea Co.*, 296 U.S. 378 (1935).

consolidation.'[19] The other 1935 case is *John A. Nelson Co. v. Helvering,*[20] in which the purchaser acquired substantially all of John A. Nelson's assets with cash and preferred stock. The US Supreme Court held that the transaction qualified as a reorganization as the preferred stock of the purchaser represented a substantial interest in its affairs and that 'the statute does not require participation in the management of the purchaser'.[21]

Commentators often construe *Minnesota Tea* and *John A. Nelson Co.* as clarifying the qualitative and quantitative components of the judicial continuity of interest requirement.[22] The qualitative component requires that the type of consideration represent a 'definite and material' interest in the transferee. The US Supreme Court, in the two cases, confirmed that the stock of the purchasing company, voting or non-voting, satisfies the qualitative test. The quantitative component was mainly set out in *Minnesota Tea,* where the court claimed that a substantial proportion of the total consideration should be a qualifying consideration. In this case, the common stock represented by the voting trust certificates was worth approximately USD 540,000, constituting about 56% of the total consideration.[23]

The two-prong test constitutes the main part of the continuity of interest doctrine. In the post-1935 era, the courts further elaborated on the type of instruments necessary to meet the qualitative requirement and the proportion of those instruments in the total consideration that suffices to meet the quantitative requirement. It has been established that the stock in the purchasing company, whether or not having voting power, is qualifying consideration, while all other instruments including debts and so-called security instruments cannot meet the test.[24] Important post-1935 cases include *LeTulle v. Scofield,*[25] where the US Supreme Court held that long-term bonds of the purchasing company were not qualifying consideration. Although the courts did not give a definite threshold for fulfilling the quantitative requirement, they decided that transactions with very low equity consideration were unqualified for the non-recognition treatment. For example, in *Kass v. Commissioner*, the Tax Court found 16% inadequate.[26]

Influenced by *Cortland* and *Pinellas Ice*, a subcommittee of the House Ways and Means Committee[27] in 1933 recommended repealing the reorganization provisions for anti-avoidance purposes. In 1934, after a heated debate on the future of the reorganization provisions, the US Congress finally decided to retain but significantly alter the statutory pattern of earlier versions of the legislation.[28] It turned the parenthetical

19. *Minnesota Tea Co.*, 296 U.S. at 385.
20. *John A. Nelson Co. v. Helvering,* 296 U.S. 374 (1935).
21. *John A. Nelson Co.*, 296 U.S. at 377.
22. Block, *supra* note 1, at 396-397; Shores, *supra* note 4, at 449.
23. *Minnesota Tea Co. v. Commissioner* 28 B.T.A. 591, 595 (1933).
24. For a review of relevant cases, *see* Meredith R. Conway, *With or Without You: Debt and Equity and Continuity of Interest*, 15 Stan. J.L. Bus. & Fin. 261, 284-287 (2009).
25. *LeTulle v. Scofield,* 308 U.S. 415, 420-421 (1940).
26. *Kass v. Commissioner*, 60 T.C. 218, 226-227 (1973).
27. The House Ways and Means Committee is the chief tax-writing committee of the US House of Representatives, *see* https://waysandmeans.house.gov/about/.
28. Regarding the codification history of the continuity of interest requirement, *see generally, e.g.*, Faber, *supra* note 4, at 244-247; Miller, *supra* note 4, at 198-201; Steven A. Bank, *Federalizing the Tax-Free Merger: Toward an End to the Anachronistic Reliance on State Corporation Laws*, 77 N.C. L. Rev. 1307, 1340-1342 (1998).

clause that had been introduced first by the 1921 Revenue Act into a separate type of reorganization, namely 'the acquisition by one corporation in exchange solely for all or a part of its voting stock of at least 80 per centum of the voting stock and at least 80 per centum of the total number of shares of all other classes of stock of another corporation; or of substantially all the properties of another corporation ...'.[29] A notable highlight of this new clause was the codified continuity of interest requirement: for a transaction to qualify as such a new type of reorganization, the consideration must be solely voting stock of the purchasing company. Similar to the *Minnesota Tea* test, this statutory requirement also has two components – qualitative and quantitative.

However, the US Congress did not impose an explicit qualifying consideration standard on each type of reorganization. According to Section 112(g)(1)(A), the predecessor of Section 368(a)(1)(A) of the current IRC, a merger or consolidation qualifies as a reorganization if it satisfies statutory merger requirements.[30] The US Congress wished that those requirements could help prevent this exceptional tax treatment from being abused, but it never expected that state statutes would evolve so fast that they very soon loosened statutory merger requirements significantly.[31] Consequently, the once thought useless judicial continuity of interest doctrine returned to the stage,[32] and after that, all types of reorganizations are subject to either judicial or statutory requirements on the quality and quantity of the consideration received by the selling parties.[33]

[2] Rationale Behind the Continuity of Interest Doctrine

The continuity of interest doctrine was first created by the US courts to combat tax avoidance. By imposing the equity consideration requirement, the doctrine prevents taxpayers from evading taxes on the gains from sales for cash.[34] However, the courts have never phrased the doctrine as a simple anti-abuse rule. The *Cortland* court treated continuity of interest as the reason for granting non-recognition treatment for mergers.

In the US, the reorganization provisions emerged due to the idea that the 'mere change in form' or 'purely paper transaction' should not trigger immediate taxes on taxpayers. In brief, the idea is that in a stock-financed reorganization, the selling parties, by replacing their stock or assets with the stock in another company, do not cash out on their investment but instead continue it in a modified corporate enterprise.[35] Since they conduct a 'purely paper transaction' and what has changed in the

29. Revenue Act of 1934 (US), § 112(g)(1). It is the predecessor of Section 368(a)(1)(B) and Section 368(a)(1)(C) of today's Internal Revenue Code.
30. Revenue Act of 1934 (US), § 112(g)(1)(A).
31. *See generally*, *e.g.*, Miller, *supra* note 4, at 200-201; Bank, *supra* note 28, at 1342-1352.
32. *Roebling v. Commissioner* finally made it clear that the judicial doctrine of continuity of interest should apply to a statutory merger or consolidation, *see Roebling v. Commissioner*, 143 F.2d 810 (3d Cir. 1944). For a detailed discussion, *see* Bank, *supra* note 28, at 1358-1360.
33. Treasury Regulations (US), § 1.368-1(e)(2)(v).
34. Miller, *supra* note 4, at 251.
35. *See* Bank, *supra* note 6, at 70.

reorganization is just the form of corporate enterprise, the tax law should allow them to postpone the recognition of gain or loss.[36]

However, both 'purely paper transaction' and 'mere change in form' are vague terms. When proposing the reorganization rule, the US Senate Committee on Finance just stated that one reason for the provision was to 'negative the assertion of tax in the case of certain purely paper transaction'.[37] After the first comprehensive reorganization provision came into existence in 1921, A.W. Gregg, a special assistant to the US Secretary of the Treasury, only clarified the meaning of 'purely paper transaction' as a reorganization that was merely a change in form and not in substance.[38]

It was until the introduction of the continuity of interest doctrine that the meanings of the two terms became clear. Since the *Cortland* decision, continuing interest in the same investment, as the defining feature of a 'purely paper transaction', has been the most important justification for the special tax treatment.[39] Professor Boris Bittker summarized the rationale behind the continuity of interest doctrine as follows:[40]

> The traditional theory of the reorganization provisions is that gain or loss should not be recognized on *changes of form* when the taxpayer's investment remains in 'corporate solution' or when 'a formal distribution, directly or through exchange of securities, represents merely a new form of the previous participation in an enterprise involving *no change of substance in the rights and relations of the interested parties one to another or to the corporate assets*'.

After several decades of development, the continuity of interest doctrine has established itself deeply in the US tax-free reorganization regime. Some US scholars described it as the 'keystone of tax-free reorganizations'[41] and 'the glue that holds the

36. Block, *supra* note 1, at 380.
37. US Senate Committee on Finance, S. REP. No. 617, 65th Cong., 3d Sess. 5 (US) (1918).
38. According to Gregg, '[Reorganization provisions] are based upon the theory that the types of exchanges specified in Section 203 are merely changes in form and not in substance...', cited in Jerome Hellerstein, *Mergers, Taxes, and Realism*, 71 Harv. L. Rev. 254, 258 (1957).
39. *Ibid.*, at 261. ('The development of the continuity of interest requirement was not an alteration, but, indeed, an implementation of the basic justification of the non-recognition provisions...') The continuity of business enterprise, which means the purchasing company continuing the target company's historic business after a reorganization, is also treated as a feature of 'purely paper transaction'. *See generally*, Thomas N. Tarleau, *Continuity of the Business Enterprise in Corporate Reorganizations and Other Corporate Readjustments*, 60 Colum. L. Rev. 792(1960). However, it is far less important than the continuity of interest. *See e.g.*, Daniel Q. Posin, *A Case Study in Income Tax Complexity: The Type A Reorganization*, 47 Ohio St. L.J. 627, 640 (1986); David F. Shores, *Continuity of Business Enterprise: A Concept Whose Time Has Passed*, 63 Tax Law. 471, 472 (2009). To certain degree, the continuity of business enterprise is subordinate to the continuity of interest. *See* Joshua D. Blank, *Confronting Continuity: A Tradition of Fiction in Corporate Reorganizations*, 2006 Colum. Bus. L. Rev. 1, 28 (2006). For the above reasons, this research does not specifically discuss the continuity of business enterprise.
40. Boris Bittker, *Federal Income Taxation of Corporations and Shareholders* (1959). (citing in part *Bazley v. Commissioner*, 331 U.S. 737, 740 (1947), emphasis added)
41. William J. Turnier, *Continuity of Interest – Its Application to Shareholders of the Acquiring Corporation*, 64 Calif. L. Rev. 902, 902 (1976).

reorganization field together'.[42] The doctrine enjoys almost sacred status mainly because it is regarded as the underlying rationale for the non-recognition treatment – if the selling parties to a merger or acquisition receive a quantum of the equity interest in the purchasing company, they will continue their interest in investment, and therefore should not incur current tax liabilities.[43]

Given the fundamental role of the continuity of interest doctrine in the special tax treatment regime, many countries that allow tax-deferred corporate reorganizations choose to adhere to this doctrine.[44] For instance, under the French Tax Code, the consideration in a form other than the stock of the purchasing company is limited to 10% of the nominal value of the newly issued stock.[45] Since the fair market value of the stock is usually much higher than its nominal value, only a tiny portion of the total consideration can be in a form other than the stock of the purchasing company. Japanese law is even more stringent. It strictly prohibits the use of any non-equity consideration in tax-deferred mergers.[46]

Some countries and international organizations explicitly endorse continuity of interest as the rationale for tax deferral. In 2000, the Tax Commission of Japan stated that 'in the case of separation type corporate division or merger, the gain or losses from old stock in the hands of shareholders of the divided company or merged company (stock in a divided company or merged company) also should generally arise. However, when shareholders keep continuing their investment, ..., that gain or loss could be deferred'.[47] The OECD also acknowledges that the reason for providing rollover relief to M&A participants is the continuity of the underlying investment.[48]

With this background in mind, it is unsurprising that the Chinese policymakers decide to follow the continuity of interest doctrine. During past decades, the Chinese central tax authorities have taken many measures to enforce the doctrine. For instance, the MOF and the STA have brought an end to the non-recognition treatment for asset swaps. In an asset swap, each of the two parties in effect first sells its assets and then uses the consideration received to purchase the other party's assets, and as a result, both parties sever connection with their original assets and break the continuity of interest. Nevertheless, under Circular 118, if in an asset swap, the monetary consideration paid by either party did not exceed 25% of the fair market value of the assets

42. Daniel Q. Posin, *Taxing Corporate Reorganizations: Purging Penelope's Web*, 133 U. Pa. L. Rev. 1335, 1371 (1984).
43. The Chinese law retains a rigid post-reorganization continuity requirement. If the target major shareholders sell the purchasing company's stock within twelve months after the transaction, the continuity of interest will be broken. *See* Caishui (2009) No. 59, Art. 5(5).
44. Frans Vanistendael, *Taxation of Corporate Reorganizations, in* 2 *Tax Law Design and Drafting* 895, 908 (Victor Thuronyi ed., 1998).
45. Hugh J. Ault & Brian J. Arnold, *Comparative Income Taxation: A Structural Analysis* 463, 468 (3rd ed., 2010). This is similar to the ratio requirement prescribed in the Merger Directive of the EU. EU Merger Directive, Art. 2.
46. Tetsuya Watanabe, *Tax-Free Treatment for Corporate Reorganizations in Japan* 20-21 (Sho Sato Conference on Tax Law, Social Policy, and the Economy, UC Berkeley, 9-10 March, 2009), https://www.law.berkeley.edu/files/sho_sato_tax_conf_web_paper--watanabe.pdf.
47. Tax Commission of Japan, *Tax Commission Paper of Japan* (2000). (cited in *ibid.*, at 19-20)
48. OECD, *Taxation of Capital Gains of Individuals: Policy Considerations and Approaches* 24, 110 (2006).

exchanged, the two parties would not recognize gain or loss at the time of the transaction.[49] After the repeal of Circular 118, the taxation of M&A transactions comes closer to the continuity of interest doctrine.

[B] Expanding the Eligibility for the Special Tax Treatment

Another basic policy with regard to M&A taxation is to make the special tax treatment more accessible. This tax policy is a part of the Chinese government's M&A stimulation package. As discussed extensively in Chapter 2, the pro-M&A policy has long been a driving force behind the development of China's M&A taxation system. Relaxing the requirements for the special tax treatment is a new addition to the whole picture.

[1] Lowering the Acquisition Percentage Threshold

In the document titled *Opinions on Further Optimizing the Market Environment for Corporate Mergers and Restructurings*, the State Council reaffirmed its commitment to encourage corporate restructurings and vowed to reduce obstacles to M&A transactions.[50] It particularly underlined the necessity to expand the eligibility for the special tax treatment.[51] The State Council believed that the minimum acquisition percentage of 75% prescribed in Circular 59 was too high and mandated the tax authorities to reduce that ratio.[52] Following the State Council's instructions, the tax authorities revised the law and cut the acquisition ratio requirement down to 50%.[53]

[2] Expanding the Scope of Qualifying Consideration

Before 2008, for a merger to qualify for the special tax treatment, a substantial portion of the consideration should be paid in the form of the purchasing company's stock. Circular 59 expands the scope of the qualifying consideration that counts towards satisfying the continuity of interest requirement by including the stock of the purchasing company's 'controlling company' (*konggu gongsi*). Article 2 of Circular 59 reads as follows:[54]

> In this circular, equity consideration refers to the consideration paid by one company in the form of its or *its controlling company's equity interest or shares* to purchase the assets or stock of another company.

---

49. Guoshuifa (2000) No. 118, Art. 5.
50. Guofa (2014) No. 14, Guanyu Jinyibu Youhua Qiye Jianbing Chongzu Shichang Huanjing de Yijian [Opinions on Further Optimizing the Market Environment for Corporate Mergers and Restructurings] (promulgated by the State Council on 7 March 2014) (PRC).
51. Guofa (2014) No. 14, Art. 4(7).
52. *Ibid.*
53. Caishui (2014) No. 109, Arts. 1, 2.
54. Caishui (2009) No. 59, Art. 2. (emphasis added)

Many commentators viewed this provision as a signal that the MOF and the STA had decided to further extend the special tax treatment to 'triangular' M&A transactions, which feature that a company uses its parent company's stock to acquire another company.[55] Compared to a typical M&A transaction that includes only two companies, a triangular transaction involves one more corporate entity, i.e., the parent of the purchasing company. In a triangular transaction, the parent company employs a subsidiary to purchase control of the target company. For example, in a triangular stock acquisition,[56] the parent company first transfers its shares to a subsidiary and then has the subsidiary purchase the target company's stock with those shares.[57] After the transaction, the parent company indirectly controls the target company through its subsidiary, and the target company's shareholders hold the parent company's shares rather than the subsidiary's. Apparently, with tax-deferred triangular transactions as an additional option, the parties would enjoy more flexibility in negotiating corporate restructurings (Figure 5.1).

Figure 5.1 Triangular Stock Acquisition

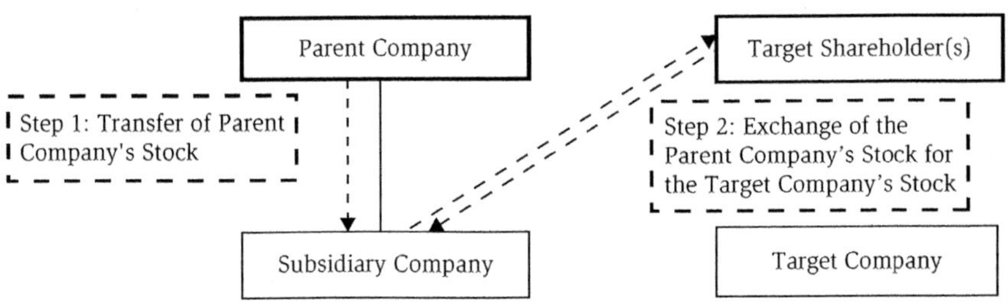

Some Chinese scholars contended that the rationale behind the continuity of interest doctrine necessitates treating the stock of the purchasing company's parent as qualifying consideration. According to them, a triangular M&A transaction satisfies the continuity of interest requirement because, after the transaction, there exists a connection - although indirect - between the transferor and its original investment.[58] However, contrary to such views, the expansion of the scope of qualifying consideration is not readily compatible with the continuity of interest doctrine. To illustrate, consider the following two hypothetical acquisitions.

55. Wei Cui, *Qiye Chongzu Shuiwu Guize Qicao Guocheng de Fansi [Reflections on the Making of the Income Tax Rules for Enterprise Reorganizations], in* 1 *Shuifa Jieshi yu Panli Pingzhu [Tax Law and Case Review]* 163, 178 (Wei Xiong ed., 2010); Wei Cui & Richard Krever, The *Tax Consequences of Corporate Reorganisations in China*, British Tax Review, no. 3, 2011, at 340, 351-352; Zhang, *supra* note 2, at 144.
56. Under the US law, it is known as a B triangular acquisition. A triangular reorganization can also be structured as a triangular statutory merger (triangular A reorganization) or a stock-for-assets acquisition (triangular C reorganization).
57. Internal Revenue Code (US), § 368(a)(1)(B)
58. Li & Yang, *supra* note 1, at 38-39; Zhang, *supra* note 1, at 146.

Acquisition #1A

Suppose Company T has a sole shareholder X. X's outstanding stock is worth RMB 2 million. P is another company that has outstanding stock worth RMB 2 million as well. P and X strike a deal in which P issues RMB 2 million worth of new stock to X in exchange for all the stock of T. After the transaction, X owns 50% of P, which, in turn, owns 100% of T. As a result of the stock offering, P's equity has a new market value of RMB 4 million. Assume P's liabilities total RMB 2 million, so its assets total RMB 6 million.

Acquisition #1B

The underlying assumptions about P, T, and X remain the same. Suppose A1 is a wholly owned subsidiary of P, having RMB 1 million worth of outstanding stock and liabilities totalling RMB 7 million. Like in the above scenario, P purchases all the stock of T from X with its RMB 2 million worth of newly issued stock. Immediately after the stock purchase, P transfers T stock to A1. As a result, P's equity is worth RMB 4 million, and its assets are worth RMB 6 million. The values of A1's equity and assets increase to RMB 3 million and RMB 10 million respectively.

As a purely stock-financed acquisition, *Acquisition #1A* doubtless satisfies the continuity of interest requirement. After *Acquisition #1A*, T stock represents 33.3% of P's assets. Thus, for every dollar worth of P stock X owns, 33.3% of such dollar reflects a continuing interest in T stock. *Acquisition #1B* is a drop-down acquisition in which the parent company issues new shares to purchase the target company's stock and subsequently drops the target company's stock down into a subsidiary. The two-step transaction is in substance a triangular acquisition where the subsidiary uses the stock of its parent to purchase control of the target company. After *Acquisition #1B*, T stock represents 20% of A1's assets, and A1 stock represents 50% of P's assets. Consequently, for every dollar worth of P stock X owns, 10% of such dollar reflects a continuing interest in T stock.

Owing to the drop-down in *Acquisition #1B*, the percentage of the value of P stock attributable to T stock plummets from 33.3% to 10%. Since X's old and new investments differ in substance, the transaction has dramatically weakened, if not eliminated, the continuity of interest by X.[59] Thus, it is evident that an indirect connection between the transferor and its original investment does not suffice to secure the continuity of interest. Furthermore, the longer the ownership chain, the weaker is the continuity of interest.

Suppose P is the ultimate parent company of an n-tier pyramidal corporate group. P owns 100% of A1, A1 owns 100% of A2, and so on. The subsidiary company at each tier of the pyramid has RMB 1 million worth of outstanding stock and liabilities totalling RMB 7 million. After the transaction with X, P transfers T stock down the chain to An. As a result, the equity and assets of each lower-tier subsidiary increase to RMB 3 million and RMB 10 million respectively. T stock represents 20% of An's assets.

59. Regarding the relationship between 'continuity of interest' and 'mere change in form', *see supra* notes 36-40 and accompanying texts.

An stock represents 30% of An-1's assets, An-1 stock represents 30% of An-2's assets, and so on. A1 stock represents 50% of P's assets. For the ultimate controller P, T stock represents 20% × (30%)n-1 × 50% of its assets. Therefore, the original investment of X contributes 10% × (30%)n-1 to the value of P stock X now owns. By setting n large enough, the percentage can approach zero. In such an extreme situation, X fails to continue its interest even though it controls the corporate group by holding 50% of P stock.[60]

Thus, the rationale behind the continuity of interest doctrine does not support the expansion of the scope of qualifying consideration. Except for making the special tax treatment more accessible, there is no other reason for the expansion. The evolution of the US triangular reorganizations also proves this observation.

Historically, in the US, the continuity of interest doctrine created a bar to multiparty reorganizations. For several decades after introducing tax-deferred reorganizations, the US tax law did not expressly permit a purchasing company to transfer the stock of its controlling or parent company in exchange for the stock or assets of the target company. The courts followed a strict textual interpretation of the statutory definitions to conclude that the exchange of the target stock or assets for stock in the parent of the purchasing company was taxable. Moreover, under the step-transaction doctrine, if the purchasing company in a tax-deferred reorganization passed the stock or assets acquired to its subsidiary subsequently, the reorganization would risk being reclassified as taxable by the court. The leading cases in this regard are *Groman v. Commissioner*[61] and *Helvering v. Bashford*[62].

Groman involved a stock acquisition followed by the target's liquidation into the purchasing company. In 1929, all the shareholders of Indiana entered into a share purchase agreement with Glidden. According to the agreement, the shareholders of Indiana transferred their shares to Ohio, a newly established subsidiary of Glidden, in exchange for a total consideration of USD 1,207,016 comprised of Glidden prior preference stock valued at USD 533,980, shares of the preferred stock of Ohio valued at USD 500,000, and USD 153,036 in cash. In filling the annual tax return, the petitioner in this case – a shareholder of Indiana – only included the cash he received in the transaction as income but ignored the shares of Glidden and the shares of Ohio.

The petitioner contended that the receipt of those shares was not taxable because Section 112(b)(3) of the Revenue Act of 1928 provided that in a reorganization, one party would not recognize gain or loss to the extent that it received stock or securities

60. One may make an analogy between the phenomenon with the one known among corporate law scholars as the separation of cash-flow and control rights through pyramids (an investor can control the company at the bottom of a corporate pyramid with only a minimal fraction of the company's cash-flow rights). *See* Lucian A. Bebchuk, et al., *Stock Pyramids, Cross-Ownership, and Dual Class Equity-The Mechanisms and Agency Costs of Separating Control from Cash-Flow Rights, in Concentrated Corporate Ownership* 298-299 (Randall K. Morck ed., 2000). In corporate law literature, an investor's cash-flow right in a company is its ownership (direct or indirect) of that company. Here, this research focuses on if the taxpayer's old and new investments are different in substance.
61. *Groman v. Commissioner*, 302 U.S. 82 (1937).
62. *Helvering v. Bashford*, 302 U.S. 454 (1938).

of another party to the transaction.[63] However, the Commissioner disagreed. It ruled that Glidden not be a 'party to a reorganization', and therefore the exchange of shares of Indiana for shares of Glidden was taxable. The US Supreme Court strictly applied Section 112(i)(2) and supported the opinion of the Commissioner. Section 112(i)(2) defined 'party to a reorganization' as including a company resulting from a reorganization and both the acquiring and target companies in a stock acquisition.[64] Glidden did not receive anything from the shareholders of Indiana, so the transaction was only between Ohio and Indiana's shareholders. Therefore, the US Supreme Court held that Glidden did not fall into the statutory definition of the term 'party to a reorganization'.[65]

The court next considered whether the corporate entity of Ohio should be treated as the alter ego of Glidden and thus be disregarded. To tackle this issue, the court referred to the purpose of the reorganization provisions in the statute. It articulated that the target shareholders were eligible for non-recognition treatment only if their historical interest in the target company 'continues to be definitely represented in substantial measure in a new or different one [company], then to the extent, but only to the extent, of that continuity of interest'.[66] As the relationship between the target shareholder and the purchasing company should be close enough to satisfy the continuity of interest requirement, the court held that treating Glidden – the parent of the purchasing company – as a party to the reorganization 'would be not only to disregard the letter, but also to violate the spirit, of the Revenue Act'.[67]

Bashford was a case very similar to *Groman*. In this case, Atlas Powder Company wanted to eliminate the competition from three rivals – Peerless Explosives Company, Union Explosives Company, and Black Diamond Powder Company. It organized a subsidiary to take over the assets of these companies. However, instead of having the subsidiary purchase the target assets directly, Atlas bought the stock in the three companies from their shareholders with cash, the stock of itself and the stock in the newly formed subsidiary and then transferred the bought stock to the subsidiary. Shortly after that, the target companies got liquidated into the subsidiary. Bashford was one of the shareholders of Peerless, who only returned the cash as income but neither the Atlas stock nor the stock of the new company. The Commissioner admitted that the stock of the new company was not taxable but insisted that the Atlas stock be taxable. The US Supreme Court cited the case of *Groman* and held that the Atlas stock did not definitely represent the interest of the shareholders of the three target companies and should be treated as taxable 'other property'.[68]

Groman and *Bashford* centre around interpreting the meaning of the statutory definition of 'party to a reorganization', but they reach far beyond the statutory language and expand the judicial continuity of interest doctrine. In context, it is clear that by referring to 'continuity of interest' and permitting tax-deferred treatment to

63. Revenue Act of 1928 (US), § 112(b)(3).
64. Revenue Act of 1928 (US), § 112(i)(2).
65. *Groman*, 302 U.S. at 85-86.
66. *Groman*, 302 U.S. at 89.
67. *Groman*, 302 U.S. at 89-90.
68. *Bashford*, 302 U.S. at 456-457.

target shareholders only to the extent they receive stock of the purchasing company, the court excluded the stock or securities of the purchasing company's parent as representing a definite continuity of interest.[69] The two cases formed the foundation of the so-called remote continuity of interest doctrine, and many lower court cases followed them.[70]

If we accept the rationale behind the continuity of interest doctrine, then the same rationale should support the US Supreme Court's decisions. As demonstrated above, if one more entity – the subsidiary of the purchasing company – were interposed between the two parties to an acquisition, the transferor's bond with its original investment would be significantly weakened.

Nevertheless, the US Congress decided to relax the continuity of interest requirement by limiting the remote continuity doctrine and allowing new types of triangular reorganizations.[71] In 1954, the US Congress allowed triangular stock-for-assets reorganizations (provided in Section 368(a)(1)(C) of the IRC). Due to the revision, the purchasing company may use the voting stock of its parent instead of its own voting stock in a tax-deferred reorganization.[72] In the report on the new provisions of the 1954 Tax Code, the US Congress claimed that the revision was 'a liberalization of prior law which modifies certain restrictive judicial interpretations as exemplified in *Groman v. Commissioner* and *Helvering v. Bashford*'.[73]

Some scholars concluded that by doing so, the US Congress intended to give companies more flexibility in choosing tax-deferred reorganizations.[74] However, the US Congress has never seriously addressed the *Groman* and *Bashford* courts' concern that consideration remoteness could break continuity. In the following years, the US Congress has introduced more types of triangular reorganizations, and as a result, the

69. David Miller argued that *Groman* and *Bashford* are merely formalistic interpretations of the term 'party to a reorganization', and the Court only intended to clarify the type of consideration that can be received tax-free but did not intend to develop the continuity of interest doctrine. *See* Miller, *supra* note 4, at 202-204. However, many commentators hold the view that the two decisions were led by the concern over continuity of interest. *See e.g.*, Daniel M. Schneider, *Groman – Or Namorg – Revisited; The Persisting Problem of Remote Continuity of Interest*, 61 Denv. L.J. 469, 480-483 (1983); David G. Levere, *Remote Continuity of Interest: The Problem Persists*, 49 Tax Law. 795, 802-804 (1995); Stephanie Hoffer & Dale A. Oesterle, *Tax-Free Reorganizations: The Evolution and Revolution of Triangular Mergers*, 108 Nw. U. L. Rev. 1083, 1089-1090 (2014).
70. For an enumeration and discussion of those cases, *see* Levere, *supra* note 69, at 804-805.
71. *See ibid.*, at 805-08; Miller, *supra* note 4, at 230-231; Hoffer & Oesterle, *supra* note 69, at 1086-1095.
72. The prior law of § 368(a)(1)(C), namely § 112(g)(1)(B) of the 1939 Code, reads as follows: the acquisition by one company in exchange *solely for all or a part of its voting stock*: ... of substantially all the properties of another company. (emphasis added). § 368(a)(1)(C) of the 1954 Code reads as follows: the acquisition by one company, in exchange solely for all or a part of its voting stock (*or in exchange solely for all or a part of the voting stock of a company which is in control of the purchasing company*), of substantially all of the properties of another company, ... (emphasis added)
73. US Congress Joint Committee on Internal Revenue Taxation, *Summary of the New Provisions of the Internal Revenue Code of 1954 (H.R. 8300)* (1955).
74. *See e.g.*, Hoffer & Oesterle, *supra* note 69, at 1089-1090.

current IRC permits a drop-down of the assets or stock acquired to a subsidiary,[75] so-called triangular B reorganizations[76] and triangular A reorganizations.[77]

§5.03 CONFLICTS BETWEEN THE TWO POLICIES

The above discussion about tax-deferred triangular reorganizations hints at conflicts between the Chinese tax policies of following the continuity of interest doctrine and expanding the eligibility for the special tax treatment. In fact, the severe clashes between the two policies have led to neither of them performing satisfactorily and produced a tax regime full of inconsistencies.

[A] Illusory Continuity of Interest Requirements

Since 2009, the statutory requirement that in tax-deferred M&A transactions, at least 85% of the total consideration should take the form of equity has remained unchanged. Given this requirement reflects the continuity of interest doctrine's two pivotal components (qualitative and quantitative), it is sensible to infer that China's M&A taxation generally keeps to the continuity of interest doctrine. However, as will be shown below, the measures to expand the eligibility for the special tax treatment have significantly weakened the continuity of interest requirements.

[1] Acquisition Percentage

The historical development of the continuity of interest doctrine seems to suggest that the only thing matters for ensuring continuity is the acquisition consideration – as long as a substantial portion of the acquisition consideration is in the form of equity, the continuity of interest requirement will be secured. However, the perception is mistaken

75. In 1954, the US Congress enacted Section 368(a)(2)(C), which reads as follows: a transaction otherwise qualifying under paragraph (1)(A) or paragraph (1)(C) shall not be disqualified by reason of the fact that part or all of the assets which were acquired in the transaction are transferred to a company controlled by the company acquiring such assets. This provision permits dropping the acquired assets or stock down to a subsidiary after an A or C reorganization.
76. In 1964, the US Congress inserted '(or in exchange solely for all or a part of the voting stock of a corporation which is in control of the acquiring corporation)' in Section 368(a)(1)(B). Prior to the revision, the purchasing company can only use its own voting stock as consideration in a B reorganization.
77. In 1968, the US Congress added Section 368(a)(2)(D), which reads as follows: the acquisition by one company, in exchange for stock of a corporation ... which is in control of the acquiring corporation, of substantially all of the properties of another corporation shall not disqualify a transaction under paragraph (1)(A) ... In 1971, the US Congress added Section 368(a)(2)(E), which reads as follows: a transaction otherwise qualifying under paragraph (1)(A) shall not be disqualified by reason of the fact that stock of a corporation ... which before the merger was in control of the merged corporation is used in the transaction... The two provisions allow taxpayers to conduct forward and reverse triangular A reorganizations.

because the ratio of assets or stock transferred in an M&A transaction also has a significant impact on the seller's continuity of interest.

Indeed, the impact of acquisition ratio is rarely mentioned in the US, which is largely due to the fact that the US tax law has imposed very rigid acquisition ratio requirements for M&A transactions to qualify as tax-deferred reorganizations: a Type A reorganization should be a statutory merger in which typically all the assets and liabilities of the target company are transferred to the purchasing company;[78] in a Type B reorganization, the purchasing company must hold at least 80% of the voting stock and 80% of all other classes of stock after the transaction;[79] and in a Type C reorganization, the purchasing company must acquire 'substantially all of the properties' of another company.[80]

China is not so rigid with regard to the acquisition ration thresholds compared to the US. Circular 59 set a relatively high acquisition ratio of 75% in the beginning; however, only five years later, the acquisition ratio threshold was slashed to just 50%. In doing so, the Chinese tax law has jeopardized the continuity of interest requirement, which will be demonstrated in hypotheticals as follows.

Acquisition #2A

Suppose a company (T) has two shareholders (X and Y), each of which owns half of the stock of T. T's outstanding stock is worth RMB 2 million. Company P, whose equity is also worth RMB 2 million, approaches X and Y about the possibility of acquiring T. After negotiation, X and Y agree to sell T to P in exchange for RMB 2 million worth of P's stock. Accordingly, each of them receives RMB 1 million of newly issued stock of P. Thus, X and Y walk away with a block of P stock, and T becomes a wholly owned subsidiary of P.

After the transaction, the value of P's equity increases to RMB 4 million. X has 25.0% ownership interest in P and 25.0% indirect ownership interest in T (which is calculated by multiplying X's ownership percentage in P and P's ownership percentage in T). Given that P's liabilities total RMB 2 million, the assets of P will total RMB 6 million, and T stock represents 33.3% of P's assets. It follows that for every dollar worth of P stock X owns, 33.3% of such dollar reflects a continuing indirect interest in T.

Acquisition #2B

The underlying assumptions of P, T, X, and Y are the same as for *Acquisition #2A*, but the acquisition ratio is different. P decides to purchase only 50% rather than all of T's stock. P transfers RMB 1 million of newly issued stock to X for half of T stock. Thus, X walks away with a block of P stock, and T is controlled by P and Y jointly.

After the transaction, P's equity has a market value of RMB 3 million. X has 33.3% ownership interest in P and 16.7% indirect ownership interest in T. Given that P's assets now total RMB 5 million, T stock held by P represents 20.0% of P's assets.

78. Internal Revenue Code (US), § 368(a)(1)(A)
79. Internal Revenue Code (US), § 368(a)(1)(B)
80. Internal Revenue Code (US), § 368(a)(1)(C)

Therefore, for every dollar worth of P stock X owns, 20.0% of such dollar reflects a continuing indirect interest in T.

Acquisition #2C

Except for the difference in equity consideration ratio, this transaction is identical to *Acquisition #2B*. X agrees to sell all of its T stock to P in exchange for a total consideration of RMB 1 million. P transfers RMB 0.85 million of newly issued stock and RMB 0.15 million in cash to X. As a result, X does not possess any T stock, and P and Y jointly control T.

Following the transaction, X has 29.8% ownership interest in P and 14.9% indirect ownership interest in T. Since P pays RMB 0.15 million cash and receives RMB 1 million of T stock, the value of its equity increases to RMB 2.85 million. Given that P's assets now total RMB 4.85 million, T stock represents 20.6% of P's assets. Thus, for every dollar worth of P stock X owns, 20.6% of such dollar reflects a continuing indirect interest in T.

Acquisition #2D

In *Acquisition #2D*, P purchases 50% and 25% of T's stock from X and Y respectively. X receives RMB 0.85 million newly issued stock and RMB 0.15 million cash. Y receives RMB 0.425 million newly issued stock and RMB 0.075 million cash. After the transaction, P and Y own T jointly.

As P pays RMB 0.225 million cash and receives RMB 1.5 million of T's stock, its equity is now worth RMB 3.275 million. X has 26.0% ownership interest in P and 19.5% indirect ownership interest in T. Given that P's assets now total RMB 5.275 million, T stock held by P represents around 28.4% of P's assets. It follows that for every dollar worth of P stock X owns, around 28.4% of such dollar reflects a continuing indirect interest in T.

Acquisition #2E

Like in *Acquisition #2D*, P purchases 50% and 25% of T's stock from X and Y respectively. However, the equity consideration ratio reduces from 85% to 75%. X receives RMB 0.75 million newly issued stock and RMB 0.25 million cash. Y receives RMB 0.375 million newly issued stock and RMB 0.125 million cash.

As P pays RMB 0.375 million cash and receives RMB 1.5 million of T's stock, its equity is now worth RMB 3.125 million. X has 24.0% ownership interest in P and 18.0% indirect ownership interest in T. Given that P's assets now total RMB 5.125 million, T stock held by P represents around 29.3% of P's assets. It follows that for every dollar worth of P stock X owns, around 29.3% of such dollar reflects a continuing indirect interest in T.

In the following table, this study uses X's indirect shareholding ratio in T (which reflects X's share of T's cash-flow rights, hereinafter symbolized as R1) and the ratio of P's T stock to its total assets (which reflects what proportion of the value of X's new investment is related to its old investment, hereinafter symbolized as R2) to compare how the five acquisitions preserve X's interest in T.

Table 5.1 Continuity of Interest in the Five Acquisitions

	Acquisition Ratio	*Equity Consideration Ratio*	*X's Indirect Shareholding in T (R_1)*	*P's T Stock to Its Total Assets (R_2)*
Acquisition #2A	100%	100%	25.0%	33.3%
Acquisition #2B	50%	100%	16.7%	20.0%
Acquisition #2C	50%	85%	14.9%	20.6%
Acquisition #2D	75%	85%	19.5%	28.4%
Acquisition #2E	75%	75%	18.0%	29.3%

Acquisition #2A and *Acquisition #2B* have the same equity consideration ratio but different acquisition ratios. A comparison of the two transactions will clearly show the impact of the acquisition ratio on a selling shareholder's continuity of interest. As can be seen from Table 5.1, both the values of R_1 and R_2 are lower in *Acquisition #2B* than in *Acquisition #2A*. Therefore, the level of interest continuity diminishes as the acquisition ratio decreases. In fact, among the five acquisitions, Acquisition #2B has the least R2 of 20%, which means only 20% of the value of X's new investment is attributable to its original investment.

Acquisition #2B and *Acquisition #2C* have the same acquisition ratio but different equity consideration ratios, a comparison between which will show how the equity consideration ratio affects the continuity of interest. It is interesting to note that in *Acquisition #2C*, where only 85% of the total consideration is in the form of equity interest, the value of R_2 is marginally higher than that in *Acquisition #2B*. A similar phenomenon can be observed in the comparison between *Acquisition #2D* and *Acquisition #2E*. However, it is too soon to claim that X better continues its interest in *Acquisition #2C* than in *Acquisition #2B* because R_2 – the ratio of P's T stock to its total assets – is an imperfect indicator of X's continuing interest.

A quick unpacking of the continuity of interest reveals two facets: (1) a substantial portion of the consideration should be paid in the form of the purchasing company's stock, and the focus here is whether the quantity of the purchasing company stock paid is sufficient to represent a 'material part of the value of the transferred assets',[81] or put differently, a substantial share of the target company's cash-flow rights; and (2) the purchasing company stock that the seller receives must have a material connection with their original investment, which can be assessed by examining the composition of the underlying assets of the purchasing company stock. Although R_2 is a reliable indicator of the second component of the continuity of interest principle, it omits the first component quantity. R_2 can be high even if a substantial portion of the consideration is in the form of cash, but under such circumstances, X apparently loses continuing interest in the old corporate enterprise. Therefore, to

81. *Minnesota Tea Co.*, 296 U.S. at 386.

accurately determine the level of X's continuity of interest, one needs to look at both R1 and R_2.

This research suggests multiplying R_1 and R_2 together to get an indicator that better reflects investors' continuing interest. Based on Table 5.1, Table 5.2 adopts this new indicator, which can be named as Continuity of Interest Index, to measure X's continuing interest in the five acquisitions.

Table 5.2 Continuity of Interest in the Five Acquisitions (Cont'd)

	Acquisition Ratio	*Equity Consideration Ratio*	*X's Indirect Shareholding in T (R_1)*	*P's T Stock to Its Total Assets (R_2)*	*Continuity of Interest Index ($R_1 \times R_2$)*
Acquisition #2A	100%	100%	25.0%	33.3%	8.33%
Acquisition #2B	50%	100%	16.7%	20.0%	3.34%
Acquisition #2C	50%	85%	14.9%	20.6%	3.07%
Acquisition #2D	75%	85%	19.5%	28.4%	5.54%
Acquisition #2E	75%	75%	18.0%	29.3%	5.27%

Compared to Table 5.1, Table 5.2 more clearly shows that a lower acquisition ratio or a lower equity consideration ratio leads to a lower level of continuity. Among the five acquisitions, *Acquisition #2C*, which barely satisfies the acquisition ratio and the equity consideration threshold under the current law, has the lowest continuity of interest index. Hence, it is clear that the continuity of interest requirement has been eroded due to the reduction of the acquisition ratio threshold from 75% to 50%. Table 5.2 also exhibits how the law inconsistently enforces the continuity of interest requirement: *Acquisition #2E* has a higher continuity of interest index than *Acquisition #2C*; however, *Acquisition #2C* is eligible for the special tax treatment, while *Acquisition #2E* is not.

[2] Qualified Equity Consideration

Circular 59 provides that 'equity consideration' – the qualifying consideration for continuity purposes – is the stock of the purchasing company or its controlling company. As mentioned earlier, most commentators believed that the term 'controlling company' referred to the company that controls the purchasing company, or simply, the purchasing company's parent.[82] However, to everyone's surprise, one year after the issuance of Circular 59, the STA enacted Circular 4, which interprets 'controlling company' in a completely different way.

Article 6 of Circular 4 provides that 'controlling company' refers to 'the company in which the purchasing company directly holds stock'.[83] Due to this official clarification, the tax-deferred triangular reorganizations commonly seen in the US are not an available option for Chinese investors, and more importantly, this unexpected definition of 'controlling company' opens a backdoor for some M&A participants that fail to continue their interest to enjoy the special tax treatment. To illustrate, consider four hypothetical stock acquisitions as shown in Table 5.3.

Table 5.3 Four Hypothetical Stock Acquisitions

Common Assumptions: Company P owns 100% of Company A, which, in turn, owns 100% of Company S. X is the sole shareholder of Company T. A approaches X about the possibility of acquiring all the stock of T.	
Acquisition #3A Company A issues new stock to X in exchange for all of X's stock in T.	*Acquisition #3C* Company A exchanges 100% of the stock in its subsidiary S for all of X's stock in T.
Acquisition #3B Company A pays cash to X in exchange for all of X's stock in T.	*Acquisition #3D* Company A uses the stock of its parent P to acquire all of X's stock in T.

Acquisition #3A is a typical stock-for-stock acquisition. Since the purchasing company (A) acquires more than 50% interest in the target corporate (T) from T's shareholder (X) solely in exchange for A's stock, the transaction meets the statutory requirements for the special tax treatment. After *Acquisition #3A*, X becomes the shareholder of A, through which X continues its interest in T. *Acquisition #3B* is a sale for cash and fails the statutory requirements for the special tax treatment. After *Acquisition #3B*, X walks away with cash, and its connection with T is severed. In *Acquisition #3C*, the requirements for the special tax treatment are satisfied since A acquires a controlling interest in T from X with the stock of A's 'controlling company'; however, after the transaction, X does not have any link with T and its new investment – the S stock – is substantially different from T stock. *Acquisition #3D* is a triangular stock acquisition which fails to meet the requirements for the special tax treatment under Circular 59 and Circular 4. After *Acquisition #3D*, X becomes the shareholder of P – the now grandparent of T – and thus keeps some weak connection with T. The following chart shows the shareholding relationship among these five companies before and after the stock acquisitions.

82. *See supra* note 55 and accompanying texts.
83. STA Gonggao (2010) No. 4, Art. 6.

Figure 5.2 Shareholding Structure Before and After Acquisition

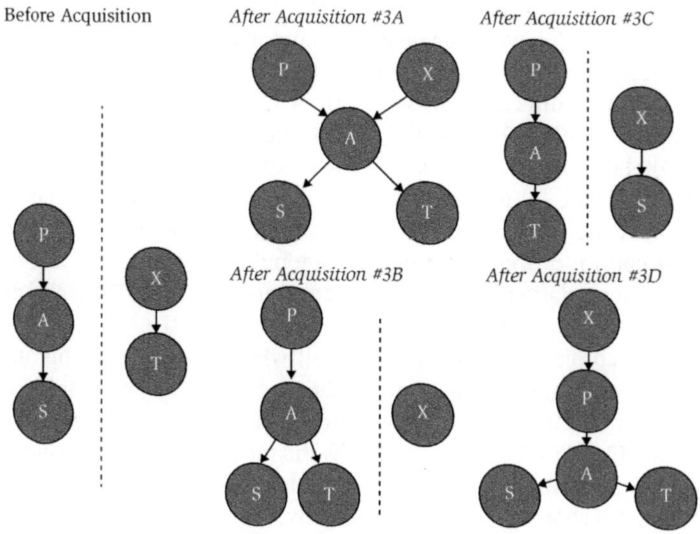

From Figure 5.2, it is evident that the Chinese tax law applies the continuity of interest requirement inconsistently. On the one hand, it allows X in *Acquisition #3C* to enjoy tax deferral benefits, even though X completely loses connection with its original investment. On the other hand, in *Acquisition #3D*, the remote connection between X and T is disregarded, and X needs to pay a current tax. Table 5.4 summarizes whether the statutory requirements for the special tax treatment are satisfied and whether X continues its interest in the four hypotheticals above.

Table 5.4 Continuity of Interest in the Four Acquisitions

	Qualified for the Special Tax Treatment	*Continuity of Interest*
Acquisition #3A	Yes	Yes (Strong)
Acquisition #3B	No	No
Acquisition #3C	Yes	No
Acquisition #3D	No	Yes (Weak)

With the special tax treatment being extended to transactions like *Acquisition #3C*, where the selling parties fail to continue their interest but can enjoy the special tax treatment anyway, many statutory requirements that are designed to ensure continuity of interest have been rendered meaningless. The interpretation of 'controlling company' provided in Circular 4 has attracted heavy criticism both within academia and among practitioners, and it has now become a consensus that 'controlling company' should be redefined as the parent of the purchasing company.[84] Nevertheless, the STA has never shown any intent to reinterpret this notion.

Many commentators seem to suggest that the STA just made a careless mistake in transplanting the US law.[85] However, a more likely possibility is that the STA deliberately interpreted the 'controlling company' as 'the company in which the purchasing company directly holds stock'. Upon closer inspection, it is not hard to find that Article 2 of Circular 59 is adapted from Section 368(a)(2)(D) of the IRC.[86] Section 368(a)(2)(D) of the IRC allows the stock of a 'controlling corporation' to count towards continuity in a type A reorganization. Unlike Article 2 of Circular 59, Section 368(a)(2)(D) of the IRC clearly defines 'controlling corporation' as the corporation 'which is in control of the acquiring corporation'. Therefore, it is unlikely that the problematic interpretation of 'controlling company' by the STA was caused by its misunderstanding of US law.

In fact, according to Professor Wei Cui, who participated in the enactment of Circular 59 as an external expert, the MOF and the STA chose to follow Section 368(a)(2)(D) of the IRC to allow for tax-deferred triangular M&A transactions by enacting Article 2 of Circular 59.[87] Then, why did the tax authorities change their mind? One possible explanation is that the tax authorities did not want to encourage a subsidiary to hold shares of its parent company.[88] According to corporate law theory, such cross-ownership of shares may impair the rights of creditors as well as those of shareholders because cross-owned companies can easily inflate capital and have greater managerial entrenchment.

Notwithstanding, the corporate law theory-based explanation is a partial one at best. The concern over cross-ownership can be easily relieved by removing the term 'controlling company' from the law, but the Chinese tax authorities do not amend the law in this way. The desire to make the special tax treatment more accessible is probably the only plausible explanation as to why the provision that recognizes the stock held by the purchasing company as qualified for the continuity of interest test is firmly upheld in China. Since the purchasing company can use any stock it holds as qualifying consideration, the parties enjoy much more flexibility in negotiating a tax-deferred transaction now than they did before 2008.

Apart from going against the continuity of interest doctrine, the problematic interpretation of 'controlling company' leads to a tax loophole. According to Circular 59, the seller in a tax-deferred transaction will take the same basis that it previously had in the assets or stock transferred as the basis in the stock received from the purchasing company, and the purchasing company's basis in the assets or stock acquired will also be the seller's historical basis in the assets or stock.[89] Such tax basis rules are sensible

84. Li & Zhou, *supra* note 1, at 21; Li & Yang, *supra* note 1, at 39; Feng Shen, *The Evolution of M&A Tax Policy and Reform Proposals*, Shuishou Jingji Yanjiu [Tax and Economic Research], no. 5, 2016, at 31, 34.
85. *See e.g.*, Li & Zhou, *supra* note 1, at 22.
86. Internal Revenue Code (US), § 368(a)(2)(D).
87. *See* Cui, *supra* note 55, at 178.
88. *See* Li & Zhou, *supra* note 1, at 20-21.
89. Caishui (2009) No. 59, Arts. 6(2), 6(3).

only in the situation where purchasing company issues new stock to the seller as consideration. Circular 4 extends the special tax treatment to transactions like *Acquisition #3C* but does not correspondingly provide a new set of tax basis rules. Consequently, taxpayers have an opportunity to evade taxes on assets exchanges permanently. Take *Acquisition #3C* as an example. Suppose that the tax basis and fair market value of T stock are both RMB 100, and S stock has a tax basis of RMB 50 and a fair market value of RMB 100. Applying the above tax basis rules to this hypothetical, T stock keeps its historical basis of RMB 100 and S stock has a stepped-up basis of RMB 100 after *Acquisition #3C*. When A and X dispose of their stock in S and T, none of them has to recognize gains, and thus the unrecognized RMB50 appreciation in the value of S stock is exempt from taxes forever.

[B] Ineffective Efforts to Expand the Eligibility for the Special Tax Treatment

This section conducts an empirical study to provide insights into whether the reduction of the acquisition ratio thresholds has effectively made the special tax treatment more accessible. As will be seen, such an amendment to Circular 59 does not work as expected. Although a more effective way to expand the eligibility for the special tax treatment is probably to reduce the equity consideration ratio threshold, the tax authorities have not embraced it as a viable option yet due to its purported adherence to the continuity of interest doctrine.

[1] Data Collection

In order to evaluate the impact of the reduction in the acquisition percentage threshold on the application of the special tax treatment, this research decides to compare how often M&A transactions get the special tax treatment before and after this reform. Owing to the lack of data on M&A transactions between closely held companies, this research has to confine itself to looking at transactions involving listed companies, and meanwhile, only those transactions happening between 1 January 2014 and 31 December 2015 are included to ensure a manageable data volume. Although short, the time window of 2014 and 2015 is perfect for the purpose of this empirical study because the reduction in the acquisition percentage threshold was rolled out at the end of 2014 – right in the middle of this two-year period.

As to the data collection process, this research first consulted a widely used electronic database for the Chinese stock market – CSMAR,[90] and the crude selection yielded a sample of 12,753 deals. To further reduce data to a manageable size, this research picked out deals based on the following criteria:

1. The transaction should be a stock acquisition, where the purchasing company purchased the stock of the target company from its existing shareholders.

90. CSMAR, http://csmar.gtadata.com/.

Since the special tax treatments for mergers and assets acquisitions are similar to that for stock acquisitions, the study on stock acquisitions is illustrative of how the special tax treatment is implemented in practice.

2. In the transaction, a part of the total consideration should be in the form of equity. In a transaction that qualifies for the special tax treatment, the sellers must receive some 'equity consideration' from the purchasing company. Thus, this research spotlighted the transactions where equity consideration was adopted. Moreover, given the serious problems surrounding the term 'controlling company', this research disregards the stock of the purchasing company's 'controlling company' as equity consideration. Put differently, 'equity consideration' as recognized in this empirical study, only includes the stock of the purchasing company.
3. In the transaction, the purchasing company purchased not less than 50% of the target's outstanding shares. Circular 59 defines stock acquisition as one company purchasing the shares of another to gain control of the latter. Although it is unclear what the minimum acquisition percentage for obtaining the right of control is, Circular 59 stipulated that only stock acquisitions where the purchasing company purchases no less than 75% of the target's outstanding shares can get the special tax treatment,[91] and this ratio has been reduced by Circular 109 to 50%.[92] This research used the 50% threshold accordingly.
4. The transaction shall be a domestic stock acquisition. Because of the additional stringent restrictions imposed by Circular 59, only cross-border M&A transactions that constitute intra-group restructurings get the opportunity to apply the special tax treatment. As intra-group restructurings generally involve a high acquisition ratio, the reduction in the acquisition percentage threshold is expected to have minimal impact on the arrangement of cross-border M&A transactions. In order to accentuate the effect of the reduction in the acquisition percentage threshold, this empirical study decides to focus on domestic transactions.

After filtering out deals that fail to meet the above criteria, the research eventually locates 585 transactions. As this empirical study is concerned with how the special tax treatment works in practice, it is necessary to differentiate transactions that qualified for the special tax treatment from those that did not. However, since the CSMAR database provides only brief summaries of these M&A transactions, this research has manually extracted relevant information from more than 500 listed company public announcements.[93]

91. Caishui (2009) No. 59, Art. 6(2).
92. Caishui (2014) No. 109, Art. 1.
93. The research searches for listed company announcements on Juchao Zixun Wang (CN Info, http://www.cninfo.com.cn), which is a website designated by the China Securities Regulatory Commission (CSRC) for listed companies to make disclosure.

[2] Empirical Findings and Analysis

Table 5.5 shows the temporal distribution of cases. Compared to 2014, the transaction volume in 2015 surged by more than 50%, which is in line with the general trend of China's M&A market. In 2014 and 2015, China's M&A transactions surged both in value and volume. According to the statistics provided by Wind Info, there were 6269 M&A deals in 2015, 54.3% more than that in 2014,[94] and the PwC reported that in 2015 the M&A deal volume in China increased by 37%, while the deal value increased by 84%.[95] Moreover, listed companies played a more active role in M&A activities. Wind Info reported that listed companies completed 310 material assets reorganizations during 2015, which outnumbered the total trade volumes of the past four years. The 2014-15 bull market was considered to have contributed to the significant growth of corporate restructurings involving listed companies.[96]

Table 5.5 Stock Acquisitions (2014-2015)

	2014	*2015*
Transactions	223	362

Table 5.6 shows the number of stock acquisitions that qualify for the special tax treatment in 2014 and 2015.[97]

Table 5.6 Frequency with Which Stock Acquisitions Got the Special Tax Treatment (2014-2015)

Year	*Number of Transactions*	*Eligible for the Special Tax Treatment*	*Ineligible for the Special Tax Treatment*	*% Eligible for the Special Tax Treatment*
2014	223	121	102	54.3%
2015	362	202	160	55.8%
Total	585	323	262	55.2%

94. Wind Info, *Binggou Langchao Xingqi: 2015 Nian Zhongguo Binggou Guimo Chuang Lishi Xingao [The Rising Tide of M&A: China's M&A Activities Hit A New Record in 2015]* (18 February 2016), http://money.163.com/16/0218/19/BG4LPIE700254UB4.html.
95. PwC, *M&A 2015 Review and 2016 Outlook* (26 January 2016), https://www.pwccn.com/en/services/deals-m-and-a/publications/ma-2015-review-and-2016-outlook.html.
96. Wind Info, *supra* note 94.
97. Apart from the above two threshold limits, a transaction also needs to meet three other requirements to gain the special tax treatment. Moreover, the STA and its local branches have the final say on this issue. Chapter 3 provides a detailed discussion on the conditions of the special tax treatment. This quantitative analysis treats a stock acquisition as eligible for the special tax treatment if it meets the threshold limits.

In counting the number of qualified deals, this study adopts the old acquisition ratio threshold – 75% – for 2014 and the new acquisition ratio threshold – 50% – for 2015. Thus, the 2014 figures indicate how the special tax treatment was applied under the old rule, while the 2015 figures show the situation after the law reform. As shown above, the rate of eligible for the special tax treatment raised slightly from 54.3% in 2014 to 55.8% in 2015. That is to say, the eligibility rate for the special tax treatment did not change significantly after the law reform.

The above findings seem to suggest that lowering the acquisition percentage requirement is ineffective in expanding the eligibility for the special tax treatment. In order to confirm this observation, this research further looks at how many transactions that were unqualified for the special tax treatment turned qualified as a result of the reduction of the acquisition percentage requirement.

Based on the acquisition percentage and the equity consideration ratio, we can classify the transactions in the sample into the following four groups. *Group A* includes stock acquisitions in which the acquisition ratio is less than 75%, and the equity consideration ratio is less than 85%. *Group B* includes stock acquisitions in which the acquisition ratio is less than 75%, and the equity consideration ratio is no less than 85%. *Group C* includes stock acquisitions in which the acquisition ratio is no less than 75%, and the equity consideration ratio is less than 85%. *Group D* includes stock acquisitions in which the acquisition ratio is no less than 75%, and the equity consideration is no less than 85%.

Table 5.7 Categorization of Stock Acquisitions (2014)

	Equity Consideration Ratio	
	[0%, 85%)	*[85%, 100%]*
Acquisition Ratio [50%, 75%)	6 (*Group A*)	12 (*Group B*)
Acquisition Ratio [75%, 100%]	84 (*Group C*)	121 (*Group D*)

Table 5.7 shows the classification of the transactions in 2014. *Group A*, *Group B*, *Group C*, and *Group D* have 6, 12, 84, and 121 transactions respectively. Under the old rule, only the 121 transactions of *Group D* were eligible for the special tax treatment. Among the remaining transactions, except for the twelve deals of *Group B*, the majority did not meet the minimum equity consideration ratio requirement. In other words, the ninety deals of *Group A* and *Group C* would always be unqualified for the special tax treatment, whatever the acquisition ratio threshold was. Only the twelve deals of *Group B* would become qualified thanks to the relaxation of the minimum acquisition percentage restriction. Those deals of Group B account for just 5.38% of all the deals of 2014. As the reform measure targeted such a small group of transactions, it was doomed to fail in its purpose.

Some might argue that the unsatisfactory figure in 2014 is due to M&A participants' unawareness of the new rule at the time of transactions, and the number of deals of Group B would probably have increased drastically had M&A participants known the new rule. In order to evaluate this hypothesis, this research analyses the transactions of 2015 in the same way as the transactions of 2014.

Table 5.8 Categorization of Stock Acquisitions (2015)

	Equity Consideration Ratio	
	[0%, 85%)	*[85%, 100%]*
Acquisition Ratio [50%, 75%)	4 (*Group A*)	17 (*Group B*)
Acquisition Ratio [75%, 100%]	156 (*Group C*)	185 (*Group D*)

Table 5.8 presents the classification of the stock acquisitions of 2015. *Group A*, *Group B*, *Group C*, and *Group D* have 4, 17, 156, and 185 transactions respectively. If the law had not changed the minimum acquisition percentage requirement, there would have been 185 qualified deals. The promulgation of Circular 109 turned the seventeen transactions of *Group B* into qualified for the special tax treatment. Those seventeen transactions of *Group B* make up less than 5% of all the transactions of 2015. As in the case of 2014, the largest portion of unqualified transactions in 2015 consisted of transactions that met the minimum acquisition percentage requirement but failed to satisfy the equity consideration ratio threshold. Those deals remained unqualified irrespective of whether the tax authorities reduced the acquisition percentage requirement. Since the stock transactions during 2014 and 2015 show similar distribution patterns, it is reasonable to conclude that the enactment of Circular 109 had limited effect in expanding the eligibility for the special tax treatment.

As shown in Table 5.9, many transactions failed to qualify as tax-deferred reorganizations because they did not meet the equity consideration ratio threshold. Thus, a reduction in the equity consideration ratio threshold should be more promising in expanding the eligibility for the special tax treatment. The table below presents a categorization of the deals over the two years based on their equity consideration ratio.

Table 5.9 Equity Consideration Ratio of the Stock Acquisitions (2014-2015)

Equity Consideration Ratio	*Transactions*	*Proportion of All Transactions*
[0%, 55%)	50	8.6%
[55%, 70%)	70	12.0%
[70%, 85%)	130	22.2%
[85%, 100%)	93	15.9%
100%	242	41.4%
Total	585	100.0%

From Table 5.9, it is immediately evident that in most transactions, more than half of the total consideration was paid in stock. About 242 transactions were paid for in pure equity, accounting for more than 40% of all transactions examined in this empirical study. Among the mixed payment transactions, the largest group is the one with equity consideration between 70% and 85%, comprised of 130 transactions, which account for about 22.2% of all transactions and about half of the unqualified transactions. In 127 out of the 130 transactions, the acquisition ratio was more than 75%. If the equity consideration ratio threshold were reduced from 85% to 70% while the acquisition ratio threshold stayed at 75%, around half of the unqualified transactions would have turned qualified. It is thus demonstrated that reducing the equity consideration ratio threshold rather than the acquisition percentage threshold is much more promising in terms of expanding the eligibility for the special tax treatment. However, since the current equity consideration ratio threshold of 85% has already become a sacred cow, the motion of scaling it down is likely to be deemed unacceptable.

§5.04 CONCLUSION

This chapter examines the underlying mechanism of the special tax treatment that takes the central role in China's income tax regime for M&A transactions. It is not intended to provide an exhaustive account of all the challenges that the regime faces. Instead, it focuses on the tensions in China's tax policies for M&A transactions and identifies, in particular, severe conflicts between two fundamental tax policies: (1) maintaining the continuity of interest as a pivotal eligibility requirement for the special tax treatment and (2) expanding the eligibility for the special tax treatment. As demonstrated in this chapter, the two conflicting policies have prevented each other from being effectively achieved and resulted in severe inconsistencies within the special tax treatment regime. Such unresolved policy conflicts are at the root of the problems in China's M&A taxation, and without addressing the conflicts, there can be little hope for establishing a consistent and neutral M&A tax system.

There are many possible solutions to the conflicts, and four possibilities are instantly obvious. First, by repealing the continuity of interest requirements, the tax authorities can take more effective measures to expand the eligibility for the special tax treatment. Second, the lawmakers may stop attempting to make the special tax treatment more accessible and instead faithfully implement the continuity of interest doctrine. Third, the law may strike a balance between the two policies and take a middle-of-the-road approach. Fourth, the tax law may abolish the special tax treatment to eradicate the mess. Then, the issue is, which is the most appropriate solution?

To make the decision, one should ask first whether the special tax treatment is normatively justified and, if so, what the justification is. The analysis in this chapter follows the traditional theory that treats continuity of interest as the rationale behind the special tax treatment. However, the traditional theory is far from an undisputed truth. If, after a thorough examination, it is confirmed that the law should and can only grant non-recognition treatment to transactions that satisfy the continuity of interest doctrine, then the second solution should be adopted. If the traditional theory is untenable, but there exists some other justification for the special tax treatment, the first solution may be more appropriate. If the special tax treatment is justifiable on multiple grounds, the third solution should succeed. If the special tax treatment is ungrounded, we should scrap it altogether, and thus all the problems above will disappear. The next chapter will deal with the issue of the normative foundation of the special tax treatment.

CHAPTER 6

Special Tax Treatment for M&A: Justifications and Prospects

§6.01 INTRODUCTION

As shown in the preceding chapter, the question of in which direction the reform to the special tax treatment should take place depends on the inquiry into its normative foundation. Hence, this chapter turns to examining the justifications for the special tax treatment and based on which to explore the direction for reforming the regime. Through such an examination, this chapter will also respond to the question raised in Chapter 5 - whether the existence of special tax treatment is a contravention of tax neutrality, the overarching principle for taxing M&A transactions.

This chapter is organized as follows. Section §6.02 will assess the traditional justifications for the special tax treatment, and the possible justifications for it derived from the principle of tax neutrality, with a view to point out whether or which of the justifications are sound. Section §6.03 draws upon the analysis of the previous section as well as the empirical findings from China's M&A market to advance some reform proposals.

§6.02 JUSTIFICATIONS FOR THE SPECIAL TAX TREATMENT

As mentioned in Chapter 3, the EITL expansively defines gross income as a company's monetary and non-monetary income from whatever source derived.[1] Alongside this tautological definition of gross income, a basic rule embodied in the EITL is that a company shall pay current taxes on the gains from sales of assets unless the law provides otherwise. The special tax treatment for M&A transactions, as one of the few exceptions to this general rule, thus fits uneasily within the framework of the Chinese

1. EITL, Art. 6.

income tax system. In order to argue the necessity of such an exceptional tax treatment, it should be demonstrated that a strong justification guaranteeing the deviation from the general recognition rule does exist. Hence, this section will be devoted to thoroughly assessing the likely justifications for the special tax treatment, which can generally be classified into two groups – the traditional justifications and those derived directly from the principle of tax neutrality.

[A] Traditional Justifications

Since the US established the non-recognition clauses for so-called reorganizations,[2] there has been a long-standing debate on the issue of whether the practice of letting certain corporate reorganizations enjoy the special tax treatment is legitimate, and many prominent academics in the US have participated in this discussion.

Professor Jerome Hellerstein is the first scholar to systematically analyse this issue. He summarized four major arguments supporting the non-recognition treatment for M&A transactions. The first argument is that in qualified M&A transactions, the exchanging shareholders continue their proprietary interest, so it is improper to tax these 'mere formal change' transactions.[3] The second argument for the non-recognition treatment is that quitting imposing taxes on certain types of corporate reorganizations can avoid the difficulty of valuing stocks received on those transactions.[4] The third reason for allowing non-recognition in M&A transactions is that the exchanging shareholders that receive little cash should face financial hardship to fulfil their tax obligations.[5] The last argument derives from the fear that levying current taxes on M&A transactions discourages business readjustments.[6]

The seminal work of Hellerstein provides an analytical framework to examine the justification for granting rollover relief to M&A participants. In the US, later academic discourse on this issue has largely developed within this framework,[7] and the impact of the four typical justifications summarized by Hellerstein has reached far beyond the US. In China, each of the four justifications has many advocates,[8] and some officials of the STA highlighted the necessity of the special tax treatment by resorting to all of the

2. 'Reorganization' is a term of art in the US tax law, referring to the tax-deferred corporate restructurings prescribed by IRC § 368. Unless specified, in this section 'reorganization' is used in its US meaning of 'tax-deferred corporate restructurings'.
3. Jerome Hellerstein, *Mergers, Taxes, and Realism*, 71 Harv. L. Rev. 254, 259-260 (1957).
4. *Ibid.*, at 281.
5. *Ibid.*
6. *Ibid.*, at 276.
7. *See e.g.*, Steven A. Bank, *Mergers, Taxes, and Historical Realism*, 75 Tul. L. Rev. 1, 5 (2000); Yariv Brauner, *A Good Old Habit, or Just an Old One? Preferential Tax Treatment for Reorganizations*, 2004 BYU L. Rev. 1, 66 (2004).
8. *See e.g.*, Continuity of interest: Lanxiang Zhou, *Continuity of Interest and Equity Consideration*, Caikuai Yuekan [Finance and Accounting Monthly], no. 5, 2015, at 90, 91; (supporting the continuity of interest argument) Haiyong Wang, *Improving M&A Tax Policies to Promote Economic Structural Reform*, Guoji Shuishou [International Taxation in China], no. 2, 2015, at 39, 39. (emphasizing the valuation difficulty); Xiaowei Hao, et al., *On Improving M&A Tax Policies*, Shuishou Jingji Yanjiu [Tax and Economic Research], no. 4, 2015, at 42, 42. (emphasizing the liquidity problem); Shusong Ba & Yafang Yu, *Coordination of Market-Oriented M&A and*

four justifications.[9] This research refines the arguments into four categories: continuity of interest, the difficulty of valuation, liquidity problem, and efficiency benefits. Considering the close relationship between the concepts of efficiency and neutrality, the first three of the justifications will be assessed under the title of 'traditional justifications' while the 'efficiency benefits' will be covered later in the subsection part about the tax neutrality-based justifications.

[1] Continuity of Interest

This justification arises from the observation that the selling shareholders in a stock-financed M&A transaction do not cash out on their investment. By replacing their stock in the target company with the stock of the acquiring company, those shareholders continue their interest in a modified corporate enterprise.[10] Since in this 'purely paper transaction', what has changed is only the form of corporate enterprise, the selling shareholders should be entitled to non-recognition of gain or loss.[11] Among the four justifications, this one is the strongest. It implies a moral norm that it is unfair to tax taxpayers who continue their interests in investment.

Before proceeding to more detailed discussions, this research finds it necessary to make a distinction between the notion of continuity of interest and the doctrine of continuity of interest. Continuity of interest, as a notion, is an assertion that a seller in an M&A transaction should be granted rollover relief if and only if it continues its interest after the transaction. The continuity of interest doctrine, in this research, refers to a set of legal rules that originates in the US and then spreads to other countries including China. Those rules indicate what the law treats as a continuity of interest. The special tax treatment can be justified from the perspective of continuity of interest only if: (1) the doctrine accords with the notion and (2) the notion is justifiable. The two conditions will be dealt with separately in the following subsection for the sake of clarity.

[a] Continuity of Interest Doctrine

This part skips introducing the continuity of interest doctrine, as Chapter 5 has already discussed it in detail. According to the continuity of interest doctrine, if the selling parties to an M&A transaction receive a quantum of the equity interest in the purchasing company, they will be deemed as continuing their interest in the original investment and can thus defer their tax liabilities arising from the transaction.

Government Policy to Address Overcapacity, Shuiwu Yanjiu [Taxation Research], no. 11, 2013, at 3, 7-8. (emphasizing the necessity to boost market efficiency)

9. *See e.g.*, Wang, *supra* note 8, at 39.
10. Bank, *supra* note 7, at 70; Xiaoguang Zhou, *Tax Deferral and Anti-Avoidance in M&A Taxation*, Shuiwu Yanjiu [Taxation Research], no. 4, 2015, at 64, 66.
11. Cheryl D. Block, *Corporate Taxation: Examples & Explanations* 380 (4th ed., 2010).

However, whether the doctrine could guarantee that only the taxpayers that continue their interests can enjoy non-recognition treatment is questionable.[12]

In many M&A transactions, especially those between big corporations and small ones, the exchanging shareholders' proprietary interests undergo significant changes. Consider the example that a large listed company (P) acquires a small closely held company (T) whose shares are exclusively held by S. In the stock acquisition initiated by P, P issues ten shares to S in exchange for all T stock that has a fair market value of RMB 10, and following the share issuance, P has 1,000 outstanding shares whose total market value is RMB 1,000. Despite that S only receives P stock as the consideration for the acquisition, its proprietary interest in T changes dramatically due to the transaction.

As the sole shareholder of T, S enjoys many rights in that company, the two most important of which are the right to participate in corporate management and the entitlement to a portion of the company's assets and earnings. Because the value of P overwhelmingly exceeds that of T, after the transaction, S owns a mere 1% of P. S used to have complete control of the corporate decisions of T, but now its role in corporate decision-making is marginalized. By exchanging the stock of a small company for the stock representing a large pool of assets, S significantly diversifies its investment and reduces the investment risk.[13]

The above hypothetical example clearly shows that the doctrine of continuity of interest, in the present form, disregards the relative size of the purchasing and the target companies and thus fails to achieve its purpose of identifying the transactions where the selling parties genuinely continue their interest.[14] S does not continue its interest despite the receipt of solely equity consideration. If the transaction consideration consisted of some cash, the connection between S and its original investment would be even weaker.

In response to a similar concern, the American Law Institute (ALI) suggested revamping the continuity of interest doctrine in 1954. In the draft Federal Income Tax Statute prepared by it, the ALI proposed to confine the non-recognition treatment to stock or asset acquisitions where the selling parties receive stock representing no less than 20% of voting power in the purchasing company.[15] In fact, the ALI was not the

12. The US doctrine of continuity of interest has been criticized from various perspectives, such as creating abuse potential, lack of clarity, uncertainty, etc. *See e.g.*, David S. Miller, *The Devolution and Inevitable Extinction of the Continuity of Interest Doctrine*, 3 Fla. Tax Rev. 187, 241-248 (1996); Joshua D. Blank, *Confronting Continuity: A Tradition of Fiction in Corporate Reorganizations*, 2006 Colum. Bus. L. Rev. 1, 19-24 (2006). The criticism here focuses on whether the doctrine can achieve its purpose of differentiating those with and those without continuity of interest.
13. The observations in this paragraph have been repeatedly articulated. See e.g., Hellerstein, *supra* note 3, at 267; William A. Lovett, *Tax Subsidies for Merger: Should Mergers be Made to Meet a Market Test for Efficiency*, 45 N.Y.U. L. Rev. 844, 850-851 (1970); Blank, *supra* note 12, at 25-31.
14. Daniel Q. Posin, *Taxing Corporate Reorganizations: Purging Penelope's Web*, 133 U. Pa. L. Rev. 1335, 1371-1373 (1984).
15. American Law Institute, *Federal Income Tax Statute (February 1954 Draft)*, § X500(f), X601, X602.

first to try to prevent the transaction where the selling parties' proportionate interest significantly plummets from qualifying as a reorganization.

In 1933, two years before the US Supreme Court delivered its decision on *Minnesota Tea*, the US Board of Tax Appeals decided that the transaction in *Minnesota Tea* not be a reorganization. The Board pointed out that the voting trust certificates merely represented 7.5% of the outstanding shares of the transferee, and therefore 'the transaction appears to be far from a continuing interest in the same property through a mere change in forms of ownership but rather an almost complete change in the essential assets owned'.[16] In 1935, the understanding of the continuity of interest requirement reached a critical fork in the road. As discussed previously, the US Supreme Court has eventually chosen to reject the Board's opinion, holding that the ratio of equity consideration to total consideration determines whether the continuity of interest is satisfied,[17] but the better route is probably the one taken by the Board. Nevertheless, the merits of the Board's route should not be overestimated because it does not address another troublesome problem – whether to treat the exchanging shareholders as an aggregate in the assessment of continuity of interest.

Since *Minnesota Tea*, an M&A transaction in the US generally will qualify for the non-recognition treatment if the composition of the overall consideration package paid to all of the sellers meets a certain standard. Such an aggregate method is both over-inclusive and under-inclusive. On the one hand, it may include shareholders whose proprietary interests have changed. That is, shareholders may get the special tax treatment just because their fellow shareholders continue their interests. Consider a stock acquisition where 95% of the consideration consists of the purchasing company's stock and the rest is cash. This transaction is apparently qualified for the non-recognition treatment; hence the law provides non-recognition to all shareholders upon their receipt of equity consideration, even though some of them receive payments mostly in cash.

On the other hand, this aggregate method may exclude shareholders who indeed continue their interest from enjoying the non-recognition treatment. For instance, if only 5% of the total consideration for target shares consists of the purchasing company's stock – a ratio far from sufficient to meet the current continuity test, the law will deny all the exchanging shareholders the non-recognition treatment. Although most people would agree that a shareholder who only receives equity consideration and whose proportionate interest does not decrease significantly in the transaction continues its interest, this shareholder cannot enjoy the non-recognition treatment as a result of the aggregate method.

It is unknown why the US Supreme Court in *Minnesota Tea* adopted this aggregate method. One plausible explanation is that the court treated companies as aggregates of their shareholders. This aggregate view of companies emphasizes that stock represents inclusion in shareholders' collective efforts to make corporate decisions. However, for the shareholders that have a minor influence on corporate

16. *Minnesota Tea Co.*, 28 B.T.A. at 595.
17. *Minnesota Tea Co.*, 296 U.S. at 385.

decision-making, their stock is merely a property interest and does not denote participation in a collective endeavour. In such circumstances, requiring continuity of other shareholders' interest in the purchasing company makes little sense as a prerequisite to one shareholder's non-recognition.[18]

If the idea that the law should only grant non-recognition treatment to sellers who continue their interest is normatively right, then the continuity of interest test must be reconstructed to examine the change in each target shareholder's proportionate interest. A proposal made by Professor Joshua Blank reflects this stance. Blank suggests that a selling shareholder should pay current taxes if its proportionate interest in the purchasing company after a transaction is less than 20% of its proportionate interest in the target company before the transaction. In other words, the non-recognition treatment is only allowed for the selling shareholder that experiences a less than 80% reduction of its proportionate interest in the underlying company.[19]

Whether Blank's proposal well conforms to the continuity of interest notion is debatable. However, one thing is for sure: the continuity of interest doctrine no doubt fails to accord with that notion.

[b] Continuity of Interest Notion

A more fundamental challenge to the continuity of interest as a justification for the special tax treatment is whether the notion itself is normatively sound. In a realization-based income tax system that has been adopted by many countries including China, taxpayers need to recognize gain or loss when there is a realization event. The most typical realization event is the sale of assets.[20] The continuity of interest notion, on the contrary, holds that the tax law should not tax certain taxpayers at the time when they sell their assets. Given the potential conflict, to examine the normative merits of the continuity of interest rationale, a study on the notion's relationship with the realization rule is needed.

The proponents of the continuity of interest notion usually deny its conflicts with the realization rule by contending that realization is not sufficient in M&A transactions where investors continue their interest.[21] Such kinds of arguments imply that transfer of ownership is not a good indicator of realization events, but discontinuity of proprietary interest is. Some fundamental issues of income taxation thus emerge: what is the justification for binding the imposition of income tax with realization events, and what are the criteria for determining realization events?

18. Stephanie Hoffer & Dale A. Oesterle, *Tax-Free Reorganizations: The Evolution and Revolution of Triangular Mergers*, 108 Nw. U. L. Rev. 1083, 1102, 1109 (2014).
19. Blank, *supra* note 12, at 50-51.
20. The EITL enumerates eight types of realization events. EITL, Art. 6.
21. *See e.g.*, Brauner, *supra* note 7, at 11; Bank, *supra* note 7, at 70.

[i] Realization as a Basic Tax Rule

As noted in Chapter 4, the Haig-Simons income tax best accords with the principle of neutrality and thus is the ideal income tax model. Under this model, taxpayers are subject to taxes on any appreciation in the value of their properties, regardless of whether they convert the appreciated assets into cash or other property.[22] Nevertheless, in most countries, only appreciation in value has never been seriously considered in the computation of gross income.

In some jurisdictions, there were episodes when the income tax law swung between accrual-based tax and realization-based tax, but without exception, all of these jurisdictions eventually returned to the realization-based tax. Take the US as an example.[23] Under the Revenue Act of 1913, which was the first modern income tax law in the US, net income is defined to include, inter alia, 'gains, profits, and income derived from ... interest, rent, dividends, securities, or the transaction of any lawful business carried on for gain or profit, or gains or profits and income derived from any source whatever'.[24] When applying this provision to the case of a stock dividend, the US Congress and the US Supreme Court used to have different ideas.

In *Towne v. Eisner*, the US Supreme Court held the opinion that an unrealized increase in the value of assets is not income. Justice Holmes stated that 'the corporation is no poorer and the stockholder is no richer than they were before [the stock dividend]'.[25] However, before *Towne* was handed down, the Revenue Act of 1913 was replaced by the Revenue Act of 1916, in which the US Congress clarified that dividends constituted income 'whether in cash or in stock'.[26] This provision explicitly authorized tax agencies to calculate income on an accrual basis.[27] However, this provision was soon declared by the US Supreme Court unconstitutional in *Eisner v. Macomber*. More importantly, the court rejected to acknowledge the existence of income derived from the property unless the income got severed from the capital.[28] *Macomber* marked a critical moment in the development of the US tax system, confirming realization as a fundamental requirement for levying an income tax.

[ii] Justifications for the Realization Rule

The realization rule, which defers tax on asset appreciation until a later disposition, is a major deviation of the modern income tax system from the Haig-Simons model that features an accrual-based tax. From a normative perspective, any deviation from the

22. Robert Murray Haig, *The Concept of Income-Economic and Legal Aspects, in The Federal Income Tax* 1, 7 (Robert Murray Haig ed., 1921).
23. For a comprehensive review of the origin of the US realization rule. *See* Bank, *supra* note 7, at 51-62.
24. Revenue Act of 1913 (US), § 2(B).
25. *Towne v. Eisner*, 245 U.S. 418, 426 (1918).
26. Revenue Act of 1916 (US), § 2(a).
27. Bank called it 'a watered-down version of the accretion tax model'. Bank, *supra* note 7, at 51.
28. *Eisner v. Macomber*, 252 U.S. 189, 207 (1920).

ideal Haig-Simons model in the process of income tax design shall be justified with strong reasons.[29]

The reasons for adopting the realization rule reside in the shortcomings of the Haig-Simons model. Taxing mere accretion, on the one hand, contributes to the normative superiority of the Haig-Simons model but, on the other hand, leads to heavy administrative burdens. The Haig-Simons model requires regular asset appraisal, which would result in substantial administrative costs.[30] Some types of assets are particularly challenging to value accurately.[31] Also, an accrual-based regime levies tax regardless of taxpayers' cash flow, resulting in taxpayers' liquidity problems.[32]

The Haig-Simons model requires modifications to become practicable. Even Professor Henry Simons himself admitted the need to make compromises to his ideal formula to reach a workable income tax system. He accepted that, in practice, taxes should be levied when actual transactions happen.[33] By relying on market prices at the time of the transaction, a realization-based system avoids the problem of valuation. In addition, the realization rule avoids the tax-without-cash problem because it collects taxes until asset exchanges happen. Hence, the realization rule could be justified as a necessary measure for reducing the tax administration burdens brought up by the Haig-Simons model,[34] and apart from this, one can hardly find any other theoretical or policy justification for it.[35]

Notwithstanding, criticizing the realization rule is a tradition among tax academics that is almost as old as the realization rule itself. Professor Robert Haig, in 1921, contended that 'practice of taxing those appreciations only irregularly as sales are consummated ... lies at the root of the present widespread dissatisfaction with the taxation of appreciations'.[36] Haig was mainly concerned with the lock-in effect caused by the realization rule. As the law only levies taxes on realization events, taxpayers tend to postpone the alienation of property to defer gain recognition and are thus

29. Because of its strong normative basis, the Haig-Simons model is often used as a benchmark of ideal tax in tax design. *See e.g.*, Noel B. Cunningham & Deborah H. Schenk, *The Case for a Capital Gains Preference* 48 Tax L. Rev. 319, 324 (1992). ('In designing an income tax system, conformity to the Haig-Simons ideal always would be preferred.')
30. Deborah H. Schenk, *Taxation of Equity Derivatives: A Partial Integration Proposal* 50 Tax L. Rev. 571, 630 (1994).
31. David J. Shakow, *Taxation without Realization: A Proposal for Accrual Taxation*, 134 U. Pa. L. Rev. 1111, 1119 (1986).
32. *See* Ilan Benshalom & Kenda Stead, *Realization and Progressivity*, 3 Colum. J. Tax L. 43, 53 (2011). For a detailed discussion on taxpayer's liquidity problem, *see* § 6.02[A][3] below.
33. Henry C. Simons, *Personal Income Taxation: The Definition of Income as a Problem of Fiscal Policy* 153 (1938). ('to demand that (taxing investors only when they get out) be abandoned outright is to display little regard for practical considerations.')
34. *See e.g.*, Deborah H. Schenk, *A Positive Account of the Realization Rule*, 57 Tax L. Rev. 355, 355-356 (2003); Shakow, *supra* note 31, at 1114.
35. A few scholars hold that there are other justifications for the realization rule, but they are not the mainstream. For example, Schizer argued that realization is a subsidy for investment, *see* David M. Schizer, *Realization as Subsidy*, 73 New York University Law Review 1549(1998). Benshalom and Stead argued that taxing personal assets on a realization basis promote tax progressivity, *see* Benshalom & Stead, *supra* note 32, at 69-72.
36. Haig, *supra* note 22, at 24.

locked into their investment.[37] Later scholars found that almost all shortcomings of current income taxation, including problems of planning, inequity, inefficiency, and complexity, are related to the realization rule. The realization rule increases deadweight loss as it causes behavioural distortions,[38] leads to inequitable allocation of the tax burden since affluent taxpayers are more likely to have income that is eligible for the realization-based deferral,[39] as well as introduces massive tax planning opportunities because taxpayers can manipulate their tax burden by timing sales.[40] Furthermore, to deal with those problems, policymakers have to introduce extremely complex tax provisions.

Although criticized by scholars for almost a century, the realization rule is perceived by most taxpayers as equitable. Some evidence from behavioural economics suggests that compared to realized gains, taxpayers regard unrealized gains as less valuable.[41] The explanation is that many taxpayers do not regard unrealized gains as real.[42] This common perception of income contributes to the persistence of the realization rule,[43] as no taxing system can afford to ignore what seems right to its taxpayers. Given that taxpayers are more willing to comply with a system that better comports with their perceptions and beliefs,[44] the realization rule may gain justification on the ground of perceptional equity.[45] For example, in the US, scholars widely see the realization rule as politically inevitable.[46] Nevertheless, it should be noted that taxpayers' perception of fairness changes over time, just like theories of taxation, and that the realization is perceived as equitable now does not mean it will remain so forever. After all, the realization rule as a pragmatic compromise should be abandoned wherever its detrimental effects outweigh its relief to tax administrative burden.

[iii] Justifications for Continuity of Interest Notion

The notion of continuity of interest is closely related to the realization rule, which stands in the middle ground between an accrual-based tax model and a consumption-based tax model.[47] If the current tax system moved away from the realization rule and

37. A more detailed account of the lock-in effect is provided in § 6.02[B][2][a] below.
38. *See* Mary Louise Fellows, *A Comprehensive Attack on Tax Deferral*, 88 Mich. L. Rev. 722, 727 (1989); *see also* David A. Weisbach, *A Partial Mark-to-Market Tax System*, 53 Tax L. Rev. 95, 100-101 (1999).
39. Terrence R. Chorvat, *Perception and Income: The Behavioral Economics of the Realization Doctrine*, 36 Conn. L. Rev. 75, 91 (2003).
40. *See* Daniel N. Shaviro, *An Efficiency Analysis of Realization and Recognition Rules under the Federal Income Tax*, 48 Tax L. Rev. 1, 4 (1992).
41. *See* Chorvat, *supra* note 39, at 77.
42. *Ibid.*
43. Schenk, *supra* note 34, at 355-356.
44. Edward A. Zelinsky, *For Realization: Income Taxation, Sectoral Accretionism, and the Virtue of Attainable Virtues*, 19 Cardozo L. Rev. 861, 903 (1997).
45. For the above reasons, some argued that perceptional equity is as important as traditional tax principles. *See e.g.*, Charles E. McLure Jr., *Comments, in Do Taxes Matter?: The Impact of the Tax Reform Act of 1986* 332, 333 (Joel Slemrod ed., 1990).
46. Shaviro, *supra* note 40, at 3; Schenk, *supra* note 34, at 355-356.
47. Steven Bank argued that the establishment of the realization rule in the US was the result of a compromise between an accrual-based tax and a consumption-based tax. Bank, *supra* note 7, at 62-66.

towards either of the two ends, it would be impossible to find any merit in the continuity of interest idea: in a pure accrual-based income tax system, all taxpayers will be taxed on asset appreciation even though they continue their interests by holding onto assets; and under a pure consumption tax model, no taxpayer will be taxed on the exchange of properties regardless of whether there is continuity of interest. Since the realization rule is not a normative requirement but merely an administratively necessary feature of modern income taxation, the continuity of interest idea, which depends on the realization rule, is even less likely to have a sound normative ground.

As mentioned previously, the proponents of the continuity of interest notion frequently rely upon the argument that realization is not sufficient in M&A transactions where investors continue their interests. This argument is untenable because the benefit of the realization rule mainly resides in mitigating valuation problems – whether or not there is sufficient realization depends on the difficulty level of valuation rather than the continuity of interest. Professor Stanley Surrey once made a thoughtful comment on the relationship between the Haig-Simons income and realization events:[48]

> 'Economic gain occurs each year as an asset appreciates. The income tax, however, does not reach that gain because the more precise measure of yearly income that would result from inclusion of the increase in value does not justify the cost to Government and taxpayer of yearly valuations. But the gain is there, and if events occur which bring about a change with respect to the asset making measurement desirable the reckoning should be made.'

Simply put, instead of creating income, realization events only serve as some convenient points in time at which it is relatively easy to measure the income of taxpayers. Therefore, valuation difficulty is the critical factor that affects the decision on what constitutes realization events, while whether investors continue their interests is not.

Some may argue that the authority might encounter valuation difficulty when taxing investors that continue their interests. This observation implies a fictional causal link between continuity of interest and valuation difficulty. The selling parties to an M&A transaction will be regarded as continuing their investment interest if they receive a substantial portion of the transaction consideration in the form of shares of the purchasing company. Admittedly certain types of shares issued by the purchasing company are indeed tricky to value, but shares that are easy to value or even have well-established market prices exist as well. In a word, the continuity of interest does not necessarily lead to valuation difficulty.

The only possible justification for the continuity of interest notion is based on perceptional equity. The special tax treatment for M&A emerged around the 1920s because the US Congress felt it necessary to exempt 'purely paper transaction' from

48. Stanley S. Surrey, *Supreme Court and the Federal Income Tax: Some Implications of the Recent Decisions*, 35 Ill. L. Rev. 779, 783-784 (1940).

taxation.[49] The concept of 'purely paper transaction' relates to the most intuitive idea of stock-financed M&A transactions – investors get no money out but merely exchange 'pieces of paper' in the old company for 'pieces of paper' in a new company.[50] This perception gets strengthened by the continuity of interest doctrine's almost one century of development and is accepted by policymakers and taxpayers in many other countries through legal transplantation. Nevertheless, it is to some extent paradoxical for one to invoke taxpayers' perception as a justification for the continuity of interest notion because the argument is derived from taxpayers' perception forged by it.

[2] Tax Administration Concern I: Difficulty of Valuation

As briefly mentioned above, it might be difficult to determine the fair market value of stocks received on M&A transactions, and based on this, some argue that valuation difficulty necessitates the special tax treatment under current law.[51] This argument can hardly hold since the valuation difficulties in M&A transactions are far from insuperable. While a simple exchange of property, such as two children exchanging toys, may occur notwithstanding that the parties have no clear idea about how much the property is worth, it is not the case for an M&A transaction. It is hard to imagine that the parties planning a corporate acquisition are oblivious to the monetary value of the property to be exchanged. In fact, most investors would require a valuation of assets before entering into an M&A transaction.

From the standpoint of the tax authorities, valuation difficulties in stock-financed M&A transactions are not exceptional compared to those in other transactions. The Chinese tax law, in most situations, imposes an immediate tax on exchanges of non-monetary properties, and in particular, Article 6(3) of the EITL provides that the gross income of an enterprise includes its gains – both monetary and non-monetary – from the disposal of assets.[52] Consequently, the tax authorities in China routinely need to deal with valuation issues emerging in the exchanges of non-monetary assets. Those who argue for the special tax treatment on the ground of valuation concern should prove that the valuation difficulties in M&A transactions are more severe than those in other non-monetary exchanges of assets, which, however, is far from easy because nothing in the nature of M&A creates unique valuation problems. If the special tax treatment for M&A transactions is justifiable on the ground of valuation difficulties, policymakers should extend similar tax treatment to other non-monetary exchanges of assets.

Contrary to the claim that the special tax treatment is necessitated by valuation difficulties, many M&A transactions that do not involve valuation problems qualify for

49. Steven Bank objected to this view. He argued that the opinion was held by the Senate, but Congress never explicitly endorsed it. *See* Bank, *supra* note 7, at 17-18. However, we can infer from the later development of the reorganization provisions that US Congress shared such opinion. See § 5.02[A][1] above.
50. Bank, *supra* note 7, at 17.
51. Wang, *supra* note 8, at 39.
52. EITL, Art. 6(3).

the special tax treatment regardless. For instance, where sellers in an M&A transaction receive publicly traded shares as consideration, the tax authorities will not encounter any valuation difficulty in taxing such a transaction.[53] A valuation problem may arise only where the sellers receive shares of a closely held company.[54] But even in such cases, there exist solutions to the valuation problem.[55]

If the purchasing company transfer closely held shares in exchange for the target company's assets, the tax authority can rely on the market price of the acquired assets to reflect the value of the closely held shares. The law has provided detailed instructions on how to establish a fair market price in a transfer of assets. For instance, in the *Implementation Rules for the Provisional Regulations on VAT of the PRC*, the MOF clarifies the steps for assessing the price of goods or services in cases where the sales revenue for calculating VAT is considered unjustifiably low. According to this circular, the tax authority in charge should first rely on the average selling price of the same goods/services recently sold by the same taxpayer. If that price is difficult to find, then the tax authority may use other taxpayers' average selling price of the same goods/services in recent periods. If both of the first two methods are difficult to apply, the tax authority can determine the price by adding a profit margin to the cost of the goods/services.[56]

If the transaction is an exchange of closely held shares for closely held shares, valuation is a bit more difficult as many valuation methods are no longer suitable.[57] The tax law has already started to tackle this problem. In the past, in order to determine the price of a closely held share, the tax authority had to find a comparable price. In 2009, the STA announced that lower-level tax authorities could determine the price of a share by looking at the value of its corresponding portion of underlying assets.[58] Furthermore, tax authorities already have considerable experience and practice in dealing with the valuation of shares. For instance, the STA issued STA Gonggao (2014) No. 67 in 2014, providing detailed guidance to local tax authorities on the method of how to assess the taxable income derived by an individual in the disposal of stock.[59]

53. Hellerstein, *supra* note 3, at 281-282.
54. For this reason, Hellerstein proposed to confine non-recognition treatment to those receiving non-publicly traded shares. Hellerstein, *supra* note 3, at 284.
55. Shakow, *supra* note 31, at 1133-1134.
56. Zhonghua Renmin Gongheguo Zengzhishui Zanxing Tiaoli Shishi Xize [Implementation Rules for the Provisional Regulations on VAT of the PRC] (promulgated by the MOF on 28 October 2011, effective 1 November 2011) (PRC), Art. 16.
57. Tax Science Research Institute of the STA, *Qiye Chongzu Qiye Suodeshui Wenti Yanjiu [On Enterprise Income Tax Issues in M&A], in Zhongguo Shuishou Yanjiu Baogao 2012-2013 [Report on Taxation in China, 2012-2013]* 14 (Tax Science Research Institute of the STA ed., 2014).
58. Guoshuihan (2009) No. 285, Guanyu Jiaqiang Guquan Zhuanrang Suode Zhengshou Geren Suodeshui Guanli de Tongzhi [Notice on Strengthening the Administration of Individual Income Tax on Income from the Transfer of Shares] (promulgated by the STA and effective 28 May 2009, repealed) (PRC), Art. 4.
59. STA Gonggao (2014) No. 67, Guquan Zhuanrang Suode Geren Suodeshui Guanli Banfa [Administrative Measures for Individual Income Tax on Income from the Transfer of Shares (for Trial Implementation)] (promulgated by the STA on 7 December 2014, effective 1 January 2015) (PRC), Arts. 11, 12, 13.

Moreover, a closer look at the rules on the special tax treatment reveals that the valuation concern is, to a large extent, illusory. The Chinese tax law expressly requires a valuation in many, perhaps most, tax-deferred M&A transactions. Under Article 6 of Circular 59, the selling parties to an M&A transaction may enjoy non-recognition treatment only to the extent of equity consideration received.[60] In calculating the taxable amount of a partially tax-deferred transaction, Circular 59 adopts the approach of proportional allocation by providing the following equation as follows:[61]

> 'Taxable gain or loss with respect to non-equity consideration = (Fair market value of shares surrendered - Aggregate tax basis of shares surrendered) × (Fair market value of the non-equity consideration received ÷ Fair market value of shares surrendered)'

Since one essential factor in this equation is the 'fair market value of the transferred assets', an accurate valuation of shares or assets transferred is a must in partially tax-deferred M&A transactions. Considering that so many M&A transactions involve non-equity consideration, the burden of valuation is, to a large extent, unavoidable. In fact, contrary to the belief that valuation difficulties are a factor contributing to the adoption of the special tax treatment, the STA has never regarded the valuation difficulties in M&A transactions as a severe issue. Under Circular 48, the participants in stock/asset acquisitions that satisfy the statutory requirements of the special tax treatment must file valuation reports of the stock/assets transferred, regardless of whether they elect the special tax treatment and whether the transaction involves non-equity consideration.[62]

However, this research does not imply that the approach taken by the STA is irreproachable. Quite the opposite, valuation problems are either omitted or not given enough emphasis in the current M&A taxation system. Despite the adoption of various valuation methods, the value of closely held shares is still hard to accurately ascertain.[63] The purpose here is to point out the paradox - the special tax treatment which is ineffective in alleviating valuation concerns has been extolled as a cure for valuation difficulties. To sum up, the valuation-based argument can at best support granting non-recognition treatment to taxpayers that receive closely held shares in M&A transactions.

[3] Tax Administration Concern II: Liquidity Problem

At first glance, the selling parties to a stock-financed acquisition receive little, or even no, cash to cover the tax liability at the time of sale, so freeing the sellers from the liquidity problem by providing non-recognition treatment seems to be a reasonable choice. It is even argued that forcing the sellers with insufficient liquidity to fulfil the

60. Caishui (2009) No. 59, Art. 6.
61. Caishui (2009) No. 59, Art. 6(6).
62. STA Gonggao (2015) No. 48, Art. 4.
63. Shakow, *supra* note 31, at 1134.

tax obligation at the time of transaction violates the principle of ability to pay.[64] Although incorrectly equating cash on hand with the ability to pay,[65] this kind of argument still exemplifies people's deep concern about the issue of liquidity problem.

The statement that the law should not force cash-poor people to settle their tax liabilities immediately is intuitively appealing. Such an intuition influenced the decision in the US landmark case of *Macomber*.[66] The core issue, in this case, was whether the issuance of a stock dividend gave rise to tax liability. Justice Pitney provided one of the most famous arguments against levying a tax on people who have no cash on hand. He said:[67]

> 'Yet, without selling, the shareholder, unless possessed of other resources, has not the wherewithal to pay an income tax upon the dividend stock. Nothing could more clearly show that to tax a stock dividend is to tax a capital increase, and not income, than this demonstration that in the nature of things it requires conversion of capital in order to pay the tax'.

Obviously, this argument that tries to provide a normative underpinning for the liquidity concern rests on two premises: (1) taxpayers should have enough funds to settle their tax liabilities, and (2) taxpayers must be able to pay off their tax liabilities with the same income on which the taxes are levied.[68] However, none of the two premises is tenable.

Linking tax liabilities to taxpayers' cash flow does not make much sense. It is possible that a wealthy capitalist has less cash on hand than an ordinary labourer, but very few people would find it reasonable to allow that capitalist to defer taxes simply for the lack of enough cash. Also, imagine two taxpayers that have similar assets. One of them conducts an asset swap and then holds onto the newly received assets, while another taxpayer sells assets for cash and subsequently consumes all the cash received. When filing the annual tax return, none of them has any cash to pay taxes on the sale or exchange of assets, but should the tax law allow them to defer tax payments until they have enough cash? If the former taxpayer is granted non-recognition treatment due to the concern over liquidity, the latter one should also be allowed to defer her tax liability.[69] However, most people would see it unacceptable to let the consumerist enjoy tax deferral and instead might even support the levy of a late payment penalty. The second premise mentioned above is even more questionable than the first one. Money is fungible, and taxpayers that invest in stock markets are likely to have various

64. *See e.g.*, Hui Li, *M&A and Individual Income Tax Policy: Theoretical Examination and Reform Proposal*, Shuiwu Yanjiu [Taxation Research], no. 4, 2017, at 108, 111.
65. For detailed discussion on ability to pay, please *see* § 4.03[C][1][b] above.
66. *Macomber*, 252 U.S. at 189.
67. *Macomber*, 252 U.S. at 213.
68. Brauner, *supra* note 7, at 8.
69. Some may argue that the former taxpayer is treated because investment is good to the economy. However, as Krever points out, consumption is equally worthy of government encouragement. *See* Richard Krever, *Structural Issues in the Taxation of Capital Gains*, 1 Australian Tax Forum, 171 (1984).

ways to earn money to settle their tax liabilities incurred by exchanges of non-monetary assets.[70]

A much stronger argument for the necessity to address the liquidity problem is provided in the debate on the pros and cons of accrual-based taxation. Some scholars argue that the liquidity problem could distort investment decisions and increase the deadweight loss in an accrual-based tax system: in order to avoid the miserable experience of struggling to sell illiquid assets to raise money for the settlement of taxes on the appreciation of such assets, investors may in the first place reduce their investments in illiquid assets that are incapable of generating sufficient cash flow.[71] Despite the plausibility of this argument, it too relies on a strict assumption that some taxpayers have almost nothing except illiquid assets. Even if there exist such taxpayers in M&A transactions, the liquidity problem faced by them can hardly justify the broad application of the special tax treatment.

In the context of M&A taxation, liquidity problem in fact only arises in limited types of transactions. In a transaction that involves a hybrid consideration of stock and cash, the selling parties can use the cash received to settle their tax liabilities. Even in a purely stock-financed M&A transaction, the liquidity problem does not necessarily arise. In particular, where the selling parties receive publicly traded shares, they can easily exchange the publicly traded shares received for cash and pay their tax liabilities.

Hence, if the special tax treatment for M&A transactions is deemed necessary for solving the liquidity problem, it should be confined to a small group of taxpayers who receive non-publicly traded shares,[72] not to mention that the special tax treatment is not the best cure for the liquidity problem.

Instead of granting rollover relief, the government may allow taxpayers to postpone taxes on the condition that they pay interest on the late payment to alleviate the liquidity problem.[73] The Chinese tax law has already adopted a similar but more lenient approach, under which taxpayers participating in exchanges of non-monetary assets can pay taxes in instalments without interest. According to Caishui (2014) No. 116, where one company makes non-monetary capital contributions to another company,[74] the contributing company may pay taxes on its non-monetary contributions in equal instalments over five years.[75] The MOF and the STA later extended the five-year tax instalment arrangement to individual investors through Caishui (2015)

70. Brauner, *supra* note 7, at 8.
71. William D. Andrews called it 'forced liquidation', *see* William D. Andrews, *A Consumption-Type or Cash Flow Personal Income Tax*, 87 Harv. L. Rev. 1113, 1143 (1973). *See also* Benshalom & Stead, *supra* note 32, at 53. ('... cash-poor taxpayers [are forced] to sell assets to pay their tax liabilities ...'); Cynthia Blum, *Rollover: An Alternative Treatment of Capital Gains*, 41 Tax L. Rev. 383, 395 (1985).
72. Hellerstein, *supra* note 3, at 281-283; Ulysses S. Crockett Jr., *Federal Taxation of Corporate Unifications: A Review of Legislative Policy*, 15 Duq. L. Rev. 1, 18-19 (1976).
73. Brauner, *supra* note 7, at 14-15.
74. Caishui (2014) No. 116, Guanyu Fei Huobixing Zichan Touzi Qiye Suodeshui Zhengce Wenti de Tongzhi [Notice on Policy Issues Concerning the Enterprise Income Tax Treatment of Non-Monetary Assets Investments] (promulgated by the MOF and the STA on 31 December 2014, effective retrospectively 1 January 2014) (PRC), Art. 5.
75. Caishui (2014) No. 116, Art. 3.

No. 41, and on top of that, individuals are allowed to pay a lump sum at the end of the five years.[76] Since the two circulars define 'non-monetary capital contributions' as covering stock-financed acquisitions where the purchasing company issues new shares to the target shareholders in exchange for the target company's non-monetary assets,[77] the liquidity problem in M&A transactions, if any, should not be a serious concern.[78]

Moreover, from the viewpoint of maintaining the consistency of the tax system, the concern over the liquidity problem is not a satisfactory justification for the special tax treatment. In many situations where no cashing-in takes place, the tax law imposes a current tax disregarding any liquidity problem that could be faced by taxpayers. For example, according to Article 25 of the EITLIR, an asset swap between two companies generally lead to current tax liabilities regardless of whether the two companies face tremendous cash-flow pressure. Under the same provision of the EITLIR, where a company pays off debts with its assets, the company will be treated as if it first sold the assets for cash and then used the cash received to settle debts.[79] A company reeling under debts is more likely to encounter a liquidity problem than those participating in M&A transactions, but it is nevertheless ineligible for any tax relief.[80]

After all, as shown by Justice Pitney's decision to *Macomber*,[81] the liquidity-based justification relates to the taxpayer's perception of fairness. The intuitive appeal of the liquidity-based justification, although it does not withstand scrutiny, has been strengthened by the media that broadcasts stories about people who allegedly quit M&A transactions due to the lack of cash to settle tax liabilities. Take the report of a failed acquisition in 2015 by the Securities Daily (*zhengquan ribao*) as an example. The purchasing company in the acquisition proposed to issue new shares to the target shareholders in exchange for all of the outstanding shares of the target company; however, two individual shareholders who held more than 60% shares in the target company eventually decided to exit the transaction. The two individuals never indicated that they gave up the deal due to tax reasons, but the report of the Securities Daily still attributed the failure of a stock acquisition to the target shareholders' lack of money to pay taxes.[82] Despite other possible explanations for the failure of the

76. Caishui (2015) No. 41, Guanyu Geren Fei Huobixing Zichan Touzi Youguan Geren Suodeshui Zhengce de Tongzhi [Notice on Policies Concerning the Individual Income Tax Treatment of Non-Monetary Assets Investments] (promulgated by the MOF and the STA and effective 30 March 2015) (PRC), Art. 3.
77. Caishui (2014) No. 116, Arts. 5, 6; Caishui (2015) No. 41, Art. 5.
78. Some asserted that the instalment payment relief is inadequate for solving the liquidity problem. *See e.g.*, Li, *supra* note 64, at 111; Feng Li & Deyin Yang, M&A Tax Policies and Continuity of Shareholder Interest, Shuiwu Yanjiu [Taxation Research], no. 8, 2015, at 37, 39. However, the analysis in this section shows that the liquidity problem may not be that severe.
79. EITLIR, Art. 25.
80. Under the current law, a taxpayer may apply for deferral if it is unable to pay taxes on time. However, the maximum deferral period is only three months, which is in no way comparable to the indefinite tax deferral under the special tax treatment.
81. *See supra* notes 66 and 67 and accompanying texts.
82. Xiaosun Gui, *Guotou Zhonglu Hungai Pengshang Heitiane-Chongzufang Jiaobuqi Geshui Chongzu Gaochui [The Restructuring of Guotou Zhonglu Failed Because of a Black Swan Event–One Party Cannot Afford Income Taxes]*, Zhengquan Ribao [Securities Daily], 3 April 2015, at C04.

transaction,[83] the report of the Securities Daily successfully evoked resonance among many scholars, and they, in turn, advocated further extending the special tax treatment to individuals to mitigate the alleged liquidity problem.[84]

[B] Justification Based on the Tax Neutrality Principle

So far, this research has examined three traditional justifications given for the special tax treatment and found that none of them is satisfactory. The remaining frequently mentioned justification – the rollover relief can encourage M&A and thus benefit the economy[85] – is also hardly tenable because it in essence advocates the proactive use of tax law as a tool for expanding economic growth. As discussed in the previous chapter, the market, in most cases, is more efficient than the government in allocating precious resources, and the tax law is often mistakenly regarded as a suitable tool for implementing economic policies.

Notwithstanding, a weaker variation of the efficiency argument, i.e., the tax law would discourage M&A transactions in the absence of the special tax treatment, is worthy of serious consideration for its obvious connection with the principle of tax neutrality. In this subsection, the necessity of the special tax treatment will be assessed against the principle of tax neutrality. Inspired by Professor Douglas Kahn's observation of two faces of tax neutrality,[86] the following discussion examines whether the special tax treatment gets support from either face of tax neutrality.

[1] First Face of Neutrality

As noted in Chapter 4, the Haig-Simons income is the normative tax base embodying the first face of neutrality, and an income tax system that better conforms to the ideal Haig-Simons model is intuitively more neutral. Hence, one step towards the Haig-Simons income is generally preferable to a further deviation from the concept. Given that the current realization-based tax system further drifts from the Haig-Simons model by providing the special tax treatment for M&A transactions, the first face of neutrality would mandate a justification for such an extension of the realization preference in the context of M&A. As has been extensively discussed previously, such a justification is hard to find.

The first face of neutrality in fact opposes the provision of any tax preference; however, it is better to think twice before declaring a tax preference as a violation of tax neutrality merely for its contravention of the first face of neutrality. The

83. Jun Wang, *Guotou Zhonglu Chongzu Gaochui Buneng Guijiu yu Shuifa [Tax Law is not to Blame for the Failure of the Reorganization of Guotou Zhonglu]*, ZhongGuo Shuiwu Bao [China Taxation News], 10 April 2015, at B02. Some speculated that the real cause for the failure is financial fraud. *See* Wei Zheng, *Guotou Zhonglu Hungai Qiake huo Lingyou Yinqing [Possible Hidden Cause of the Failure of Guotou Zhonglu Reorganization]* (12 April 2015), http://www.changjiangtimes.com/2015/04/500261.html.

84. *See e.g.*, Li, *supra* note 64, at 112-113; Li & Yang, *supra* note 78, at 40.

85. *See e.g.*, Hellerstein, *supra* note 3, at 280; Brauner, *supra* note 7, at 4.

86. *See* § 4.03[B][1] above.

appropriateness of the first face of neutrality as the benchmark for evaluating a specific tax provision faces severe challenges from the second-best theory, which contends that where one of the conditions for an optimum is not satisfied, the remaining conditions for the optimum also become no longer desirable. In other words, a further departure from the conditions for an optimum may not necessarily deteriorate the situation.[87]

Influenced by the second-best theory, tax scholars have made a distinction between de novo tax design and the reform of existing tax laws.[88] The Haig-Simons model is crucial in de novo tax design because it provides a blueprint for the basic structure of a proposed system.[89] For instance, when framing his proposal for an accrual-based tax, Professor David Shakow started by accepting the Haig-Simons model as the general framework.[90] However, the Haig-Simons model plays a minimal role in the piecemeal reforms of the existing tax system. The current tax system departs far from the optimal Haig-Simons model, and the only possible way to satisfy all the conditions inherent in the Haig-Simons model is to redesign a system from scratch. According to the second-best theory, a small step pushing the current tax system towards the ideal model may increase tax bias,[91] while a step away from the ideal model may reduce tax bias.

The promulgation, the amendment as well as the repeal of the special tax treatment fall into the scope of tax reform rather than drafting a tax law from scratch.[92] Unless we abolish the realization-based income tax system, the first face of neutrality is not suitable for examining the special tax treatment. The significant shortcomings of the realization rule have driven some scholars to advance alternatives to the widely adopted realization-based income tax system[93] and some countries to incorporate 'mark-to-market' rules into their income tax systems,[94] but the realization rule is still indispensable for keeping administrative burdens at a reasonable level. In particular, the valuation difficulty resulting from the abolishment of the realization rule is hard to

87. R. G. Lipsey & Kelvin Lancaster, *The General Theory of Second Best*, 24 The Review of Economic Studies 11, 11 (1956).
88. *See e.g.*, Martin Feldstein, *Compensation in Tax Reform*, 29 National Tax Journal 123, 124 (1976); Cunningham & Schenk, *supra* note 29, at 324; Edward A. Zelinsky, *Efficiency and Income Taxes: The Rehabilitation of Tax Incentives*, 64 Tex. L. Rev. 973, 996-998 (1986).
89. Cunningham & Schenk, *supra* note 29, at 325.
90. Shakow, *supra* note 31, at 1119.
91. Feldstein, *supra* note 88, at 124.
92. All discussions about specific tax preferences are arguably belong to the discourse of tax reform. *See e.g.*, Cunningham & Schenk, *supra* note 29, at 324-325.
93. For example, Professor David Shakow once proposed to replace the realization-based system with an accrual-based tax system. Under his proposal, taxpayers recognize gains on the appreciation of nearly all assets every year. Only the assets that are particularly hard to value, such as the stock of certain closely held companies, are excluded from this accrual tax system. *See* Shakow, *supra* note 31, at 1119.
94. Income Tax (Trading and Other Income) Act 2005 (UK), § 236 ('(1) This section applies if there is a change of basis from – (a) not recognising a profit or loss on an asset until the asset is realised, to (b) bringing assets into account in each period of account at a fair value.'); Internal Revenue Code (US), § 475 ('(a)(2) In the case of any security which is not inventory in the hands of the dealer and which is held at the close of any taxable year – (A) the dealer shall recognize gain or loss as if such security were sold for its fair market value on the last business day of such taxable year…')

solve: in the US, the mark-to-market approach currently only applies to the taxation of financial instruments,[95] and even scholars who are most averse to the realization rule can hardly completely exclude it from their proposed tax models.[96] Under the persistent shadow of the realization rule, the first face of tax neutrality is far from becoming an appropriate benchmark for examining the special tax treatment.

[2] Second Face of Neutrality

Compared to the first face of neutrality, the second face of neutrality, which focuses on the best solution to reduce tax-induced bias in a less than ideal system, or, simply put, the second-best solution to tax-induced bias, is much more suitable for examining the special tax treatment. This subsection will therefore assess the special tax treatment against the second face of neutrality to see if it could be justified as proper mitigation to the distortive effects - particularly the lock-in effect - caused by the realization-based tax system.

[a] Lock-In Effect and Solutions

A realization-based tax system is inherently non-neutral since it allows taxpayers to defer paying taxes on the accretion in the value of assets until a realization event - which is usually a sale of assets - takes place. Due to the realization requirement, the tax liabilities of investors vary depending on whether they decide to sell assets or not. This practice of hinging tax liability to realization events has created a severe tax bias between realized and unrealized gains and thus distorts the economic behaviour of taxpayers. In order to benefit from the tax deferral, taxpayers tend to hold onto assets with accumulated unrealized gains.[97] This tax-induced bias which is known as the lock-in effect, provides disincentives for taxpayers to switch their current investments to those with a higher return because the tax imposed on the transfer of assets may entirely or partially offset the increase of before-tax yields.

More specifically, the lock-in effect distorts the economy in three significant ways. First, it prevents an asset from being transferred to an owner who can use it more efficiently and productively and thus hinders the full utilization of resources.[98] Second,

95. Internal Revenue Code (US), §§ 475, 1256. § 475 of the IRC applies the mark-to-market approach to the taxation of non-investment securities held by dealers. § 1256 of the IRC applies the approach to the taxation of options and futures.
96. For example, Professor Edward A. Zelinsky correctly points out that despite being described as the 'taxation without realization', the accrual tax system proposed by Professor Shakow retains many relics of the realization rule and is in essence, a hybrid of accrual-based tax and realization-based tax. *See* Zelinsky, *supra* note 44, at 876-877.
97. Alan J. Auerbach, *Retrospective Capital Gains Taxation*, 81 The American Economic Review 167, 167 (1991).
98. *See e.g.*, Walter J. Blum, *A Handy Summary of the Capital Gains Arguments*, 35 Taxes 247, 256-258 (1957); Michael J. Waggoner Michael J. Waggoner, *Eliminating the Capital Gains Preference – Part I: The Problems of Inflation, Bunching and Lock-In*, 48 U. Colo. L. Rev. 313, 366 (1976); Cunningham & Schenk, *supra* note 29, at 344-345; OECD, *Taxation of Capital Gains of Individuals: Policy Considerations and Approaches* 24, 52 (2006).

it hinders the efficient allocation of capital across industries and firms, and as a result, the cost of capital is much higher for young enterprises than for the enterprises whose owners get locked into their shareholdings.[99] Third, the lock-in effect may discourage taxpayers from optimally diversifying their portfolios.[100] Those general observations on the lock-in effect also apply to the specific context of M&A transactions because investors may quit M&A transactions which they would have conducted in the absence of the lock-in effect.

In order to address the lock-in problem, it is necessary to establish conformity between the tax treatments of realized gains and unrealized gains. There are two opposite approaches to achieving conformity. One approach is to increase the tax burden on unrealized gains, and the other approach is to reduce the tax burden on realized gains.

Figure 6.1 Two Directions for Addressing the Lock-In Effect

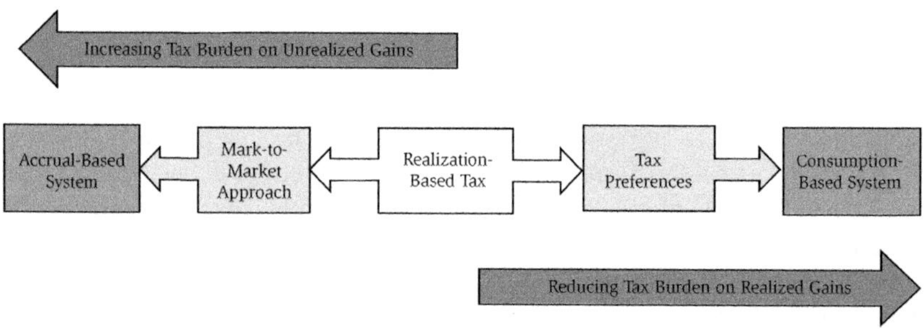

As shown in Figure 6.1, when taken to the extreme, the two approaches lead to an accrual-based and a consumption-based system respectively, representing the ends of a continuum. There is no lock-in effect in both two systems. In an accrual-based system, the appreciation in the value of assets is always subject to current taxes irrespective of whether it is realized or not, and thus taxpayers will not obtain any tax benefits by merely holding onto appreciated assets.[101] In a typical consumption-based system, investment proceeds are left out of the tax base so long as taxpayers do not use them for consumption,[102] and as a result, the disparity in treatment between unrealized and realized gains vanishes.

However, as the realization rule is unlikely to be abolished,[103] the above two solutions, although successful in eliminating the lock-in effect, are impractical. A real-world solution to the lock-in problem lies along the continuum between the two extremes. Under the approach of imposing taxes on unrealized gains, a less extreme

99. *See e.g.*, Blum, *supra* note 98, at 257.
100. *See e.g.*, Cunningham & Schenk, *supra* note 29, at 345; OECD, *supra* note 98, at 51-52.
101. *See* Cynthia Blum, *Rollover: An Alternative Treatment of Capital Gains*, 41 Tax L. Rev. 383, 394-397 (1985).; *see also* Cunningham & Schenk, *supra* note 29, at 346.
102. *See* Blum, *supra* note 101, at 397-399.
103. *See* § 6.02[A][1][b][ii] above.

solution is to adopt a partial mark-to-market regime that can prevent taxpayers from being locked into certain investments. For example, in the US, investors are subject to taxes on the appreciation in the value of specified financial instruments at the end of each year, so whether to sell those kinds of financial instruments makes no difference from a tax perspective. The mark-to-market method's counterpart under the approach of reducing taxes on realized gains is to provide tax breaks for capital gains.

Compared to the mark-to-market method, preferential measures for capital gains can be applied in a broader scope and a more flexible manner, so they have been widely adopted around the world to address the lock-in effect. Commonly used preferential measures for capital gains include tax exemption, tax reduction, favourable tax rate, as well as rollover relief which are the focus here.

[b] Rollover Relief for M&A and Tax-Induced Biases

The special tax treatment for M&A transactions introduces a rollover relief for capital gains on the disposal of assets beyond the year when the gains arise. By extending the non-recognition treatment of unrealized gains under the realization-based system to gains realized in M&A transactions, the rollover relief helps to alleviate the lock-in problem in the context of M&A. That is why some scholars regard providing the rollover relief as a measure to 'neutralize' the tax consequences of M&A transactions.[104]

Nevertheless, it is too hasty to assert that the special tax treatment passes the scrutiny of the second face of tax neutrality. It is common that a reform plan aiming to remove one tax bias leads to a new bias or magnifies other existing biases. For this reason, Professor Douglas Kahn notes that the mere existence of a tax bias is not a sufficient justification for introducing a corrective tax policy.[105] While the special tax treatment helps alleviate the lock-in effect, it creates or exacerbates two other distortions. First, since the special tax treatment only applies to M&A transactions, the tax law discriminates against taxpayers' income arising in various kinds of economic activities other than M&A transactions. Second, because an M&A transaction is qualified for the special tax treatment only if the transaction consideration consists mainly of the purchasing company's stock, the tax law creates a bias against cash-financed M&A transactions. In order to justify the special tax treatment as enhancing tax neutrality, we must conduct a cost-benefit analysis to prove that the distortion removed by it outweighs the distortion that it creates or increases.[106]

The concept of tax elasticity is of great use for such a cost-benefit analysis. Tax elasticity depicts the likelihood of economic decisions being affected by taxes, and an

104. *See e.g.*, Vanistendael, *supra* note 44, at 908; Chunyan Zhang, *Binggou Jiaoyi Suodeshui Falv Zhidu Yanjiu-Jiyu dui Liyi Chixu Yuanze de Kaoliang [Research on the Mergers and Acquisitions Income Tax Law-Based on the Continuity Doctrine]* 23 (2015); Zhou, *supra* note 10, at 66; Li & Yang, *supra* note 78, at 37.

105. Douglas A. Kahn, *The Two Faces of Tax Neutrality: Do They Interact or Are They Mutually Exclusive* 18 N. Ky. L. Rev. 1, 14 (1990).

106. *Ibid.*

economic decision is regarded as highly tax-elastic if it is prone to be substituted by another decision because of tax reasons.[107] One crucial element that determines the tax elasticity of an economic decision is how convenient it is for the decision-maker to avoid tax liabilities. Where taxpayers can avoid their tax liabilities with great ease, the levy of taxes will tend to cause a significant substitution effect. Therefore, the bias against a tax-elastic decision is more detrimental than the bias against a tax-inelastic one.

Among various types of economic activities, investing activities that generate capital gains are arguably the most tax-elastic. Under the realization-based tax system, investors can easily avoid capital gains tax by holding onto their investments rather than selling them. The high tax elasticity of realizations of capital gains is evidenced by the fact that capital gains tax has a low revenue maximizing rate.[108] Given the effects of tax elasticity, it is understandable for the law to provide some tax preferences for capital gains,[109] which may include the rollover relief for M&A transactions.

Another factor matters in the cost-benefit analysis is whether the social and economic benefits resulting from the alleviation of the lock-in effect are greater than the social and economic losses resulting from the creation or exacerbation of other tax distortions.[110] Due to the alleviation of the lock-in effect, taxpayers are supposedly more active in the M&A market. Hence, the more beneficial M&A transactions can be to the society and the economy, the more likely the special tax treatment can pass the cost-benefit analysis and thus be proved to satisfy the second face of tax neutrality.

[c] *Rollover Relief for M&A: A Second-Best Solution*

There is rich non-tax literature on the pros and cons of M&A transactions. Since Professor Henry Manne first recognizes the positive effects of mergers on the economy,[111] numerous scholars have discussed the benefits of M&A transactions. Professor Roberta Romano provides a comprehensive account of how M&A transactions can be beneficial to the economy.[112]

According to Romano, M&A transactions are beneficial in two ways. First, M&A transactions can create synergy effects, which are the value of the combination of the purchasing company and the target company exceeding the value of the two firms running separately. The synergy gains are derived from achieving economies of scale

107. Shaviro, *supra* note 40, at 30-32.
108. Cunningham & Schenk, *supra* note 29, at 351-353. For most types of taxes, if its rate is elevated beyond certain point, the amount of tax collected will drop rather than increase. The phenomenon is known as the 'Laffer Curve'. The tax rate that results in the most revenue is the revenue maximizing rate.
109. Based on this tax-elasticity argument, Cunningham & Schenk contended that capital gains preferences as a second-best solution. *Ibid.*, at 350-73.
110. Kahn, *supra* note 105, at 14.
111. Henry G. Manne, *Mergers and the Market for Corporate Control*, 73 Journal of Political Economy 110(1965) (arguing that the takeover scheme helps ensure efficient management and thus protect small, non-controlling shareholders.)
112. Roberta Romano, *A Guide to Takeovers: Theory, Evidence, and Regulation*, 9 Yale J. on Reg. 119(1992). (providing a comprehensive review of the theories of takeovers)

or scope, better using managerial capacity, or from reducing capital costs. Second, M&A transactions help to reduce the agency cost of management. The corporate control market created by M&A transactions provides a mechanism for addressing the conflict of interest between corporate management and shareholders, as poorly managed companies are prone to hostile takeovers. There are also arguments emphasizing the negative implications of M&A transactions on the economy. For instance, some scholars consider takeovers as a mechanism that increases the wealth of the target company's shareholders by expropriating the wealth of other stakeholders including bondholders and employees. But as pointed out by Romano, those opinions on the negative implications of M&A transactions are outside the mainstream.[113]

It is worth noting that in order to sensibly examine the pros and cons of M&A transactions, the specific social and economic context in which the transactions take place should be taken into account. Take the third M&A wave in the US, which started in the mid-1950s and lasted through the 1960s, as an example. This M&A wave featured the development of large conglomerates through the absorption of small enterprises.[114] At that time, there was a widely shared concern over the concentration of economic power and oligopolistic tendencies.[115] The concern kept growing as the pace of conglomerates accelerated over time, and consequently, tax scholars' attitudes towards the rollover relief became more and more negative. In 1957, Professor Hellerstein suggested that given the risks of oligopoly, the rollover relief should only apply to mergers between closely held companies.[116] In 1970, Professor Lovett criticized the rollover relief as defying the antitrust efforts and asserted that 'it would be foolish to continue substantial merger subsidies which work at cross purposes with antitrust efforts.'[117] In 1976, after reviewing the problem of booming conglomerates' mergers and the legislative responses, Professor Crockett claimed that the rollover relief was unjustified and policymakers should remove it from the tax law.[118] With the third M&A wave going down in the mid-1970s, the risk of monopolization of the economy became less significant, and thereafter very few tax scholars continued to criticize the rollover relief as encouraging M&A transactions detrimental to economic development.[119]

In the unique context of the Chinese economy, M&A transactions should generate more positive than adverse effects in China. First, Chinese firms – particularly SOEs – have for long faced severe problems with corporate governance, and the main reason behind the poor corporate governance is the lack of supervision of management.

---

113. *Ibid.*, at 133-143, 148-150.
114. M&A transactions in the US are commonly divided into five waves. They occurred during the following time periods respectively, the 1890s-1903, the 1910s-1929, the 1950s-1973, 1981-1989, and 1993-2001. *See* Marina Martynova & Luc Renneboog, *A Century of Corporate Takeovers: What Have We Learned and Where Do We Stand?*, 32 Journal of Banking and Finance 2148, 2149-2152 (2008).
115. *See e.g.*, Hellerstein, *supra* note 3, at 279-281; Lovett, *supra* note 13, at 844-847; Crockett, *supra* note 72, at 13.
116. Hellerstein, *supra* note 3, at 280-281.
117. Lovett, *supra* note 13, at 873-874.
118. Crockett, *supra* note 72, at 30.
119. The development of antitrust laws also alleviates the concern over the creation of monopoly or oligopoly. *See* Romano, *supra* note 112, at 142.

Although the Company Law provides that shareholders have the power to monitor managers,[120] for many years in the listed companies with the state as the majority shareholder, the monitoring pressure from shareholders is minimal.[121] In order to enhance the monitoring of the management, policymakers in China have incorporated into the Company Law many new measures, such as the supervisory board[122] and the independent directors,[123] but unfortunately, they all have proved to be ineffective in achieving the purported function.[124] Because the monitoring of management in China is quite unsatisfactory, the value of M&A transactions in lowering agency costs has become particularly prominent. Second, as China is shifting from a planned economy to a market-oriented economy, resources are still allocated in a highly inefficient manner. Hence, M&A transactions stand out as a pivotal mechanism for optimizing the allocation of scarce resources.[125]

Given the significant benefits of M&A transactions in the Chinese context, it appears that the tax bias created by the special tax treatment is likely to be less detrimental than the lock-in effect alleviated by it. Another tax bias caused by the introduction of the special tax treatment is the discrimination effect on cash-financed M&A transactions. Since the special tax treatment is only applicable where the purchase price for an M&A transaction consists mainly of equity consideration, the selling parties are encouraged to enter into stock-financed transactions rather than cash-financed ones. In the corporate law and economics literature, however, cash-financed transactions are generally superior, or at least not inferior, to stock-financed transactions in terms of overall effects.[126] Nevertheless, compared to the lock-in effect that may refrain taxpayers from entering into M&A transactions in the first place, the tax discrimination between different types of consideration used in M&A transactions should result in less deadweight loss.

Based on the above analysis, the following assertion, counterintuitive as it seems, may hold true: if the special tax treatment were abolished, China's tax system would advance closer to the ideal Haig-Simons model, but in the meantime, the abolishment would generate more tax distortions than it could resolve. That is to say, in the Chinese context, the introduction of the rollover relief for M&A transactions is likely to satisfy the second face of neutrality and thus constitute a second-best solution to the distortive effects of taxation on M&A decisions. Moreover, as suggested in the above cost-benefit analysis, the rollover relief for M&A transactions should be made more accessible where the lock-in effect is severe or where the benefits of M&A transactions are significant.

---

120. Company Law, Art. 37 (listing the powers of the shareholders' meeting).
121. Hui Huang, *China's Takeover Law: A Comparative Analysis and Proposals for Reform*, 30 Del. J. Corp. L. 145, 162-163 (2005).
122. Company Law, Art. 51.
123. Company Law, Art. 122.
124. Huang, *supra* note 121, at 163; Li Guo, *Revisiting the Chinese Styled Board of Supervisors-How It Gets Failed? An International Comparative Perspective*, Bijiaofa Yanjiu [Journal of Comparative Law], no. 2, 2016, at 74, 76-78.
125. Huang, *supra* note 121, at 164.
126. For a comprehensive review of those studies, *see* Brauner, *supra* note 7, at 26-31.

[C] Rethinking the Continuity of Interest Requirements

The preceding analysis suggests that while the continuity of interest doctrine has shaped the existing special tax treatment regime in China, the doctrine itself has no normative basis and fails as a justification for providing rollover relief to M&A participants. Having said that, the two essential components of the doctrine, namely the qualitative and quantitative requirements on consideration, do not necessarily thus become undesirable.

In the absence of those requirements, the rollover relief would be inappropriately generous that the selling parties to M&A transactions can postpone the recognition of gain or loss on the exchange of their stock or assets for any non-cash consideration. As discussed earlier, the rollover relief conforms to the tax neutrality principle only if the lock-in effect removed by it outweighs the new distortions created by it. If used in an excessive manner, the rollover relief is likely to generate more distortions than it solves. In addition, a too broad application of rollover relief can establish a heavy burden on tax administration as the tax basis of some properties - especially the fungible ones - is difficult to track. Therefore, despite the shift in the rollover relief's primary rationale from the continuity of interest to tax neutrality, the qualitative, and quantitative requirements on consideration still have some merits as a tool for confining the application scope of the rollover relief.

Notwithstanding, since the continuity of interest doctrine is no longer relevant, there is no need for the tax law to provide stringent qualitative and quantitative requirements on the consideration used in tax-deferred M&A transactions. Instead, the requirements should be deemed appropriate so long as they reflect the severity of the lock-in effect or the magnitude of benefits generated by M&A transactions. For instance, in a country where the lock-in effect is severe or where M&A transactions produce significant benefits to the economy, the requirements should be more lenient.

Australia sets an excellent example in this regard. As noted in Chapter 3, during Australia's late-1990s tax reform, the Review of Business Taxation emphasized the necessity to remove tax barriers to M&A transactions to facilitate the development of a more efficiently functioning capital market.[127] Due to the deep concern about the lock-in effect and the acknowledgement of the benefits of M&A transactions, the Review of Business Taxation proposed a 'scrip-for-scrip' rollover mechanism which later became a part of the Australian Income Tax Act. Among many countries that provide rollover relief for M&A transactions, the Australian scrip-for-scrip rollover is outstanding for having relatively low consideration eligibility criteria.

Under Subdivision 124-M of the Income Tax Assessment Act 1997, a selling shareholder may opt for the scrip-for-scrip rollover if the following conditions are satisfied.[128] First, the shareholder should exchange the original interests for interests of the same or similar kind.[129] Since the original interests are the stock in the target

127. *See* Chapter 3 above.
128. The Australian tax law provides additional conditions for some special situations, such as acquisitions between related parties or involving foreign resident selling shareholders.
129. Income Tax Assessment Act 1997 (Australia), § 124-780(1)(a).

company, the selling shareholder should receive stock in another company. Second, the exchange should happen under a 'single arrangement'. Third, as a result of the single arrangement, the purchasing company should end up owning at least 80% of the voting stock in the target company.[130] Fourth, the arrangement should allow all owners of the voting stock in the target company to participate in[131] and provide substantially the same terms for the shareholders owning the same class of stock.[132] Fifth, the stock received by the selling shareholder should be the stock of the purchasing company or the ultimate holding company of the wholly owned group in which the purchasing company is a subsidiary.[133]

Out of the five conditions, only the first and the fifth conditions contain requirements on the consideration received in an acquisition. The requirements are merely qualitative – the selling shareholder should receive the stock of the purchasing company or the ultimate controlling company of the acquirer. As long as the five conditions are satisfied, a selling shareholder can enjoy rollover relief on a scrip-for-scrip exchange, regardless of whether cash consideration is also used or what the ratio of equity consideration to total consideration is. Such a lenient rollover relief mechanism matches well with the Australian government's strong desire to reduce the lock-in effect and its full acknowledgement of the benefits associated with M&A activities.

§6.03 PROSPECTS OF THE SPECIAL TAX TREATMENT

Given that the only defensible rationale behind the rollover relief is that it is in accord with the tax neutrality principle, the Chinese tax law no longer needs to adhere to the continuity of interest doctrine but should shift its focus towards enhancing tax neutrality which requires the rollover relief for M&A transactions to be more accessible in cases where M&A activities are notably beneficial or where the lock-in effect is severe.

As discussed previously, the benefits of M&A transactions are profound in the particular context of China's further transition to a market-oriented economy. Also, there is supporting evidence that the lock-in problem is severe in China. The Shanghai Stock Exchange found that many companies had terminated M&A transactions due to tax concerns,[134] and an anonymous Chinese investment banker revealed that in 2014 nearly one-third of the M&A transactions which he advised on eventually failed because investors were unwilling to bear heavy tax burdens.[135]

Thus, under the mandate of the principle of tax neutrality, expanding the eligibility for the special tax treatment for M&A transactions turns out to be a justifiable measure for addressing the inconsistencies within China's M&A taxation. While

130. Income Tax Assessment Act 1997 (Australia), § 124-780(2)(a)(i).
131. Income Tax Assessment Act 1997 (Australia), § 124-780(2)(b).
132. Income Tax Assessment Act 1997 (Australia), § 124-780(2)(c).
133. Income Tax Assessment Act 1997 (Australia), § 124-780(3)(c).
134. Lifen An, *Shuishou Cheng Binggou Chongzu Lanluhu [Taxation Becomes an Obstacle to M&A Transactions]* (12 March 2015), http://m.21jingji.com/article/20150312/34bf0ea0a7a6dad9b5450e1f293e8312.html.
135. *Ibid.*

reforming the special tax treatment in this direction, one must not forget to prevent the regime from being abused for tax avoidance purposes.

[A] Expanding the Eligibility for the Special Tax Treatment

[1] Obstacles in Access to the Special Tax Treatment

In order to effectively expand the eligibility for the special tax treatment, it is essential to identify the main factors that keep M&A transactions from eligible for this tax relief. The high equity consideration ratio threshold is the first to blame. As evidenced by the empirical findings presented in Chapter 5, many transactions failed to qualify as tax-deferred reorganizations because the ratio of equity consideration to total consideration in them was lower than 85%.

Another less obvious obstacle in access to the special tax treatment relates to the dual-track income tax system in China. As discussed in Chapter 3, China's income tax laws for companies and individuals run along separate tracks so that only corporate taxpayers can enjoy the special tax treatment for M&A transactions. Since individuals and partnerships engaging in an M&A transaction always need to recognize gain or loss at the time of the transaction, regardless of whether the transaction meets the requirements of a tax-deferred reorganization, they are presumably less keen on receiving equity consideration than corporate taxpayers in M&A transactions. One natural speculation, given the preceding, is that many transactions fail to qualify as tax-deferred reorganizations because non-corporate taxpayers receive too much non-equity consideration. If this speculation is confirmed, there will be additional options for making the special tax treatment more accessible.

In order to test the above speculation, the first step is to examine whether the identity of target shareholders has any impact on the possible tax treatment of an M&A transaction.

Table 6.1 Identity of Shareholders of the Target Company (2014-2015)

Identity of Shareholders	*Number of Acquisitions*	*Eligible for the Special Tax Treatment*	*Ineligible for the Special Tax Treatment*	*% Eligible*
Company	190	174	16	91.6%
Non-company	169	48	121	28.4%
Company & Non-company	226	113	113	50.0%
Total	585	335	250	57.3%

Table 6.1 classifies the 585 stock acquisitions in the sample into three groups according to the identity of the selling shareholders. The first group includes acquisitions where all the selling shareholders were companies. The second group includes acquisitions where all the selling shareholders are non-companies, namely individuals or partnerships. The last group includes acquisitions which have both corporate and non-corporate selling shareholders.

During the period from 2014 to 2015, there were 190 stock acquisitions where the exchanging shareholders were comprised solely of enterprises. The overwhelming majority of those transactions had no less than 85% of the total consideration paid with the purchasing company's stock, which may be prima facie evidence of corporate shareholders' strong preference for equity consideration. In contrast, for the 169 stock acquisitions without corporate shareholders, the eligibility rate was only 28.4%. Moreover, where a transaction involved two types of shareholders, the probability that such a transaction could get the special tax treatment was 50.0%, falling between the rates for the two groups of transactions that had only one type of selling shareholders.

It is thus evident that the transactions with companies as exchanging shareholders are more likely to get the special tax treatment than those only involving non-corporate shareholders. One possible explanation for this phenomenon is that non-corporate shareholders' preference for cash consideration over equity consideration has dramatically dragged down the equity consideration ratio, thereby rendering acquisitions ineligible for the special tax treatment. An alternative explanation is that non-corporate shareholders did not exhibit a preference for cash but were nevertheless not as keenly interested in equity consideration as corporate shareholders.

To be sure, the best way to ascertain how the identity of selling shareholders may affect the preference for the type of consideration is to examine the consideration composition of each shareholder in the sample. However, since the data set size is too large to handle, this research decides to treat shareholders in the same transaction of the same identity as one single entity. Such a treatment of data is valid because, in nearly all transactions, shareholders of the same identity received the same ratio of equity-to-total consideration. As a result of the data treatment, we have a smaller-sized data set that contains 416 corporate shareholder groups and 395 non-corporate shareholder groups.

Table 6.2 Composition of Consideration Received by Corporate Shareholder Groups (2014-2015)

Equity Consideration Ratio	*Number of Corporate Shareholder Groups*	*%*
0%	11	2.6%
(0%, 20%]	3	0.7%
(20%, 40%]	2	0.5%
(40%, 60%]	32	7.7%
(60%, 80%]	52	12.5%
(80%, 100%)	77	18.5%

Equity Consideration Ratio	*Number of Corporate Shareholder Groups*	*%*
100%	239	57.5%
Total	416	100.0%

In Table 6.2, this research divides corporate shareholder groups into seven categories based on the consideration composition. It is first noticeable that those groups display a strong preference for equity consideration. Around 95% of them were paid more with stock than cash. However, caution is warranted when generalizing these findings because there is a considerable amount of purely cash-financed acquisitions left out of the sample.

Another eye-catching characteristic of these corporate shareholder groups is that many of them received pure stock payment – 239 groups, or around 57% of the total number, received nothing but shares of the purchasing company. Since the higher the equity consideration ratio, the more a transaction is likely to be eligible for the special tax treatment, corporate shareholders naturally have a strong motive for receiving as much equity consideration as possible to ensure the special tax treatment. Empirical findings underscore this observation. As shown in Table 6.2, the number of corporate shareholder groups increases with the equity consideration ratio. Nearly 70% of the groups received more than 85% of the total consideration in the form of the acquiring company's stock.

Table 6.3 Composition of Consideration Received by Non-corporate Shareholder Groups

Equity Consideration Ratio	*Number of Non-corporate Shareholder Groups*	*%*
0%	3	0.8%
(0%, 20%]	0	0.0%
(20%, 40%]	4	1.0%
(40%, 60%]	56	14.2%
(60%, 80%]	140	35.4%
(80%, 100%)	85	21.5%
100%	107	27.1%
Total	395	100.0%

Like Table 6.2, Table 6.3 divides non-corporate shareholder groups into seven categories according to the consideration composition. In a similar way to corporate shareholders, less than 15% of the non-corporate shareholder groups received more cash than stock. Therefore, the speculation that non-corporate shareholders generally have a strong preference for cash consideration is ungrounded. Again, due to the data selection bias, caution is warranted when generalizing that non-corporate shareholders prefer equity consideration outside of this sample.

Notwithstanding, non-corporate shareholders were apparently less willing to accept pure equity payment than corporate shareholders. Around 27% of non-corporate shareholder groups received nothing other than the purchasing company's stock, while the same figure for corporate shareholder groups was 57%. Compared to corporate shareholders, non-enterprise shareholders had a much smaller proportion that received more than 85% of the total consideration in the form of the purchasing company's stock.

It is interesting to note that 234 (around 59%) non-corporate shareholder groups received a below 85% ratio of equity consideration to total consideration. Among the seven categories, the largest one (around 36%) consists of non-corporate shareholder groups receiving an equity-to-total consideration ratio between 60% and 80%. Up to this point, it is quite clear that many acquisitions failed to qualify as tax-deferred reorganizations because, to a large extent, relatively few non-corporate shareholders receive more than 85% of their consideration in the form of equity. In many cases, non-corporate shareholders in effect hold veto power over the acquisition being tax-deferred.

[2] Reform Proposals

The above analysis shows that the access to the special tax treatment is mainly blocked by two factors, i.e., the high equity consideration ratio threshold of 85% and the denial of rollover relief's application to non-corporate shareholders. Correspondingly, there are three possible approaches to reform the special tax treatment: (1) reducing the equity consideration ratio threshold, (2) extending the special tax treatment to non-corporate taxpayers, and (3) decoupling the tax treatments of different taxpayers.

[a] Reducing the Equity Consideration Ratio Threshold

Reducing the equity consideration ratio threshold is the most straightforward way to expand the eligibility for special tax treatment. With a lower equity consideration ratio threshold, it is more unlikely that non-corporate taxpayers can veto a tax-deferred reorganization. The empirical findings presented in Chapter 5 confirm that if the equity consideration ratio threshold had been reduced, many acquisitions would have turned from ineligible for the special tax treatment to eligible.

Under this approach, the most critical issue is what an appropriate ratio threshold might be. There is far from consensus on this matter,[136] and probably, it is never possible to reach one. No one can justify why a percentage of, say, 50% is more

136. Scholars have proposed many different numbers such as 50% and 75%. *See e.g.*, Weiping Li, *The Incentive Effect of the Tax System on M&A Activities*, Caijing Wenti Yanjiu [Research on Financial and Economic Issues], no. 4, 2007, at 72, 74; Li & Yang, *supra* note 78, at 40; Feng Shen, *The Evolution of M&A Tax Policy and Reform Proposals, Shuishou Jingji Yanjiu [Tax and Economic Research]*, no. 5, 2016, at 35.

appropriate than 51% in separating taxable and tax-deferred transactions. Despite the inevitable arbitrariness of this kind of line-drawing, it is possible to identify several key numbers that policymakers need to consider in setting the equity consideration ratio threshold.

As presented in Table 6.3, non-corporate shareholder groups that received an equity consideration ratio between 60% and 80% made up the largest of the seven categories, and thirty-one (around 7.8%) non-corporate shareholder groups had an equity consideration ratio of more than 80% and less than 85%. Why did many non-corporate shareholders prefer the equity consideration ratios of 70% or 80% to that of 85%? To what extent was the 5% or 10% more cash consideration crucial for them? As non-corporate shareholders always need to recognize gain or loss at the time of the transaction, the only tax consideration that could possibly contribute to this phenomenon is whether this is enough cash to settle taxes. Where a non-corporate selling shareholder, such as an individual, receives plenty of cash from the purchasing company, the tax arising in the transaction can be easily paid with the cash received. In contrast, in the transactions where none or only a small fraction of the consideration is paid in cash, the non-corporate shareholders involved have to use cash from other sources to fulfil their tax liabilities, but they may be unwilling to do so in the first place. Therefore, it is reasonable to assume that non-corporate shareholders tend to ensure they can receive enough cash consideration to cover their tax liabilities.

In terms of ensuring enough liquidity, what is the minimum cash consideration ratio acceptable to this shareholder? Individuals and partnerships are likely to give different answers because the tax rules applicable to them vary significantly. Therefore, this research will examine the two groups of shareholders' preference for cash consideration separately. Suppose that the purchasing company acquires the target company's shares from an individual (X) and a partnership (Y), and both of them receive mixed payments. X receives C1 worth of consideration, rx of which is the stock of the purchasing company, and Y receives C2 worth of consideration, ry of which is equity consideration. Moreover, the tax basis of X's and Y's stocks in the target company are B1 and B2 respectively. X and Y both make profits in this transaction; that is to say, C1 is larger than B1, and C2 is larger than B2.

For X, the taxable income is the amount of her total consideration (C1) minus the tax basis of her target stock (B1). The IITL separates 'gains from transferring property', which include the proceeds of selling securities, from other types of income, and sets the tax rate for them at 20%.[137] Therefore, X's tax payable is 20% of her taxable income. In order to guarantee X receives enough cash to pay taxes, the cash consideration must at least be equal to X's taxes payable. Consequently, an equation is derived as follows: $20\% \times (C1\text{-}B1) = (1\text{-}rx) \times C1$. We can simplify this equation into the following one:

137. IITL, Art. 3(3).

$$r_x = 0.8 + 0.2 \times \frac{B_1}{C_1}$$

Since B1 is less than C1, the maximum value of $0.2 \times \frac{B_1}{C_1}$ is 20%. Accordingly, r_x has a maximum value of 100%. Moreover, because the tax basis of X's target stock, B1, is no less than zero, the minimum value of r_x is 80%. Therefore, for any individual shareholder who receives less than 80% of her consideration in the form of stock, the cash paid by the purchasing company will always be enough to cover her tax liability.

In the case of Y, which is a partnership, the relevant tax rules are much more complicated. Under the current law, partnerships are not taxable entities, and the tax authorities collect income taxes at the partner level. A partnership may have two types of partners, namely individual partners and corporate partners. As aforementioned, the tax deferral treatment for enterprises provided by the special tax treatment cannot pass through partnerships.[138] Therefore, when a partnership participates in an acquisition as a target shareholder, its partners, regardless of their identities, cannot defer their tax liabilities arising in the transaction. In other words, both two types of partners may insist on enough cash consideration to cover their tax liabilities. The preference of individual partners and corporate partners will be examined separately since two different sets of rules apply to them.

Assume that partnership Y has only one partner, which is a resident company. According to the EITL, resident companies are generally subject to a single tax rate of 25%.[139] In a stock acquisition, the corporate partner has taxable income that is equal to the amount of its consideration received (C2) minus the tax basis of the target stock traded (B2), and that taxable income is subject to the tax rate of 25%. Let the cash consideration be equal to the enterprise income taxes payable; the following equation will be derived: 25% × (C2-B2) = (1-ry) × C2. A simplified version of this equation is as follows:

$$r_y = 0.75 + 0.25 \times \frac{B_2}{C_2}$$

The maximum and minimum values of r_y are 75% and 100% respectively. Thus, if Y receives no more than 75% of the consideration in the form of stock, the cash received in the acquisition is always enough for its corporate partner to fulfil its income tax liability.

Instead, assume that partnership Y has an individual as its sole partner. Where a partnership sells securities, the tax law will treat the gains allocated to the partnership's natural person partners as the 'income from conducting trade or business' rather than the 'income from transferring property'.[140] The IITL stipulates a progressive rate structure for this category of income, and the marginal tax rate is 35%.[141] In order to

138. *See* § 3.04[C][2] above.
139. EITL, Art. 4.
140. IITL, Arts. 3(2), 3(3); Caishui (2000) No. 91, Art. 4.
141. IITL, Art. 3(2).

find out the maximum equity consideration ratio acceptable to the individual partner, it is assumed that the individual partner of Y needs to pay taxes at the marginal rate of 35%. Accordingly, the taxes payable in this scenario are 35% × (C2-B2). Suppose the cash received in the acquisition barely covers the taxes payable; we derive an equation: 35% × (C2-B2) = (1-ry) × C2. This equation can be simplified into the following one:

$$r_y = 0.65 + 0.35 \times \frac{B_2}{C_2}$$

The value of r_y between 65% and 100%. Hence, provided that the equity consideration ratio is not greater than 65%, the individual partner will always have enough cash to pay taxes.

The three maximum equity consideration ratios, 65%, 75%, and 80%, are in the interval [60%, 80%], which corresponds to the largest category of non-corporate shareholders in the data set. It thus seems that non-corporate shareholders' need for cash to cover tax liabilities could be a plausible explanation for why many of them declined an equity consideration ratio of more than 85%. Although further study is needed to confirm this explanation, the above analysis suffices to show that 65%, 75%, and 80% are critical numbers worthy of consideration in the adjustment of the equity consideration ratio threshold.

[b] Extending the Special Tax Treatment to Non-corporate Taxpayers

Another approach for expanding the eligibility for the special tax treatment is to extend the treatment to non-corporate taxpayers. Given the broad participation of non-corporate shareholders in M&A transactions (non-corporate shareholders were involved in 395 out of 585 acquisitions in the data sample, and in 169 out of the 395 acquisitions, all the selling shareholders are non-companies), if this method is adopted, non-corporate shareholders will be more willing to receive equity consideration, and therefore, many more tax-deferred transactions will emerge even if the equity consideration ratio threshold is kept at 85%.

This method has been enthusiastically advocated by many scholars in China, mainly because it is believed to be able to reduce the discrepancy between the income tax rules for companies and individuals.[142] However, contrary to this widely held view that extending the special tax treatment to non-corporate taxpayers would improve the integrity of the tax system, this research argues that the adoption of this method would create tax loopholes.

The Chinese income tax treatments for individuals and companies differ in many aspects. In some cases, the tax rules for companies are more preferential than those for individuals. One example of this is the special tax treatment for M&A. However, there are also many favourable tax rules applying exclusively to individuals. For instance, as mentioned in the previous section, an individual taxpayer may choose to pay taxes on her non-monetary contribution to a company in a lump sum five years after the

142. Hao, et al., *supra* note 8, at 45-46; Li & Yang, *supra* note 78, at 40.

contribution,[143] while a company in a similar situation is only allowed to pay taxes in equal instalments over five years.[144] Given that there are numerous differences between the income tax rules for companies and individuals, a minor attempt to reduce the discrepancy between the two sets of rules may be counterproductive to the aim. This is what the second-best theory tells us.[145] In order to avoid making things even worse, it is necessary to look at the broad picture of how the law (including but not limited to tax law) treats the transfer of shares, rather than blindly extending the special tax treatment to non-corporate taxpayers.

Take the income tax treatment for selling listed stock by individuals as an example. Individuals are generally subject to income tax at the rate of 20% on gains arising from selling shares of PRC resident companies; however, shortly after China's securities markets came into operation,[146] the MOF and the STA issued Caishui (1994) No. 40 to exempt individual investors' income from disposals of listed shares from individual income tax.[147] This exemption of individual income tax on gains from transferring listed shares has later been extended twice and is still valid until this day.[148] Assume that individuals were allowed to defer recognition on gains from M&A transactions while the aforementioned tax exemption remains unchanged; for those who receive listed stock in tax-deferred M&A transactions, the taxes on their gains would be in effect permanently exempted. Therefore, if the Chinese lawmakers are about to extend the application scope of the special tax treatment to non-corporate shareholders, they should also scrutinize other existing tax rules to avoid creating tax avoidance opportunities like the exemplified one.

[c] Decoupling Tax Treatments of Different Taxpayers

Under the current Chinese law, the selling shareholders in M&A transactions are entitled to non-recognition treatment only if a certain percentage of the total consideration is equity consideration. In other words, the current Chinese law treats all selling shareholders of a transaction as a simple aggregation in determining whether the transaction is eligible for the special tax treatment. Where a selling shareholder fails to receive enough equity consideration, the remaining sellers face the risk of losing access

143. Caishui (2015) No. 41, Art. 3.
144. Caishui (2014) No. 116, Art. 3.
145. *See* § 6.02[B][1] above for a detailed discussion of the second-best theory.
146. China established two national stock exchanges in the early 1990s. The Shanghai Stock Exchange and the Shenzhen Stock Exchange started trading on 19 December 1990 and 3 July 1991 respectively.
147. Caishuizi (1994) No. 40, Guanyu Gupiao Zhuanrang Suode Zanbu Zhengshou Geren Suodeshui de Tongzhi [Notice on the Exemption of Individual Income Tax on Income from Transfer of Shares] (promulgated by the MOF and the STA and effective 20 June 1994, repealed) (PRC).
148. Caishuizi (1996) No. 12, Guanyu Gupiao Zhuanrang Suode 1996 Nian Zanbu Zhengshou Geren Suodeshui de Tongzhi [Notice on the Exemption of Individual Income Tax on Income from Transfer of Shares in 1996] (promulgated by the MOF and the STA and effective 9 February 1996, repealed) (PRC); Caishuizi (1998) No. 61, Guanyu Geren Zhuanrang Gupiao Suode Jixu Zanmian Zhengshou Geren Suodeshui de Tongzhi [Notice on the Continuation of Exemption of Individual Income Tax on Income from Transfer of Shares] (promulgated by the MOF and the STA on 30 March 1998, effective retrospectively 1 January 1997) (PRC), Art. 8.

to non-recognition treatment. Given that the current law prescribes a relatively high equity consideration ratio threshold and confines the special tax treatment to corporate taxpayers, that risk is quite significant.

While the two reform methods discussed above defuse the situation, the only way to eliminate that risk is to change the underlying mechanism of the special tax treatment and treat taxpayers engaging in an M&A transaction as independent actors. In other words, under this method, the tax authorities will determine the eligibility for non-recognition treatment on a shareholder-by-shareholder basis. In the US, some proposed alternatives to the tax rules on reorganizations suggest decoupling the tax treatment of one target shareholder from another,[149] and the Australian scrip-for-scrip rollover relief also reflects this method.[150]

[B] Minimizing Tax Avoidance Opportunities

As noted previously, to make the taxation system for M&A transactions better conform to the principle of tax neutrality requires controlling the tax avoidance opportunities related to the special tax treatment. Anyone with knowledge of M&A taxation will recognize that there are many complex issues to be addressed under this subject. In what follows, this research selects one of the most significant tax avoidance problems within this topic, i.e., tax basis adjustment without gain recognition.

During the past few decades, the Chinese tax law has been oscillating between applying fair market value basis rules and carry-over basis rules in determining the tax basis of assets or stock transferred in tax-deferred M&A transactions. As discussed in detail in Chapter 2, before 2003, the Chinese tax law applied carry-over basis rules and strictly prohibited the purchasing company in tax-deferred mergers from adjusting the original tax basis of the transferred assets.[151] However, in 2003 the STA repealed the carry-over basis rules and allowed the purchasing company to use fair market value as the basis for the transferred assets.[152] With the issuance of Circular 59 in 2009, the MOF and the STA have re-established the carry-over basis rules: Article 6 of Circular 59 provides that assets or stock transferred in tax-deferred M&A transactions shall retain their original tax basis.[153]

Some Chinese scholars and practitioners criticize the current carry-over basis rules and contend that the tax law should allow the purchasing company in tax-deferred transactions to have a fair market value basis in the transferred assets or stock. Their main argument is that the current tax basis rules preserve realized gains in two places and thus lead to the problem of double taxation. More specifically, the tax law requires both the purchasing company and the selling parties in tax-deferred transactions to keep the original tax basis of the transferred assets or stock. Thus, the

149. *See e.g.*, Hoffer & Oesterle, *supra* note 18, at 1102, 1109; Blank, *supra* note 12, at 50-51.
150. For a discussion on the Australian scrip-for-scrip rollover relief, *see* § 6.02[C] above.
151. Guoshuifa (1993) No. 139, Art. 1(2); Guoshuifa (1997) No. 71, Art. 1(1).
152. Guoshuifa (2003) No. 45, Art. 6(2).
153. Caishui (2009) No. 59, Arts. 6(2)(1), 6(3)(1), 6(4)(1).

appreciation inherent in the assets or stock will be subject to double tax, once in the hands of the sellers and once more in the hands of the purchasing companies.[154]

This research concurs with the view that the carry-over basis rules create a double tax. However, it objects to applying the fair market value basis rules to all types of tax-deferred transactions. To make this point, let us consider the consequences of allowing the purchasing company in tax-deferred M&A transactions to have fair market value as the basis of transferred assets or stock. Imagine that there is a multistep sale of assets. The first step is a tax-deferred asset acquisition in which a company issues shares to its parent company in exchange for the latter's assets, and the second step is that the subsidiary company sells the transferred assets to another company for cash. Based on the current carry-over basis rules, the subsidiary will incur taxes in the second step, and therefore, this complicated multistep transaction structure makes little sense from a tax benefit perspective.

However, if the step-up in tax basis is allowed, many taxpayers will adopt such a transaction structure to avoid taxes because the subsidiary in the above hypothetical scenario can step up the basis of the assets transferred from its parent to the fair market value and thus no gain will arise upon the target company's subsequent selling of the assets to the ultimate purchaser for cash. Provided that the subsidiary company retains the cash received from the ultimate purchaser in its business and the parent company keeps the shares that the subsidiary issues to it, the realized but unrecognized gains from the appreciation in the value of the transferred assets, although preserved in the basis of the shares of the subsidiary company, will enjoy a de facto tax exemption. That is to say, all the gains arising in the two-step transaction will escape taxes permanently.

Thus, if the fair market value basis rules are reintroduced into the Chinese law, the application of such rules should be confined to tax-deferred M&A transactions between unrelated parties so as to prevent the tax avoidance scheme illustrated above. In this regard, the Australian tax law provides valuable lessons. Under the Australian scrip-for-scrip rollover regime, the ordinary cost basis rules generally apply in determining the tax basis of interests acquired by a purchasing company. However, where the selling shareholder is either a significant stakeholder or a common stakeholder for the transaction arrangement, the tax basis of the target company's shares in the hands of the purchasing company will be equivalent to the original tax basis of those shares.[155] This exceptional tax basis rule applies if the selling shareholder, together with associates, has either a 30% or more stake in the target company before the transaction and in the purchasing company after the transaction; or together with other entities, at least an 80% holding common to both the target and the purchasing companies.[156]

Although lawmakers in China can learn from the Australian experience and create different tax basis rules for tax-deferred M&A transactions between related

154. *See e.g.*, Xiaohui Hong, *The Problem of Double Taxation in M&A Transactions*, Xin Kuaiji [Modern Accounting], no. 7, 2015, at 69, 70; Yunbin Gao, *Does the Special Tax Treat Lead to Double Taxation?*, Caiwu yu Kuaiji [Finance & Accounting], no. 6, 2013, at 34, 35.

155. Income Tax Assessment Act 1997 (Australia), § 124-782(2).

156. Income Tax Assessment Act 1997 (Australia), § 124-783.

parties and unrelated parties, this research would like to point out that they do not have to do so. Under the current law, the special tax treatment permits the parties to an M&A transaction to defer taxes otherwise payable, but only at the cost of preserving the unrecognized gains once more through the mechanism of a carry-over basis. Therefore, the double tax in tax-deferred transactions is in effect the consideration paid by taxpayers to the government for permission to enjoy tax deferral benefits. Moreover, as the law allows M&A participants to elect between the ordinary and the special tax treatments, taxpayers who are worried about a potential double tax can choose the ordinary tax treatment.

The real problem with the carry-over basis rules, however, is not the double tax but the duplication of tax losses. As just described, the dual substituted tax basis rules under Circular 59 effectively preserve the unrecognized gain from a tax-deferred M&A transaction for potential later taxation in both the purchasing company's and the selling parties' hands. Symmetrical application of the rules would result in a similar potential for duplication of unrecognized losses. Imagine, for example, that a parent company sells all the stock in its wholly owned subsidiary with a basis of RMB 100 and a fair market value of RMB 50 in exchange for RMB 50 worth of stock in the purchasing company. If the parties to this stock acquisition choose the special tax treatment, the parent company's RMB 100 substituted tax basis in the stock of the purchasing company will preserve the RMB 50 built-in loss for recognition upon a subsequent sale of the stock. The purchasing company will also take an RMB 100 basis in the stock of the subsidiary company. If the purchasing company later were to sell the acquired stock, it too would recognize the RMB 50 loss.

The US loss restriction rules provide a valuable reference regarding how to prevent the doubling of built-in losses. In order to prevent taxpayers from duplicating tax losses through the Section 351 tax-deferred capital contributions, the US tax law has introduced Section 362(e)(2), which provides that the transferee company's tax basis in the assets received in a Section 351 exchange 'shall not exceed the fair market value of such property immediately after such transaction'.[157] As such, the previously unrecognized loss is preserved in the selling parties' hands but not in the purchasing company's. The Chinese lawmakers may consider including a similar rule to limit the purchasing company's basis in the acquired stock to its fair market value so as to guarantee a single loss result in tax-deferred M&A transactions.

§6.04 CONCLUSION

In the foregoing chapter, it was suggested that the direction for reforming the special tax treatment depends on the inquiry into its normative foundation. This chapter then began to investigate what the justification for the special tax treatment is. There are traditionally two groups of justifications supporting providing rollover relief to M&A participants. One is the continuity of interest theory; the other is two tax administration concerns, including the difficulty of valuation and the liquidity problem.

157. Internal Revenue Code (US), § 362(e)(2)(A).

The continuity of interest theory suffers serious problems. First, under the continuity of interest doctrine that originates in the US and then spreads to other countries including China, many M&A participants who do not genuinely continue their interest can enjoy rollover relief. Second and more important, the notion that taxpayers who continue interests in the transferred business enterprise after M&A transactions should be granted rollover relief does not have much normative plausibility because it depends on the realization rule, which is not a normative requirement but merely an administratively necessary feature of the modern income taxation. Also, the two administration concerns cannot justify the establishment of the special tax treatment as they are neither unique to M&A transactions nor insurmountable in the absence of rollover relief.

It is argued that the principle of tax neutrality, or more accurately, the second face of neutrality, may give grounds for the provision of rollover relief to M&A transactions. Rollover relief can be a second-best solution to the distortive effects – in particular the lock-in effect – caused by the realization-based tax system, on the condition that the distortion removed by it outweighs the distortion that it creates or increases. This condition is in essence a cost-benefit analysis, which is likely to give a positive result in the Chinese context. Thus, supported by the principle of tax neutrality, expanding the eligibility for the special tax treatment for M&A transactions turns out to be a proper measure for addressing the severe inconsistencies within China's M&A taxation.

Chinese taxpayers' limited eligibility for the special tax treatment is largely due to two factors – the high requirement on the ratio of equity consideration to total consideration and the denial of access to rollover relief for non-corporate shareholders. There correspondingly are three possible approaches to make the special tax treatment more accessible to taxpayers, which include reducing the equity consideration ratio threshold, extending the special tax treatment to non-corporate taxpayers, and decoupling the tax treatments of different taxpayers. While all of them can help make the special tax treatment more accessible, cautions are warranted with respect to whether they fit well into the income tax system. Moreover, since tax avoidance is the worst enemy of the neutrality of a tax system, the flaws of the special tax treatment, in particular, the problematic basis adjustment mechanism, should be addressed to prevent taxpayers from abusing rollover relief for tax avoidance purposes.

CHAPTER 7

Neutral Tax Treatment of Asset and Stock Acquisitions

§7.01 INTRODUCTION

As pointed out in Chapter 4, apart from providing the contrasting ordinary and special tax treatments, the current Chinese tax law also affects the choice between alternative transaction options and thus contravenes the principle of tax neutrality by allowing the distinction in tax consequences between stock and asset acquisitions. This chapter will, therefore, focus on how the Chinese tax law would be improved to ensure various forms of acquisitions are subject to taxes in a similar manner.

This chapter proceeds as follows. Section §7.02 will comprehensively review the problem of disparity in tax treatment between asset acquisitions and stock acquisitions. Section §7.03 will investigate the causation of the problem and identify a promising direction to solve the problem. Section §7.04 will trace the historical development of Section 338 in the US IRC. Since the US has rich experience in equalizing the tax treatments of stock acquisitions and asset acquisitions, this will provide the basis for subsequent discussion. Section §7.05 will critically compare and analyse various methods of conforming stock acquisitions and asset acquisitions, intending to determine if they suit the particular needs of China. Section §7.06 will discuss how the taxation of liquidation affects the discontinuity between stock and asset acquisitions and determines the direction for solving the discontinuity. Section §7.07 will give some suggestions for China on how to improve the parity between asset acquisitions and stock acquisitions.

§7.02 DISPARATE TAX TREATMENTS OF ASSET AND STOCK ACQUISITIONS

Under the current Chinese tax law, a taxable asset acquisition triggers immediate taxable gain or loss to the target company on its transfer of assets to the purchasing company. After the disposal of assets, the target company may liquidate or continue operating. In either case, the target company's shareholders are likely to incur tax liabilities upon receiving distributions. By contrast, a stock acquisition only results in current tax to the selling shareholders of the target company.

Nevertheless, a stock acquisition is not necessarily more tax-attractive than an asset acquisition. In an asset acquisition, the corollary of the corporate level recognition is a cost basis in the transferred assets which reflect their fair market value. Where the transferred assets have appreciated in value, a cost basis means an increase in the tax basis of the transferred assets, which will allow the purchasing company to have more depreciation deductions in subsequent years. A stock acquisition, on the contrary, does not produce such benefits as the target company's assets retain their original tax basis.

The above crude comparison suggests that a buyer prefers to purchase the assets of a company while the seller favours a stock sale. However, such an assertion is over-simplistic and potentially misleading for two reasons. First, when considering the impact of taxation on transaction decision-making, the tax consequences to the seller are inseparable from those of the buyer. Since the parties to a transaction can make price adjustments in response to tax detriments or benefits, instead of focusing on one particular party's tax treatment, it is more meaningful to look at the overall tax consequences of the transaction. Second, because there does not exist a unified rule applying universally to all types of taxpayers, one must be cautious not to overgeneralize taxpayers' preference for one form of acquisition over the other.

The remaining part of this subsection presents a series of hypothetical case studies to explore the difference in tax treatment between asset acquisitions and stock acquisitions.

[A] Gain Case

Suppose that a company (S) owns all of the outstanding stock of T, another company that engages in manufacturing and selling electronic gadgets. S wants to withdraw investment in the electronics industry by having T sell its all assets to the purchasing company (P), which in turn continues the original business of T.

Assume for the moment that those assets have a fair market value of RMB 200 and a combined tax basis of RMB 100 in the hand of T and that S has a tax basis of RMB 100 in its T stock. Besides, P expects to use those assets to produce RMB 220 worth of electronic gadgets and sell them to consumers. S, T, and P are all subject to the standard enterprise income tax of 25%.[1] They may structure the transaction as an asset acquisition or stock acquisition.

First, let us consider the tax consequences of an asset acquisition. Suppose that P agrees to pay RMB 200 in cash for T's assets. At Time 0, when P buys those assets, T incurs an immediate tax of RMB 25 on its gain of RMB 100 (i.e., 200-100). The tax basis of the transferred assets correspondingly increases from RMB 100 to RMB 200. In the future, the RMB 200 basis will translate into a depreciation deduction, which will reduce P's taxable income from selling gadgets to RMB 20 (i.e., 220-200). For the sake of convenience, this research deems that the RMB 20 is a one-off gain recognized at Time 1, and thus P will pay an RMB 5 tax on the gain.

There is another way to view the process. We can see P as first paying an RMB 55 tax on the RMB 220 gross profit and then receiving an RMB 50 payment from the government for the depreciation deduction. While the amount of depreciation deduction may vary with the form of acquisition, the value of products to be sold by P is always RMB 220. In other words, P will inevitably incur a tax of RMB 55, regardless of which form of acquisition it takes. As this research focuses on the difference between the tax treatments of asset and stock acquisitions, it will disregard the RMB 55 tax in the following discussion. Therefore, this research sees the asset acquisition as generating a tax benefit of RMB 50 to P at Time 1. As a corporate shareholder, S receives T's RMB 75 after-tax profits as tax-free inter-corporate dividends.[2] Following the distribution of dividends, the value of T stock drops to RMB 100. S may sell the T stock without realizing any gain or loss.

Second, the parties may choose to conduct a stock acquisition in which S sells its stock in T to P. After the stock sale, T becomes P's subsidiary. Suppose for now that P decides to pay RMB 200 for the stock. The research will explain more about the purchase price but tentatively set the price at RMB 200. At Time 0, S is subject to an RMB 25 tax on its gain of RMB 100 (i.e., 200-100), and P receives the T's stock with a stepped-up basis of RMB 200 while T retains the historical basis of RMB 100 in its assets. At Time 1, T can claim an RMB 100 depreciation deduction and recognize a taxable gain of RMB 120 (i.e., 220-100). As before, we deem that T pays an RMB 55 tax on selling RMB 220 worth of products and receives an RMB 25 payment from the government for the tax basis depreciation of RMB 100. Again, we omit the RMB 55 tax and thus see the stock acquisition as bringing T an RMB 25 tax benefit.

Table 7.1 represents the amounts of taxes payable resulting from the two transaction options.

1. EITL, Art. 4.
2. Assume T meets requirements on the distribution of dividends under the Company Law.

Table 7.1 Tax Consequences of Asset and Stock Acquisitions (Corporate Shareholders – Gain Case)

	Time 0	*Time 1*	*Total*
Asset Acquisition	25	-50	-25
Stock Acquisition	25	-25	0

Note: Negative numbers represent tax benefits enjoyed by taxpayers.

An examination of the table shows that the form of acquisition selected by the parties under normal conditions will be asset acquisition. Asset acquisition is preferred because it avoids a deferred corporate-level tax that would result from a stock acquisition. Viewed from another perspective, in an asset acquisition, the purchasing company pays a tax on the appreciation of the target company's assets in exchange for a step-up in the basis of those assets. The increase in tax basis will allow the purchasing company to claim more depreciation deductions. In contrast, a stock acquisition incurs a tax burden of the same amount, but the basis of the target's assets remains unchanged.

The above analysis's assumption that P pays RMB 200 for the stock of the target company has an implicit premise – S is with strong bargaining power and is keen on a stock acquisition, so P has to bear the full amount of the tax increase compared to conducting an asset acquisition. However, in most cases, the purchase price tends to be less in a stock acquisition than in an asset acquisition because the increase in tax liability will be shared by the buyer and the seller. In other words, the choice of stock acquisition in the above scenario tends to make each party worse off.

[B] Loss Case

As Professor David Weisbach points out, 'what is bad for taxpayers in the case of gains is usually good for taxpayers in the case of losses'.[3] Investors in our hypothetical will find the stock acquisition appealing if T's stock and assets have depreciated rather than appreciated. Suppose that the assets of T have a combined tax basis of RMB 220 in the hands of T and that S has a tax basis of RMB 220 in its T stock. All other assumptions remain unchanged.

In an asset acquisition, T sells its assets to P and realizes a deductible loss of RMB 20. Assume that shortly after the disposal of the assets, T makes a profit of RMB 20 from some other sources. Since the profit can exactly offset the loss arising in the disposal of the assets, T realizes no gain or loss and cannot make any non-liquidating distribution. Company S will not report any gain or loss on selling T's stock since the value of the stock now is RMB 220 – equal to its tax basis. Hence, the asset acquisition in effect generates an RMB 5 tax benefit at Time 0. As to P, it receives the assets with a fair

3. David A. Weisbach, *The Irreducible Complexity of Firm-Level Income Taxes: Theory and Doctrine in the Corporate Tax*, 60 Tax L. Rev. 215, 237 (2006).

market value basis of RMB 200 and will enjoy an RMB 50 tax benefit by claiming depreciation deduction at Time 1.

If they conduct a stock acquisition, S recognizes an RMB 20 loss on selling T's stock. The loss can be immediately deducted against the taxable income of S and produce an RMB 5 tax benefit. P receives T stock with a fair market value basis of RMB 200, whereas T retains the RMB 220 basis in its assets. The RMB 220 tax basis will generate a tax benefit of RMB 55. The net result is that the parties derive RMB 60 of total tax benefits from the stock acquisition.

Table 7.2 presents the amounts of taxes payable in the loss scenario. It is evident that the stock acquisition now proves to be more tax-efficient.

Table 7.2 Tax Consequences of Asset and Stock Acquisitions (Corporate Shareholders – Loss Case)

	Time 0	*Time 1*	*Total*
Asset Acquisition	-5	-50	-55
Stock Acquisition	-5	-55	-60

Note: Negative numbers represent tax benefits enjoyed by taxpayers.

The two forms of acquisition produce the same benefit at the time of the transaction, but they lead to different tax bases in T's assets. In the asset acquisition, the tax basis of the assets is reduced to the fair market value, whereas in the stock acquisition, the assets retain the historical basis. As a result, the RMB 20 loss inherent in T's assets survives the stock acquisition, even though S has already recognized a shareholder-level loss. The built-in loss will be recognized again in the hands of T, producing another RMB 5 tax benefit. The possibility of duplicating losses creates an opportunity for loss trafficking and thus increases the attractiveness of the stock acquisition. Due to the potential benefit of a second loss, S would likely charge more than RMB 200 for T's stock.

To sum up, the gain and loss examples show that stock acquisitions create the possibility of multiple realizations of the same economic gain or loss.

§7.03 AN ANALYSIS OF THE DISPARITY BETWEEN TAX TREATMENTS

Professor Weisbach convincingly argues that the roots of the inconsistency between taxing stock and asset sales lie in the problem of dual ownership.[4] The term dual ownership, as used by Weisbach, means that a company can possess assets either directly or through a subsidiary. Due to the existence of dual ownership, a company has two options to sell its assets. One option is to transfer its assets straightforwardly; the other is to transfer the stock of its subsidiary. The tax law must impose the same tax burden on asset and stock sales to prevent easy avoidance.

4. *Ibid.*

In order to achieve this goal, it is necessary to coordinate the corporate-level and the shareholder-level tax consequences. In Weisbach's words, 'to make the tax consequences of stock sales and asset sales identical, there must be a system of basis adjustments in which any gain or loss in the stock of a firm has to be reflected in the basis of the firm's assets, and any gain or loss in the assets has to be reflected in the stock'.[5]

Shortly put, in an M&A transaction, the law should ideally adjust both the tax bases of the assets and the stock of the target company. Such a two-level basis adjustment is also essential for avoiding multiple taxes on the same income. In the following part of this section, an in-depth analysis of the tax treatments of asset and stock acquisitions will be conducted, with a focus on the tax basis coordination. The analysis will present a new perspective for understanding the disparity in the tax treatment of asset and stock acquisitions and shed light on how to solve the disparity problem.

[A] Gain Case

In the asset acquisition, while T's basis in its assets, or the inside basis, is increased from RMB 100 to RMB 200, the basis of T's stock, or the outside basis, remains at RMB 100. In the absence of an exceptional rule, there would likely be multiple realizations of the same RMB 100 gain. To illustrate, suppose that in the previous example, the inter-corporate dividends exemption rule does not apply. When receiving dividends from T, S is subject to a tax on the already-taxed income of RMB 75.

The above process can be repeated multiple times if there are multiple layers of corporate ownership. T's after-tax profits would be taxed again to the shareholders of S upon the receipt of distributions, yet again to the shareholders in the next layer of the pyramid, and so on up to the ultimate shareholders. Thus, the problem of double taxation evolves into multi-tiered taxes. Imagine that Sn ultimately controls T via n-1 layers of intermediate wholly owned subsidiaries. If those intermediate subsidiaries liquidate sequentially, Sn will receive an after-tax profit of RMB 75 $\times$ 0.75^{n-1}.[6] As n approaches infinity, the after-tax profit of Sn approaches zero. That is, in an extreme case, the tax authority expropriates all the gains arising in the asset acquisition.

In order to avoid repeated taxation of the same economic gain, the taxable event of T should be reflected in both the bases of T's assets and stock. If the basis in T's stock is increased by the amount of T's after-tax profits, S will be entitled to an extra basis offset of RMB 75 in the subsequent sale of T's stock. Since the fair market value of T's stock remains at RMB 100 after T makes distributions, when S sells T's stock subsequently, it will realize a loss of RMB 75, which perfectly offsets its taxable gain from receiving T's after-tax profits. Thus, S reports no gain, and the RMB 100 gain in T's assets is subject to tax only once.

5. *Ibid.*
6. Given a tax rate of 25%, the after-tax return rate is 75%. Each company in the pyramid recognizes an after-tax gain that equals 75% of its subsidiary's after-tax gain. In the end, Sn receives 0.75n-1 of T's RMB 75 after-tax gain.

Consider, we combine the two steps of first increasing the basis in T's stock and then reducing it to offset the distribution of T's after-tax gains into one. One method to do this is to leave the basis in T's stock unchanged and treat the distribution of T's after-tax gains as a non-taxable event. That is precisely the approach adopted by the current Chinese law.[7] By exempting inter-corporate dividends from income tax, the law provides an equivalent to the two-step basis adjustment, and the consequent conformity between inside and outside tax bases ensures T's after-tax profits will not be taxed again to S.

By contrast, in the stock acquisition, there lacks a mechanism that provides two-level tax basis adjustments. Upon the transfer of T's stock, S is subject to a shareholder-level tax, and T's outside basis is stepped up to the fair market value. However, T's inside basis is not increased correspondingly. The carry-over of T's historical basis in its assets leads to an extra, although implicit, corporate-level tax, but the step-up in the basis of T's stock does not generate any tax benefit at Time 1. As a result, the stock acquisition probably leads to a double-tiered tax or even a multi-tiered tax in the case of a long corporate ownership chain[8] on the same gain.

[B] Loss Case

The perspective of outside-inside basis conformity is also applicable for analysing the disparity problem in the loss case. Before delving into the discussion, it is essential to understand how the recognition of loss affects a taxpayer's tax burden. When a company makes profits, a portion of its earnings will be taken away by the government. Symmetrically, if the company incurs losses, the government will shoulder a portion of the deficit by forgoing some future revenues. From the viewpoint of the company, the recognition of loss is identical to receiving money directly from the government. Let us assume for a moment that there is an absolute symmetry between gain and loss realizations. That is, a company actually receives money from the government as soon as it incurs losses.

In the stock acquisition, S suffers a loss of RMB 20 and therefore receives RMB 5 from the government. The recognition of loss does not bring about an adjustment to the basis of T's assets, so T keeps the RMB 20 unrealized loss, for which the government will pay another RMB 5. As a result, the nonconformity between the inside and outside basis creates an opportunity for loss duplication. Moreover, the loss can be replicated multiple times in the case of a pyramidal ownership structure.[9]

7. The EITL allows exemption on the dividends between PRC tax resident companies. EITL, Art. 26(2).
8. The example involving 'n-1 layers of intermediate subsidiaries' can be used to illustrate how the stock acquisition results in multi-tiered tax. Suppose Sn sells its stock in Sn-1 to Pn, then Sn-1 sells its stock in Sn-2 to Pn-1, and so on, until S1 sells its stock in T to P1. Eventually, T disposes of its assets. P1, P2, ..., and Pn are companies independent from each other. Thus, a gain of RMB 100 is realized n + 1 times, resulting in RMB 100n additional gains.
9. Suppose that in the hypothetical example discussed in texts accompanying note 8 above, T has a built-in loss rather than built-in gain of RMB 100 in its assets. The stock transactions result in RMB 100n additional losses as P1, P2, ..., and Pn each realizes RMB 100 loss upon the liquidation of their respective subsidiary.

A similar problem occurs in asset acquisition as well. Based on our assumptions, the government pays RMB 5 to T because T experiences a loss of RMB 20 from selling assets to P. However, there is no corresponding adjustment to the basis of T's stock. Upon the sale of T's stock, which is now worth RMB 205, S realizes a loss of RMB 15, which equals the amount of T's 'after-tax losses'. Despite the actual deficit of RMB 20, taxpayers recognize an RMB 35 loss in aggregate. Given an extreme long ownership chain, the government will fully compensate T's ultimate owner for the RMB 20 loss.[10]

The most straightforward way to tackle the problem is to adjust both the inside and outside tax bases. If in the stock acquisition, T's inside basis decreases to RMB 200, there will not be a replication of the loss inherent in T's assets. If in the asset acquisition, T's outside basis is stepped down to RMB 205, no shareholder-level loss will arise from the sale of T's stock by S. However, the law adopts an alternative approach, under which a company can only utilize its losses through offsetting gains earned by it.[11] Unlike our assumption that a company can recognize loss even though it has no profit, making gains becomes a prerequisite to deriving tax benefits from losses.

This alternative approach relieves the need for adjusting the outside basis of the target company in the asset acquisition. To recognize the loss from selling its assets, T must have made gains from some other source. In our hypothetical loss case, T is assumed to make a profit of RMB 20 shortly after the sale of assets. T's taxable income is zero because the RMB 20 profit and the loss from the asset sale cancel each other out. We can separate the process into two parts: paying taxes on the profit and deriving benefits from the loss. As discussed, when T derives a tax benefit from the built-in loss in assets, its outside basis should be decreased, and when T pays taxes on the profit, its outside basis should be increased. Overall, T's outside basis stays unchanged.[12]

However, this alternative approach dealt ineffectively with the problem of loss duplication in the stock acquisition. S sells T's stock that has depreciated in value, thereby realizing a loss of RMB 20, and the built-in loss of RMB 20 will also reduce the taxable gain of T by RMB 20. But as the ownership link between S and T no longer exists, the recognition of loss by T will not have any tax implications on S. Therefore,

10. The loss is reduced by 25% each time one company makes liquidating distribution to its parent company. After liquidations of T and n-1 layers of intermediate subsidiaries, the ultimate shareholder - Sn - bears a loss of RMB 15 0.75n-1. As n approaches infinity, the limit of that expression is zero.
11. EITL, Art. 18. Such loss realization mechanism is widely adopted around the world.
12. Researchers often omit that in the reality the recognition of losses occurs in tandem with the recognition of equal amount gains, and therefore tend to exaggerate the possibility of loss duplication in asset acquisitions. For instance, in explaining how the US tax treatment of distributions leads to double loss, Weisbach asserts that, after a subsidiary realizing loss and distributing remaining assets, the parent company can claim a second loss from selling its stock in the subsidiary for zero. *See e.g.*, Weisbach, *supra* note 3, at 240. However, given that the subsidiary's utilization of loss implies that it has earnings from some other source, the distribution of which will have tax implications, and therefore the parent company in fact cannot easily claim a second loss. For similar reasons, it has been argued that the seriousness of loss duplication in tax-free incorporation is overstated, *see* Douglas A. Kahn and Jeffrey H. Kahn, *Prevention of Double Deductions of a Single Loss: Solutions in Search of a Problem*, 26 Va. Tax Rev. 1, 43-45 (2006).

in the stock acquisition, we still need to make an additional adjustment to T's inside basis. Otherwise, taxpayers would recognize the loss in T's assets twice, just like the taxable income gets doubled in the gain case.

[C] Direction for Addressing the Disparity Problem

The Chinese tax law does not include a system dedicated to coordinating the tax bases of the target company's assets and stock. But by allowing dividends to be distributed tax-free between companies and regarding profit-making as a prerequisite for loss recognition, the Chinese tax law provides an alternative approach to adjusting the outside and the inside tax bases of the target company. Notwithstanding, such an alternative mechanism only functions in asset acquisitions; however, in stock acquisitions, the tax basis of the target company's assets – or the inside basis – is immune from any effective adjustment under the current law.

The lack of outside-inside basis coordination causes stock acquisitions to result in double or even multiple realizations of the same gain. By contrast, gain or loss recognized in asset acquisitions will not be taxed again since both the outside and inside bases of the target company reflect the recognition. As discussed previously, to address the disparity in the tax treatment of stock and asset acquisitions, the law should always adjust both the outside and the inside tax bases of the target company. Hence, the proper direction for reform is allowing the target company of a stock acquisition to adjust its inside tax basis. Besides, as the current law has already provided a dual basis adjustment mechanism for asset acquisitions, the outside basis of the target company can be kept unchanged following asset acquisitions.

§7.04 ADDRESSING THE DISPARITY PROBLEM: THE US EXPERIENCE

As a pioneer in the field of M&A taxation, the US has developed extensive tax rules for equalizing the tax treatments of stock acquisitions and asset acquisitions. The core of those rules is allowing the target company in a stock acquisition to adjust its inside tax basis to the fair market value of its assets. Since this is precisely the approach that this research has suggested for consideration, a review of the US regime will be helpful for further discussion. This subsection will therefore investigate the US rules to provide insights for a feasible solution to the disparity problem in the Chinese context.

[A] General Utilities Doctrine and the Pre-1986 Section 338

How to achieve parity between stock and asset acquisitions has, for a long time, been a core issue in corporate tax reform discourse in the United States. The US tax law's effort in this regard dates back to 1950 when the case of *Kimbell-Diamond Milling Co. v. Comm'r* came before the tax court.[13] In this case, the purchaser bought 100% of the

13. *Kimbell-Diamond Mill. Co. v. Comm'r*, 14 T.C. 74 (1950).

target company's stock and liquidated the target shortly afterwards. Under the then law, the purchaser was entitled to inherit the historical basis of the target's assets, which was higher than their fair market value. However, the Commissioner argued that since the purchaser had decided to liquidate the target company before the transaction, the stock purchase and the subsequent liquidation in their entirety constituted an asset acquisition. The court supported the Commissioner's contention, leaving the purchaser with a lower cost basis in the target's assets.[14]

Three years later, the US Congress enacted the old Section 334(b)(2) of the IRC, which codified the principles derived from *Kimbell-Diamond*.[15] Under this clause, the purchasing company in a stock acquisition would obtain a cost basis for the target company's assets, provided that it acquired at least 80% of the target's stock during a twelve-month period and liquidated the target according to a plan of liquidation adopted within two years after the date of the stock acquisition.[16] In other words, if a stock acquisition satisfied those conditions, the realization of gain or loss by the selling shareholders would be reflected in the new basis of the target company's assets. The purchasing company would thus be relieved from an additional recognition of gain or loss, and the acquisition only led to a shareholder-level tax.

In the meantime, asset acquisitions would also be tax-free at the corporate level if certain conditions were satisfied. Such a tax treatment had its roots in the General Utilities doctrine, a once fundamental principle of the US corporate income taxation. The General Utilities doctrine took its name after the landmark case of *General Utilities & Operating Co. v. Helvering*.[17] In this case, General Utilities distributed its highly appreciated assets – shares of another company – to its shareholders. The US Supreme Court held that General Utilities did not need to pay taxes on the appreciation in the value of the distributed assets. To a large extent, the General Utilities doctrine is derived from the perception that a distributing company should not be subject to any tax because it receives nothing in exchange for the distribution.[18]

Under that doctrine, a company would not realize any gain upon distributing appreciated assets to its shareholders. In 1954, through the establishment of the old Section 337, the US Congress extended the doctrine to cover asset sales followed by a complete liquidation.[19] According to the old Section 337, a sale of assets would not

14. Despite the government's victory, the decision could be favourable to those taxpayers who intended to acquire target companies with appreciated assets. For a list of the cases in which Kimbell-Diamond doctrine was applied in favour of the taxpayer, *see* Harold Dubroff & Robert L. Daileader Jr., *Kimbell-Diamond Revisited: A Critique of Judicial Analysis of the Exclusivity of Section 334(b)(2)*, 43 Alb. L. Rev. 739, 743 (1978).
15. For a historical account of the enactment of the clause, *see ibid.*, at 753-757.
16. Internal Revenue Code (US), § 334(b)(2). (before repealed in 1982).
17. *General Utilities & Operating Co. v. Helvering*, 296 U.S. 200 (1935).
18. Glenn E. Coven, *Taxing Corporate Acquisitions: A Proposal for Mandatory Uniform Rules*, 44 Tax L. Rev. 145, 150 (1988).
19. In the same year, the US Congress enacted the old § 311 and § 336, which were also derived from the General Utilities doctrine, to provide corporate level non-recognition treatment for non-liquidating and liquidating distributions. They, along with the old § 337, codified the General Utilities doctrine. Internal Revenue Code (US), §§ 311, 336, 337. (1982)

cause recognition of gain or loss to the selling company as long as the company was liquidated shortly afterwards and its shareholders were subject to taxes.[20]

By exempting the corporate-level tax in both stock and asset sales, the then US law narrowed the discontinuity in tax treatments of the two forms of transactions. For this reason, some scholars regard the old Section 334(b)(2) as an extension of the General Utilities doctrine and argue that the doctrine was a vital feature of the historic effort to achieve neutrality between the treatment of stock and asset acquisitions.[21] In a similar vein, the successor of the old Section 334(b)(2) – Section 338 – allows an adjustment to the tax basis of the target company's assets following a stock acquisition.[22] However, unlike its predecessor, Section 338 does not require a complete liquidation of the target company, and it is explicitly elective.[23] If the purchaser made a Section 338 election, the target company would be deemed to have engaged in a sale and repurchase of all of its assets.

According to the pre-1986 version of Section 338(a)(1), the old Section 337 applied to the deemed asset sale.[24] That is to say, a Section 338 deemed sale of assets would not lead to a corporate-level tax. Thus, despite the replacement of the old Section 334(b)(2) by Section 338, the US law continued to exempt the company level tax in both stock and asset acquisitions and kept controlling the disparity in the tax treatments of the two forms of acquisitions. However, such a mechanism ceased to exist after 1986 when the US Congress repealed the General Utilities doctrine.

[B] Section 338 in the Post-General Utilities Era

In the post-General Utilities era, an asset acquisition always triggers recognition of gain or loss at the corporate level, irrespective of whether the target company subsequently winds up according to a plan of complete liquidation.[25] When the target company eventually gets liquidated, its shareholders will realize gains or losses on the receipt of liquidating distributions. We will return to how the US treats liquidating distributions later on, but for the time being, it is enough to know that an asset acquisition followed by a liquidation of the target company incurs both a shareholder-level tax and a corporate-level tax.

A stock acquisition with a Section 338 election also results in a corporate-level tax since the 1986 tax reform severed the link between Section 338 and the old Section 337.[26] Under the current Section 338 election, if taxpayers conduct a 'qualified stock

20. Internal Revenue Code (US), § 337. (before repealed in 1986)
21. *See e.g.*, Coven, *supra* note 18, at 151-152; Lori Farnan, *A Mandatory Section 338: Can It Be Implemented*, 42 Fla. L. Rev. 679, 681-685 (1990).
22. Internal Revenue Code (US), § 338. Section 338 replaced the old Section 334(b)(2) in 1982.
23. For a detailed comparison of the old Section 334(b)(2) and Section 338, *see* R. Lawrence Heinkel, *Section 338 – An Analysis and Proposals for Reform*, 59 Notre Dame L. Rev. 158, 165-170 (1983).
24. Internal Revenue Code (US), § 337. (1982)
25. Unless specified otherwise, M&A transactions discussed in this chapter are all taxable transactions.
26. Consistent with the repeal of the old Section 337, the current Section 338(a)(1) removed the reference to Section 337.

purchase',[27] they may choose to treat the target company as if it first sold all of its assets at the fair market value and purchased those assets on the next day as a new company.[28] In the deemed assets sale and repurchase, the target company will recognize gain or loss, and the purchasing company effectively adjusts the basis of acquired assets to the fair market value.[29] As shareholders of the target company also need to recognize gain or loss on the sale of stock, a stock acquisition with a Section 338 election leads to two-tier taxes, just like what happens in an asset acquisition followed by the liquidation of the target company.

It is evident that, despite the significant revision of the US tax code in 1986, Section 338 still helps to bridge the gap in the taxation of stock and asset acquisitions. Nevertheless, the pre-1986 and current Section 338 operate in opposite directions. Before 1986, Section 338 tackled the disparity problem by exempting the corporate-level tax in stock acquisitions, while after the repeal of the General Utilities doctrine, Section 338 election has imposed an instant corporate-level tax on stock acquisitions, thereby aligning the tax treatment of stock acquisitions with the tax treatment of asset acquisitions. Because taxpayers always prefer to pay lower taxes, the once appealing Section 338 election diminishes in attractiveness after the 1986 revision.

In his article, Professor Weisbach analyses how the current US law taxes various forms of acquisitions differently. He compares the tax consequences of an asset sale followed by the liquidation of the target company, a stock sale without Section 338 election and a stock sale with Section 338 election. The comparison demonstrates clearly that among the three forms of transactions, the stock sale without Section 338 election turns out to be the most tax-efficient,[30] which casts doubt on to what extent the elective provision of Section 338 is helpful in solving the disparity problem. Being aware of this, some US scholars have considered the possibility of turning the elective Section 338 into mandatory.[31]

[C] Section 338(h)(10)

In the case where the target company is a subsidiary of another company, a special rule to Section 338 applies. Under this special rule, i.e., Section 338(h)(10), if the purchasing company makes a 'qualified stock purchase' from its consolidated group or affiliate,

27. 'Qualified stock purchase' is defined as a stock transaction or series of stock transactions, after which the purchaser possesses more than 80% of both the total voting power and the total value of the target company's stock. For series of transactions, they must take place during a twelve-month period. Internal Revenue Code (US), §§ 338(d)(3), 338(h)(1), 1504(a)(2).
28. Internal Revenue Code (US), §§ 338(a)(1), 338(a)(2).
29. Internal Revenue Code (US), § 338(b).
30. Weisbach, *supra* note 3, at 245-247. It should be noted that Weisbach deals with a case where the assets of the target company are appreciated. If the target company's assets are depreciated, the conclusion will be different, *see* Section 2 of this chapter for a detailed analysis. In the following discussion, unless specified otherwise, it is assumed that the target company owns appreciated assets.
31. *See e.g.*, Farnan, *supra* note 21, at 687-690.

the parties to the acquisition can jointly make an election[32] so that they will only be subject to a corporate-level tax and have the tax basis of the target company's assets stepped up to the fair market value. In other words, the target company will recognize gain as if it sold all of its assets in a single transaction, and the selling shareholders incur no gain on the sale of stock.

§7.05 EXISTING PROPOSALS FOR SOLVING THE DISPARITY PROBLEM

Inspired by the US experience, some Chinese scholars suggest introducing Section 338 of the IRC into China. This section starts with an examination of this law reform suggestion and then investigates other possible measures that might help solve the disparity problem.

[A] Transplantation of the US Section 338

In the US, stock acquisitions are generally more tax-efficient than asset acquisitions. In stock acquisitions, taxpayers can defer the recognition of gain on the appreciation of the target company's assets. By contrast, in asset acquisitions, the target company is subject to a tax on the appreciation of its assets, and shareholders of the target company need to recognize the gain on the appreciation of their stock upon the target company's liquidation. Briefly speaking, an asset acquisition leads to an immediate double tax, while a stock acquisition results in an immediate shareholder-level tax and a deferred corporate-level tax.

To bridge the discontinuity in the tax treatments of asset and stock acquisitions, Section 338 of the IRC transforms the deferred tax on the appreciation in the targets' assets in stock acquisitions into an immediate one. Upon a Section 338 election, taxpayers need to pay both corporate-level and shareholder-level taxes for a stock acquisition, as they do for asset acquisitions. As designed to impose an additional tax on stock acquisitions, Section 338, in most cases, will not be elected by taxpayers, but it nevertheless offers a possibility for achieving parity in the tax treatments of the two types of transactions.

However, it is doubtful whether a Chinese version of Section 338 carries even a remote possibility of solving the disparity problem. An analysis based on the hypothetical example discussed in Section 2 above helps illustrate this point. In that hypothetical example, if the parties choose to conduct an asset acquisition at Time 0, the target company (T) will pay a tax of RMB 25 on its RMB 100 gain, and P will have an RMB 200 tax basis in the acquired assets. The RMB 200 basis will translate into a depreciation deduction that reduces P's taxable income from RMB 220 to RMB 20. Thus, the asset acquisition will bring an RMB 50 tax benefit to P at Time 1.

If they conduct a stock acquisition at Time 0, S will recognize a gain of RMB 100, and P will receive T's stock with a stepped-up basis of RMB 200. Moreover, T will carry

32. The definition of 'qualified stock purchase' is provided in § 338(d)(3). Internal Revenue Code (US), § 338(d)(3).

forward the historical basis of RMB 100 in its assets. In the subsequent business operation, T can claim depreciation deductions for its assets and recognize a taxable income of RMB 120. The net result in the stock acquisition is that S pays an RMB 25 tax at Time 0, and T derives an RMB 25 tax benefit at Time 1.

Now, let us consider the impact of a Section 338 election in the Chinese context. If a Section 338 election follows the stock acquisition, S will pay an RMB 25 tax, and the tax basis of T's stock will be increased to RMB 200. The law will treat T as if it first sold its assets and, shortly after that, repurchased those assets. In the deemed sale, T will recognize the gain on the RMB 100 appreciation in its assets and pays an RMB 25 tax. Upon the completion of the process, T will transform into a new company that is unrelated to the old one. None of the old T's tax attributes, including the earnings and profits from the deemed sale, will survive the deemed repurchase, and the new T will take a cost basis in its assets. At Time 1, T will enjoy an RMB 50 tax benefit for claiming an RMB 200 depreciation deduction.

Table 7.3 summarizes the tax consequences of the three types of transactions.

Table 7.3 Tax Consequence of Section 338 Election (Corporate Shareholders – Gain Case)

	Time 0	*Time 1*	*Total*
Asset Acquisition	25	-50	-25
Stock Acquisition	25	-25	0
Section 338 election	50	-50	0

Note: Negative numbers represent tax benefits enjoyed by taxpayers.

As discussed in §7.02, asset acquisition is preferred because it allows P to derive more benefits from depreciation deduction on the acquired assets. In the asset acquisition, built-in gains in the target company's assets are subject to taxes, and the purchasing company can increase the tax basis of the acquired assets to the fair market value. In the stock acquisition, however, the target company recognizes a gain of the same amount, but its assets retain the historical basis. Therefore, compared to the asset acquisition, the stock acquisition leads to an extra implicit corporate-level tax on the appreciation of T's assets.

An examination of the table also reveals that a Section 338 election allows P to have an extra RMB 25 benefit at Time 1, matching the tax consequence of the asset acquisition. However, such an extra benefit comes at the cost of an additional tax of the same amount at Time 0. Compared to the stock acquisition without a Section 338 election, the stock acquisition with an election shifts the payment of the RMB 25 tax on the appreciation in T's assets to an earlier date. Therefore, in the Chinese context, the Section 338 election will widen rather than narrow the gap between the tax treatment of asset acquisitions and stock acquisitions.

[B] Other Possible Measures

The US first allowed the purchasing company, through a stock purchase, to obtain a cost basis in the target's assets without having the target company recognize gain on its unrealized appreciation in assets, but then it moved towards requiring the target company to recognize gain in exchange for a step-up basis in its assets. This reform by no way suggests, however, that the current US Section 338 election is necessarily superior to its predecessor.

Instead, as already demonstrated, the current and the past versions of Section 338 elections were each tailored to a particular set of corporate tax doctrines, and none of them would continue to be useful if the underlying doctrines changed. The current US law permits two types of elections, prescribed in Section 338 and Section 338(h)(10) respectively. Some commentators who advocate learning from the US experience do not even note Section 338(h)(10) election, let alone differentiate the two types of elections.

Given this background, this subsection will be devoted to further exploring the possible options for China to establish an effective regime that aligns the tax treatments of stock acquisitions and asset acquisitions. Generally speaking, when adjusting both the inside and outside tax bases in stock acquisitions, we can impose a double-tiered tax or a single-tiered tax either at the corporate or the shareholder level. The Section 338(h)(10) election, the old Section 338 election, and the current Section 338 election in the US correspond with the three options for adjusting the tax bases in stock acquisitions with a view to solving the disparity problem.

First, a current Section 338 election leads to two layers of taxes. The target company and its shareholders recognize gain on the deemed asset sale and the stock sale respectively. Second, following an election under Section 338 (h)(10), the target company recognizes the gain on the appreciation in its assets. The unrealized appreciation in the target company's stock, however, will never be taxed. Finally, in a stock acquisition followed by an election under the old Section 338, the target company is exempted from paying tax on the asset appreciation, whereas its shareholders are obliged to recognize gains on the stock sale.

If, after further examination, all of the above three measures are proved unsuitable for China, we will face another question: what prevents them from fulfilling the purpose of aligning the tax treatments of stock acquisitions and asset acquisitions. The answer must lie somewhere else in the corporate income tax system.

[1] Section 338(h)(10) Election

The mechanism of Section 338(h)(10) election is similar to that of the election under Section 338. If the shareholders of the target company and the purchasing company jointly make a Section 338(h)(10) election, the law will treat the old target company as selling all of its assets to the new target company at the fair market value, and T will accordingly recognize a gain of RMB 100. The new T will take a fair market value basis of RMB 200 in its assets. At the shareholder level, P will receive T's stock with a stepped-up basis of RMB 200, and S will not recognize any gain on the stock sale. Moreover, the law treats the old T as if it liquidated tax-free into S immediately after the deemed asset sale.

In the above scenario, at Time 0, S is subject to an RMB 25 tax on the gain from T's deemed asset sale at Time 0, and at Time 1, the new T can use the RMB 200 basis in its assets to offset its receipts from selling products, thereby reporting a net gain of RMB 20. Again, this research disregards the RMB 220 income from the sale of products and treats the new T as receiving an RMB 50 payment from the government for the depreciation deduction of RMB 200.

[2] Old Section 338 Election

If the parties to a stock acquisition make an old Section 338 election, the basis of T's assets will increase from RMB 100 to RMB 200. Unlike in the case of a Section 338 election, where the basis increase of T's assets comes at the cost of a tax imposed on T, an old Section 338 election does not induce any extra tax burden to T. The step-up in the basis of T's assets will translate into an increase in depreciation deductions against T's gross income. Consequently, an old Section 338 election will bring T an extra RMB 25 benefit at Time 1. S and P are unaffected by the election. At Time 0, S is subject to a tax of RMB 25, and P takes T's stock with a fair market value basis of RMB 200.

Table 7.4 compares the tax consequences of the various types of transactions.

Table 7.4 Tax Consequences of Section 338(h)(10) and Old Section 338 Elections (Corporate Shareholders – Gain Case)

	Time 0	*Time 1*	*Total*
Asset Acquisition	25	-50	-25
Stock Acquisition	25	-25	0
Section 338 Election	50	-50	0
Section 338(h)(10) Election	25	-50	-25
Old Section 338 Election	25	-50	-25

Note: Negative numbers represent tax benefits enjoyed by taxpayers.

Unlike the current Section 338 election, the Section 338(h)(10) election and the old Section 338 election effectively reduce the tax burden of the stock acquisition. They both allow P, without incurring a second layer of tax, to obtain a fair market value basis in the acquired assets. In our example, they help address the discontinuity in tax treatment between asset acquisitions and stock acquisitions. However, as will be seen, their effectiveness is confined to a small cluster of situations.

[3] Effectiveness of Other Possible Measures

Our discussion up to this point rests on the premise that the target company only has corporate shareholders. In reality, however, the shareholders of a company may consist of both individuals and companies. Would the measures discussed above still be valid in situations where individuals get involved in M&A transactions? The answer is likely to be negative.

The tax consequences of asset acquisitions change with the identities of the target company's shareholders. In an asset acquisition, the target company recognizes gain on the sale of assets, and then the shareholders pay taxes on the receipt of liquidating distributions from the target company. While the identity of shareholders has no impact on the corporate-level tax liability, it significantly affects the amount of tax at the shareholder level. The law intentionally creates a double tax on individual shareholders, as corporate distributions do not result in tax liabilities to corporate shareholders but are fully taxable to individual shareholders.

Given the impact of the identity of the target company's shareholders, the delicate equilibrium between asset acquisitions and stock acquisitions achieved through Section 338(h)(10) and the old Section 338 elections can easily break down if some of the target company's shareholders are individuals. To illustrate, let us come back to the hypothetical case, but now we suppose that S is an individual shareholder. The tax consequences of the two forms of acquisitions are described in detail as follows.

Asset Acquisition

If at Time 0, P buys the assets of T, T is subject to a tax of RMB 25 on the RMB 100 built-in gain in its assets. P will accordingly step up the basis of the acquired assets to RMB 200. In the following years of operation, P can claim depreciation deductions to the extent of that RMB 200 tax basis. Due to the depreciation deductions, P derives an RMB 50 benefit at Time 1. When T distributes its after-tax profit of RMB 75, S will be subject to an RMB 15 tax.[33] When selling T's stock, S will deduct its RMB 100 tax basis in the stock and recognize no gain or loss.

Stock Acquisition

When selling T's stock to P, S needs to pay a tax of RMB 20 for the recognition of RMB 100 of gain.[34] P has a fair market value basis of RMB 200 in the acquired stock, and T retains its historical basis of RMB 100 in its assets. The RMB 100 tax basis will translate into depreciation deductions, which bring P an RMB 25 tax benefit. Overall, the tax consequence is an RMB 20 tax at Time 0 and an RMB 25 tax benefit at Time 1.

33. Under the IITL, the tax rate for dividend income is 20%. IITL, Art. 3(3).
34. *Ibid.* Under the IITL, the tax rate for capital gains is also 20%.

Possible Measures for Solving the Disparity Problem

If S and P make a Section 338(h)(10) election in the stock acquisition, the law will disregard the gain from the stock sale. The transaction is treated as if T sold its assets at the fair market value, and therefore an RMB 25 tax arises at the time of the transaction. In contrast, if the parties make an old Section 338 election, S will recognize gain on the stock sale, and T will take a fair market value basis in its assets without recognizing any gain. The only difference between the two types of elections lies in the tax liability at Time 0. Whichever measure is taken, the tax basis of T's assets will be stepped up to the fair market value. The increase in the basis will bring T an additional depreciation deduction of RMB 100, which can produce RMB 25 more tax benefits. Table 7.5 presents the result.

Table 7.5 Tax Consequences of Section 338(h)(10) and Old Section 338 Elections (Individual Shareholders – Gain Case)

	Time 0	*Time 1*	*Total*
Asset Acquisition	40	-50	-10
Stock Acquisition	20	-25	-5
Section 338(h)(10) election	25	-50	-25
Old Section 338 election	20	-50	-30

Note: Negative numbers represent tax benefits enjoyed by taxpayers.

The table shows that the stock acquisition generates RMB 5 less benefit than the asset acquisition. One may accordingly conclude that, where the target company's shareholders are individuals, an M&A transaction is likely to take the form of asset acquisition. However, this assertion is inaccurate because it neglects the time value of money. It usually takes time for P to depreciate the target's assets fully, so the RMB 25 more benefit in the asset acquisition at Time 1 has a present value less than RMB 25 or even less than RMB 20 at Time 0. Therefore, without further information, it is difficult to determine which form of transaction is more tax-efficient.

Nevertheless, we can notice that both the Section 338(h)(10) election and the old Section 338 election fail their purpose in this modified scenario. These measures increase the basis of the target's assets, thereby allowing the purchasing company to claim more depreciation deductions. However, the taxpayers incur little or even no additional tax for that basis increase. The net result is a single level tax on all gains. Given that the Chinese tax law imposes a double-tiered tax on individual shareholders of companies, the two types of elections cause stock acquisitions to be under-taxed. If applied widely, they would create a tax avoidance problem.

Even in the case where the target company only has corporate shareholders, the two types of elections alleviate the disparity problem by coincidence. In the previous discussion, we assume that T's inside and outside basis match with each other and that T can make distributions to the extent of its after-tax profits from the sale of assets. If we change those assumptions, the two types of elections will no longer alleviate the disparity problem.

Let us suppose now that S has an RMB 40 basis in T's stock, and T has accumulated retained profits of RMB 40. The remaining assumptions in the original example remain in place. If the parties conduct an asset acquisition, T will pay an RMB 25 tax on its RMB 100 gain. When T distributes its earnings, S will receive an RMB 115 tax-exempted dividend. Upon selling T's stock for RMB 60, S will recognize a gain of RMB 20 and thus incur an RMB 5 tax. P faces the same tax consequence as before.

In the case of a stock acquisition without any election, S is subject to an RMB 40 tax on the RMB 160 appreciation in T's stock. Following the acquisition, the basis of T's assets remains at RMB 100. Thus, as seen above, T will obtain an RMB 25 benefit at Time 1. If S and P jointly make a Section 338(h)(10) election, the stock acquisition will lead to only one layer of tax, which is the tax on T's deemed sale of its assets. S will not recognize gain for selling T's stock, but it will be obliged to pay an RMB 25 on the taxable gain arising in the deemed asset sale by T. Because there is no shareholder-level tax liability, the change in the tax basis of T's stock does not affect the tax consequence of the acquisition. Therefore, the stock acquisition with a Section 338(h)(10) election brings the taxpayers an RMB 25 tax liability at Time 0 and an RMB 50 tax benefit at Time 1.

In contrast, an election under the old Section 338 results in a tax on the appreciation of T's stock. It does not incur any tax liability on T but allows T to increase the tax basis of its assets from RMB 100 to RMB 200. At Time 0, the only tax to be paid is that owing by S when it recognizes a capital gain of RMB 160 upon exchanging T's stock for cash. Moreover, the new RMB 200 basis of T's assets will generate an RMB 50 tax benefit at Time 1. Table 7.6 summarizes the tax consequences of this new scenario.

Table 7.6 Tax Consequences of Stock and Asset Acquisitions (Corporate Shareholders – Gain Case – Variation)

	Time 0	*Time 1*	*Total*
Asset Acquisition	30	-50	-20
Stock Acquisition	40	-25	15
Section 338(h)(10) Election	25	-50	-25
Old Section 338 Election	40	-50	-10

Note: Negative numbers represent tax benefits enjoyed by taxpayers.

As is evident, in the new scenario, neither the Section 338(h)(10) election nor the old Section 338 election can solve the disparity problem. The stock acquisition followed by a Section 338(h)(10) election only leads to a single-tiered tax. However, the asset acquisition triggers a double-tiered tax. To be specific, in the asset acquisition, added to T's tax on the appreciation of its assets, S must recognize gain to the extent that the post-distribution value of T's stock exceeds the tax basis of T's stock. Thus, compared to the asset acquisition, the stock acquisition followed by a Section 338(h)(10) election results in RMB 5 more benefit to the taxpayers. For the same reason, the stock acquisition followed by an old Section 338 election, in which the taxpayers recognize gain in T's stock, results in less benefit than does the asset acquisition.

Thus far, we have discussed all the possible options derived from the US law for solving the disparity problem. Unfortunately, none of them is suitable for China. What prevents them from fitting well in the Chinese tax system? A quick answer is that they are incompatible with the Chinese tax treatment of corporate distributions. The following section will further discuss this point.

§7.06 DISPARITY PROBLEM AND TAX TREATMENTS OF CORPORATE DISTRIBUTIONS

[A] US Tax Treatment of Liquidating Distributions and Section 338

It is evident from the US legislative history that Section 338 of the IRC operates in conjunction with the rules on liquidating distribution. When the US Congress revised the rules on liquidating distributions, it amended Section 338 accordingly. Therefore, it is particularly meaningful to take a further look at how Section 338 interacts with the US tax treatment of liquidating distributions. For the sake of convenience, let us assume that Section 338 is mandatory rather than elective.

Generally speaking, liquidation is a process through which a company winds up its affairs, pays debts and then distributes remaining assets to its shareholders. Under the current US law, making liquidating distributions, in most cases, are taxable events for both the distributing company and its shareholders. Section 331 of the IRC provides that 'amounts received by a shareholder in a distribution in complete liquidation of a corporation shall be treated as in full payment in exchange for the stock'.[35] Accordingly, for shareholders of a liquidating company, receiving liquidating distributions is analogous to collecting the consideration for selling their shares back to the company. The shareholders will compute gains on the sale in the same way that they would do for selling shares to someone else. The amount of taxable gain equals the difference between the basis of their stock and the purchase price,[36] which is the fair market value of the company's remaining assets.

The tax treatment for a liquidating company is provided in Section 336 of the IRC. According to Section 336(a), a liquidating company should recognize gain or loss on the distribution of property in complete liquidation as if it sold the property to its shareholders at the fair market value. Just like Section 331, which treats the shareholders as if they sold their stock to the liquidating company in exchange for the company's remaining assets, Section 336 treats the company as if it sold the remaining assets in exchange for its outstanding stock. Therefore, the liquidation also results in a

35. Internal Revenue Code (US), § 331.
36. The Treasury Regulations explicitly provides that the gain or loss to a shareholder from a liquidating distribution should be determined under Section 1001 by subtracting the basis of the stock from the amount of the distribution. Treasury Regulations (US), § 1.331-1(b).

corporate-level gain recognition, which is calculated by subtracting the basis of the distributed assets from their fair market value.

It is worth noting that the US law provides very different tax treatments for liquidating distributions and non-liquidating distributions. According to Section 301(c), if a company makes distributions during its lifetime, the distributions may fall into three categories. First, a distribution constitutes a dividend to the extent of the company's retained earnings and profits.[37] Second, the amount of distribution over the company's retained earnings and profits applies against and reduces the tax basis of the company's stock. Third, if the tax basis of the company's stock has been reduced to zero after the first two steps, the law will treat any remaining portion of the distribution as a taxable gain of the recipient.[38]

Whether a distribution constitutes a dividend has broad implications on the recipient's tax burden.[39] One crucial implication is due to the tax deduction on inter-corporate dividends. To ease the problem of multi-tax, Section 243 of the IRC allows a corporate shareholder that receives a dividend from a domestic US company to deduct a proportion of the dividend. The standard deduction rate is 50%[40] and will be higher in situations where a distribution meets certain conditions. For example, the deduction rate for dividends paid between members of an affiliated group is 100%.[41]

Since the US tax law treats a liquidation as a sale and purchase transaction, liquidating distributions in the US do not constitute dividends. Therefore, a corporate shareholder receiving liquidating distributions is ineligible for the Section 243 deduction. The US is among the few countries that do not attempt to categorize a portion of liquidating distributions as dividends. In many other countries, such as Canada, liquidating distributions are classified into three groups, namely dividends, free-recovery of capital, and capital gains, just like how the US law treats non-liquidating distributions. Section 84(2) of the Canadian Income Tax Act sees a liquidating company as having paid a dividend equal to the excess of the amount of the liquidating distribution over the amount of the company's paid-up capital.[42] If the paid-up capital equals the tax basis of the company's stock, the distributee will receive it tax-free. Otherwise, the distributee will realize a capital gain or loss on the difference between them.[43]

Because of the unique rules for liquidating distribution, in the US, an asset acquisition followed by a liquidation of the target company always leads to a double tax on the same gain, regardless of whether the shareholders are companies or individuals.

37. Internal Revenue Code (US), § 316. Section 316 provides a definition of dividend. According to it, any distribution paid out of a company's accumulated earnings and profits or out of current earnings and profits will be regarded as dividend.
38. Internal Revenue Code (US), § 301(c).
39. For instance, if treated as a dividend, the distribution will be taxed in full. In contrast, the distribution that is not a dividend only reduces the tax basis of the shareholder's stock and does not bring any tax liability.
40. Internal Revenue Code (US), § 243(a)(1).
41. Internal Revenue Code (US), §§ 243(a)(3), 243(b)(1).
42. Income Tax Act (Canada), § 84(2).
43. Income Tax Act (Canada), § 54.

Similarly, if the parties conduct a stock acquisition with a current Section 338 election, they will also be subject to both corporate-level and shareholder-level tax.

To achieve the aim of solving the disparity problem, Section 338 should be compatible with the tax treatment of liquidating distributions. Suppose that the US revives the General Utilities doctrine but maintains the current Section 338 unchanged. While stock acquisitions followed by an election under Section 338 results in a double tax, asset acquisitions, on the contrary, are not taxable at the corporate level as long as the target company distributes its assets in complete liquidation.[44] Despite that both types of transactions provide the purchasing company with a step-up basis in the target company's assets, a Section 338 election will fail to harmonize the tax treatment of asset and stock acquisitions because the basis increase in stock acquisitions comes at an extra price of a corporate-level tax.

Moreover, because the US tax law contains exceptional rules for taxing liquidating distributions, Section 338 is not always helpful in solving the disparity problem. One prominent exception to the standard tax treatment for liquidating distributions applies in the context of the winding-up of subsidiaries.[45] Provided that a transaction meets the criteria prescribed in Section 332(b), Section 332(a) allows a company to receive another company's liquidating distributions tax-free.[46] Under Section 332(b), the recipient's ownership of stock of the other company should meet the requirements of Section 1504(a)(2). That is, the shareholder must possess at least 80% of the total voting power and at least 80% of the total value of the liquidating company's stock.[47] If the parent company receives in kind property, that property will remain its basis as if it were still in the hands of the subsidiary.[48] For the liquidating subsidiary, the rule is quite straightforward. Section 337(a) provides that 'no gain or loss shall be recognized to the liquidating corporation on the distribution to the 80-percent distributee of any property in a complete liquidation to which section 332 applies'.[49] Thus, the liquidation of a subsidiary leads to a deferred tax on the appreciation of the subsidiary's assets.

Because of those exceptional rules, a company is subject to only one layer of tax on the sale of its subsidiary's assets. Consider two alternatives for a company to sell assets in its subsidiary. First, the subsidiary can sell all of its assets directly to the purchasing company and then go into liquidation. In this arrangement, the asset sale is taxable, but the liquidation is not – the parent company will receive liquidating distributions tax-free according to Section 332. Second, the parent company can liquidate the subsidiary and then sell the subsidiary's assets. According to Sections 332 and 337, the liquidation is neither taxable to the parent company nor the subsidiary –

44. On how asset acquisitions are taxed before the repeal of the General Utilities doctrine, *see* § 7.04[A] above.
45. The major rationale for the exception is that Congress hopes to encourage the simplification of complex corporate structure, *see* John A. Busterud, *The Liquidation of Subsidiaries under Section 112(b)(6)*, 58 Yale L. J. 1050, 1050-1051 (1948).
46. Internal Revenue Code (US), § 332(a).
47. Internal Revenue Code (US), §§ 332(b)(1), 1504(a)(2).
48. Internal Revenue Code (US), § 334(b).
49. Internal Revenue Code (US), § 337(a).

the parent company receives the subsidiary's assets with their historical tax basis so that the built-in gain in those assets is preserved and will be taxed in the subsequent asset sale. In either case, the seller of assets is only subject to only one layer of tax.

From the above analysis, it is evident that in transactions where the target company is a subsidiary of another company, Section 338 does not help solve the disparity problem. In response to the problem, the US Congress enacts Section 338(h)(10), which exempts the built-in gain in the subsidiary's stock from taxes, just like Section 332 exempts from taxes the income of a company arising in its subsidiary's asset sale and liquidation.

[B] Chinese Tax Treatment of Corporate Distributions

The Chinese tax rules for non-liquidating distributions are relatively simple: all non-liquidating distributions are categorized as dividend income and taxed at rates of 20% for individual shareholders and 25% for corporate shareholders. In the preceding sections, we assume that following an asset acquisition, the target company makes non-liquidating distributions, and then the target's shareholders sell their stock in the target. Indeed, the target company's shareholders can alternatively liquidate the target company and receive liquidating distributions. The focus here is on the tax treatment of liquidating distributions.

The EITL only has two articles relating to the taxation of corporate liquidations. Article 53 of the EITL requires a liquidating company to treat the liquidation period as a separate tax year,[50] and Article 55 of the EITL briefly mentions that a liquidating company shall pay tax on the taxable income arising in the liquidation period.[51] Based on Article 55 of the EITL, Article 11 of EITLIR further defines the 'taxable income arising in the liquidation period' and sketches out the tax treatment for recipients of liquidating distributions.[52]

These articles are too skeletal to provide sufficient guidance on how to decide the tax consequences of corporate liquidations. To make them workable in practice, the MOF and the STA jointly issued Caishui (2009) No. 60. This circular, in a detailed manner, regulates the tax treatment of liquidating companies and their shareholders. Since its enactment in 2009, Circular 60 has become the central regulation for taxing corporate liquidations. Liquidation, in Article 1 of Circular 60, is described as the process by which a company ceases business operations, disposes of all its assets, settles all its liabilities, and distributes remaining assets to its shareholder.[53] This description is in line with the corporate liquidation procedure prescribed in the Company Law.[54] Nevertheless, liquidation in Circular 60 is a term of art with a unique tax law meaning. According to Article 2 of Circular 60, the term covers not only those

50. EITL, Art. 53.
51. EITL, Art. 55.
52. EITLIR, Art. 11.
53. Caishui (2009) No. 60, Art. 1.
54. Company Law, Art. 186.

liquidations conducted in conformance with the Company Law but also some deemed liquidations taking place in corporate restructurings.[55]

In some corporate restructurings, the Company Law may not require the target company to liquidate, but the tax law treats the target company as undergoing liquidation. Circular 59, the centrepiece of China's M&A taxation system, specifies three types of deemed liquidation events. First, if a company is converted into a non-legal person reorganization such as sole proprietorship or migrates to another tax jurisdiction, the law will treat the company as being liquidated.[56] Second, a deemed liquidation occurs in the context of corporate mergers. In a taxable merger, the target company is treated to be wound up. Third, demergers of companies also trigger deemed liquidations.

Both statutory liquidation and deemed liquidation are taxable to the liquidating company. Article 3 of Circular 60 prescribes the steps that a liquidating company must follow to determine its tax liability. First, the liquidating company must recognize the unrealized gain or loss in all its assets. For assets which the liquidating company disposes of, the company computes the taxable income by subtracting the tax basis of it from the sale price. If an asset is not sold but used to pay off liabilities or make a distribution in kind, the liquidating company will recognize a gain equal to the tax basis of the asset less than the realizable value. Second, the liquidating company needs to recognize gain or loss on debt recovery and settlement of liabilities. In general, the company will not have a gain or loss if it fully recovers all debts and settles all liabilities. Where the liquidating company fails to recover all debts, it will realize a loss.[57] If the liquidating company derecognizes liabilities, it will realize gains.[58]

Third, when calculating the taxable income, the liquidating company can, on the one hand, subtract prepaid expenses, and it must, on the other hand, add back deductions claimed for accrued expenses.[59] Prepaid expenses are expenses that have been paid but have not yet been used up. Generally, a company needs to spread the deduction for a prepaid expenditure over the period during which benefits arise out of that expenditure.[60] However, as the liquidating company ceases to be a going concern, it can deduct prepaid expenses one-off at the liquidation. For the same reason, the law requires the company to add back the deductions for accrued expenses, which are expenses that have been recorded in books but not yet paid. Finally, to arrive at the amount of taxable income, the liquidating company is entitled to deduct liquidation period expenses as well as loss carry forwards. The liquidation period, no matter how short or how long, is treated as a separate tax year. At the end of the liquidation period, the liquidating company files its last tax return.[61] After paying tax on taxable income, the liquidating company distributes the remaining assets to its shareholders.

55. Caishui (2009) No. 60, Art. 2.
56. Caishui (2009) No. 59, Art. 4(1).
57. EITLIR, Art. 32.
58. EITLIR, Art. 22.
59. Caishui (2009) No. 60, Art. 3(3).
60. EITLIR, Arts. 68, 69, 70.
61. EITL, Arts. 53, 54.

In determining a shareholder's taxable gain or loss on liquidation, China, like many other countries, distinguishes dividend income from the rest of the distributions. The Chinese tax treatment of liquidating distributions is also analogous to how the US tax law treats non-liquidating distributions. Based on Article 5 of Circular 60, any distribution made out of the liquidating company's accumulated retained earnings and capital reserves constitutes a dividend. The remaining portion of the distribution provides for a tax-free recovery of the shareholder's tax basis in the liquidating company's stock, and the shareholder has to recognize a capital gain or loss where the remaining portion is in excess of or short of the tax basis.

Moreover, the tax consequences of a liquidation hinge on the identity of the recipients. A resident corporate shareholder is in general not subject to income tax on the receipt of dividends from another resident company. A corporate shareholder, no doubt, would like as much of the liquidating distributions as possible to be treated as dividends. However, unlike corporate shareholders, individual shareholders are fully taxed on dividends income at a flat rate of 20%. Although individuals are subject to the same rate for dividends and capital gains, they tend to prefer the liquidating distributions to be classified as capital gains rather than dividends, especially when there are built-in losses in the liquidating company's stock. Such a preference arises because, on the one hand, individual shareholders are not eligible for a tax-free return of their original investment upon receiving liquidating distributions, and, on the other hand, they cannot use capital losses to offset other taxable gains.

To illustrate, imagine that individual shareholder A owns all the stock of a company with a tax basis of RMB 200, the paid-up capital of the company is RMB 100, and the company's assets consist solely of RMB 200 cash. Under the current law, when the company liquidates, RMB 100 out of the total RMB 200 distribution will be treated as a dividend. Shareholder A will recognize a gain on the full amount of the dividend. The remaining RMB 100 liquidating distribution allows A to recover half of the original investment. Although shareholder A can never recover the other half of her investment, she cannot recognize a loss for that. As a result, shareholder A recognizes a gain of RMB 100. If, instead, the law treated none of the liquidating distributions as a dividend, shareholder A would fully recover the investment cost and recognize no gain or loss on receiving liquidating distributions.

Because under the Chinese tax law, distributions, whether made in the liquidation process or not, are taxed as dividend income to the extent of the distributing company's retained earnings, the two choices after an asset acquisition, namely the target company making distributions and then liquidating and the target company making liquidating distributions, lead to the same tax consequences. For this reason, this research will simplify the hypothetical cases discussed above by supposing that the target company liquidates after selling its assets.[62]

In Part A of this section, we have demonstrated that the tax treatment of corporate distributions is a crucial factor to consider when designing a rule to address

62. The two approaches are not equivalent in cases where an individual shareholder has unrealized loss in the target's stock. However, we disregard those exceptions, as they result from the defects of the IITL.

the disparity problem. As the Chinese tax law on corporate distributions differs significantly from its US counterpart, it is no wonder that the elections currently or previously available under the US law are not appropriate for China.

§7.07 SOLVING THE DISPARITY PROBLEM: SUGGESTIONS FOR CHINA

Although the elections provided by the US law have been proved not suitable for China, the underlying logic of the US elections is still valuable for China to tackle the disparity problem. From the historical development of the US law, we can generalize the mechanism that underlies the US approach for addressing the disparity problem: letting the target company in stock acquisitions have a fair market value basis in its assets and imposing taxes as if the target company made liquidating distributions to its original shareholders. This approach is hopeful for mitigating the disparity problem in China. However, as will be shown, the impact of the tax treatment of corporate distributions is more far-reaching than previously acknowledged, and even a sophisticated design in this direction can be inadequate. Additional rules are necessary for dealing with the disparity problem.

Before proceeding further, one caveat is in order: the suggestions that this research is going to make do not address the question of whether it is indeed desirable to have a set of rules more complicated than the US one. We may eventually decide to tolerate the disparity problem or to solve the problem by revamping the corporate tax system. Whatever the final decision is, it is necessary to have a thorough understanding of how to solve the disparity problem without changing the essential features of the present corporate tax system.

[A] Revisiting the Disparity Problem

On the surface, tax implications are more straightforward in stock acquisitions than in asset acquisitions. That is, stock acquisitions are only taxable to the target's shareholders. While the shareholders realize gain or loss for selling their stock in the target, the target itself is unaffected and keeps all tax attributes. In asset acquisitions, however, both the target and the target's shareholders can incur tax consequences.

This observation, though correct, overlooks the broader implications of stock acquisitions. After a stock purchase, the purchasing company may eventually liquidate the target company. The tax consequence of that liquidation would likely affect taxpayers' choice between asset acquisitions and stock acquisitions. Therefore, this part will re-examine the cases presented in Section 2 to research further how the treatment of corporate distributions affects the tax consequences of stock acquisitions, which in turn affects the parity in tax treatments of asset and stock acquisitions.

Here is a brief recapitulation of the facts of the two hypothetical cases. T and P are companies that pay income tax at a rate of 25%. S owns all the stock of T, and P wants to acquire T. After the acquisition, P will use the acquired assets – either held directly by it or indirectly through T – to produce RMB 220 worth of products. In the gain case, S has an RMB 100 basis in T's stock, the value of which has appreciated to RMB 200;

T has an RMB 100 basis in its assets, which are valued at RMB 200 as well. In the loss case, T's stock and assets both have a tax basis of RMB 220 and a fair market value of RMB 200.

As corporate and individual shareholders face different tax treatments, the discussion can be divided into two scenarios – where S is a corporate shareholder and where S is an individual shareholder. The following subsections focus on the tax consequences of the liquidation of the target company coming after stock acquisitions.

[1] Target Company with Corporate Shareholders

S is a company. If the parties choose to conduct an asset acquisition, then as discussed earlier: in the gain case, T incurs taxes of RMB 25 at Time 0, and P enjoys an RMB 50 tax benefit at Time 1; in the loss case, T and P enjoy tax benefits of RMB 5 at Time 0 and RMB 50 at Time 1 respectively. If they conduct a stock acquisition, the tax consequences are as follows.

Gain Case

At Time 0, S incurs taxes of RMB 25 for selling stock. When T vends RMB 220 worth of products at Time 1, it can be treated as paying an RMB 55 tax on selling products for RMB 220 and receiving an RMB 25 payment from the government for the tax basis depreciation of RMB 100. The RMB 55 tax on selling products is omitted in the comparison between asset acquisition and stock acquisition since it always occurs regardless of the type of acquisition. After settling taxes, T has RMB 190 of cash left. If the paid-up capital of T is assumed to be RMB 100 – the same as the basis of T's assets, on the winding-up of T, the distribution of RMB 90 will be regarded as a dividend, which is not subject to any further tax; P will realize an RMB 100 loss, which equals the amount that the paid-up capital of T (i.e., RMB 100) is less than its basis in T stock (i.e., RMB 200), and the loss can be deducted against P's future taxable income, producing a tax benefit of RMB 25 at Time 2.

Table 7.7 represents the tax consequences of the two types of acquisitions.

Table 7.7 Tax Consequences of Stock and Asset Acquisitions (Corporate Shareholders – Gain Case – Revisited)

	Time 0	*Time 1*	*Time 2*	*Total*
Asset Acquisition	25	-50	0	-25
Stock Acquisition	25	-25	-25	-25

Note: Negative numbers represent tax benefits enjoyed by taxpayers.

The two forms of acquisitions produce the same total nominal taxable income. However, it does not mean that they are rigorously equivalent in terms of tax consequences. In the stock acquisition, the parties bear an implicit corporate-level tax of RMB 25, the present value of which is RMB 25 at Time 1, but the recognition of the shareholder-level loss comes last in the sequence of events, generating tax benefit with a present value less than RMB 25 at Time 1. Therefore, the stock acquisition still results in a higher overall tax burden than the asset acquisition. Where P can claim depreciation immediately while the liquidation of T occurs after an extremely long time, the value of the loss recognition at Time 2 vanishes and the parties in the stock acquisition pay RMB 25 more tax.

Loss Case

At Time 0, S suffers a loss of RMB 20 and therefore receives RMB 5 tax benefit for selling stock. When T vends RMB 220 worth of products at Time 1, it can be treated as paying an RMB 55 tax on selling products for RMB 220 and receiving an RMB 55 payment from the government for the tax basis depreciation of RMB 220. Assuming the paid-up capital of T is RMB 220 – the same as the basis of T's assets. When T makes liquidating distributions, none of its RMB 220 cash left will constitute a dividend. Thus, P will recognize an RMB 20 gain and pay a tax of RMB 5. Table 7.8 represents the tax consequences.

Table 7.8 Tax Consequences of Stock and Asset Acquisitions (Corporate Shareholders – Loss Case – Revisited)

	Time 0	*Time 1*	*Time 2*	*Total*
Asset Acquisition	-5	-50	0	-55
Stock Acquisition	-5	-55	5	-55

Note: Negative numbers represent tax benefits enjoyed by taxpayers.

In total, the stock acquisition leads to an RMB 55 tax benefit, as does the asset acquisition. However, since the liquidation comes after T manufactures and sells products, the tax paid by P at Time 2 has a present value less than RMB 5 at Time 1. The stock acquisition still proves to be more tax-efficient in this scenario. Moreover, the distortion becomes stronger as P can postpone the realization of the RMB 20 offsetting gain simply by keeping T as a subsidiary. If T liquidates after a long time, the present value of the RMB 20 offsetting gain on T's liquidation will reach close to zero. In this way, P turns the extra RMB 5 tax benefit temporarily enjoyed by T at Time 1 into a permanent one.

[2] Target Company with Individual Shareholders

Whether S is an individual or a company makes no difference to the tax consequences at Time 1 and Time 2, and the Time 0 tax consequences in the gain case have already been provided in Section 5. Therefore, here we only need to examine the Time 0 tax consequences in the loss case. If S and P decide to conduct an asset acquisition, T can enjoy an RMB 5 tax benefit. If a stock acquisition is elected, the loss suffered by S will produce no tax benefit because the current law does not allow individuals to recognize losses.

Tables 7.9 and 7.10 represent the tax consequences in the two scenarios.

Table 7.9 Tax Consequences of Stock and Asset Acquisitions (Individual Shareholders – Gain Case – Revisited)

	Time 0	*Time 1*	*Time 2*	*Total*
Asset Acquisition	40	-50	0	-10
Stock Acquisition	20	-25	-25	-30

Note: Negative numbers represent tax benefits enjoyed by taxpayers.

Table 7.10 Tax Consequences of Stock and Asset Acquisitions (Individual Shareholders – Loss Case – Revisited)

	Time 0	*Time 1*	*Time 2*	*Total*
Asset Acquisition	-5	-50	0	-55
Stock Acquisition	0	-55	5	-50

Note: Negative numbers represent tax benefits enjoyed by taxpayers.

Where the target shareholder is an individual, the discontinuity between the two forms of acquisitions appears more severe after we consider the broader picture. Interestingly, in the gain case, the stock acquisition, which was previously thought of as inferior, turns out to be more tax-efficient. The reason is that following the stock acquisition, a distribution from T to its shareholder, which used to be taxable, is now tax-free. In the loss case, the stock acquisition is less appealing because S is unable to claim any loss.

[B] Proposed Solutions

At the start of this section, we mention that treating the target company in a stock acquisition as if it were liquidated is insufficient for solving the problem. However, such a method alone will create new discontinuities. To illustrate, we can apply this method to the gain case. If this method is adopted, the parties to the stock acquisition will recognize a corporate-level gain at Time 0 and increase the tax basis of T's assets to fair market value. The increase in tax basis will produce an extra benefit of RMB 25. While the method successfully equalizes the tax consequences of stock and asset acquisition at Time 0 and Time 1, it does not deny P the RMB 25 benefit from the increase in the basis of T's stock. It seems that this method overcorrects for the perceived problem, leading to a disparity in the opposite direction.

In order to solve the disparity problem, the broader picture should be taken into account. No matter how close the tax consequences of asset and stock acquisitions are to each other at Time 0 and Time 1, as long as P needs to recognize gain or loss at Time 2, the disparity in the tax treatment of the two forms of acquisitions will never disappear. The aforementioned method only focuses on the adjustment of the tax basis in T's assets and neglects the impact of P's receipt of liquidating distributions.

Given that the US elections follow a similar approach that does not change the tax status of the purchasing company, one may be curious about how they can effectively solve the disparity problem. The key lies in the fact that the US tax law provides a unique definition of dividends. According to Section 316, a company can only make a distribution of dividends out of its accumulated or current earnings and profits, which are distinct from the concept of 'retained earnings' for purposes of the corporate balance sheet.[63] The US tax law determines a company's earnings and profits by making certain adjustments to the company's taxable income.[64] If taxpayers make an election under Section 338, the target company, after the deemed sale and repurchase of its assets, is treated as a new company that has no earnings and profits. Moreover, since the tax basis of its assets has been stepped up to fair market value, when selling those assets subsequently, the target company will not realize taxable income and thus will not generate earnings and profits. Therefore, T following the election cannot distribute dividends to P, which, in turn, will recognize no gain or loss on the winding-up of T.

In China, the concept of dividends has the same meaning under the tax law as it does under the Company Law. A company can distribute dividends as long as it has retained earnings or capital surplus on the balance sheet. Adjustments to tax basis impact only corporate taxable income but not the accounting earnings. Therefore, T, in our example, can distribute the accounting profit from selling its assets to P as tax-free dividends. The amount of the dividends is equal to subtracting the paid-up capital of T from its net assets, and the paid-up capital of T, when distributed to P, will first be used to recover P's tax basis in the stock of T. If the paid-up capital of T is abundant to recover the tax basis fully, P will recognize gain to the extent of the remaining portion of the paid-up capital; if the paid-up capital is less than the tax basis, P will recognize losses.

In general, under the current Chinese tax law, the tax liability of P at Time 2 depends on two elements.[65] One is P's tax basis in T's stock, and the other is the amount of T's paid-up capital. P realizes gain or loss on the difference between them. The tax law should eliminate such a difference to prevent P from recognizing gain or loss at Time 2. The method described above, however, only adjusts the tax basis of T's assets but leaves the above two elements unchanged. Therefore, additional rules are

63. Internal Revenue Code (US), § 316.
64. The purpose of the adjustment is to more accurately reflect corporate economic gain and loss. Internal Revenue Code (US), § 312(n).
65. This research does not consider the possibility of overhauling the rules on corporate distribution, including the definition of dividend.

required for equalizing the tax basis of T's stock and T's paid-up capital. There are two options to do so.

The first one is to adjust the amount of T's paid-up capital to be equal to the tax basis of T's stock. This option lacks feasibility. Unlike 'tax basis', 'paid-up capital' is not in the realm of tax law jargon. It is, instead, a corporate law term, which refers to the assets that have been received by a company through issuing shares of stock to its shareholders. Changing the target's paid-up capital goes beyond the boundaries of tax law. From the corporate law perspective, a stock acquisition results in a change of the ownership of the target company, but the target company itself is not affected and maintains the same amount of paid-up capital. One can boldly imagine that the corporate law would change its stance and treat T as if it were reincorporated in the stock acquisition. However, it goes against the fundamental principle of corporate law that a company is a distinct entity from its shareholders. In this sense, this option is even more unrealistic than an overhaul of the tax rules on corporate distributions.

Therefore, the second option, which is to change P's tax basis in T's stock, is more promising. Let us suppose that P obtains T's stock with a basis equal to the amount of T's paid-up capital. Then, when P decides to liquidate T, it will recognize no gain or loss upon receiving distributions. In this way, the law can narrow the gap between the tax treatments of asset acquisitions and stock acquisitions. More importantly, this option is also necessary for combating dividend stripping practices.

Briefly speaking, dividend stripping refers to a transaction in which a shareholder transfers the right to receive a dividend to another entity before the declaration of the dividend. The underlying reason is that the tax law imposes different tax burdens on the transferor and the transferee for receiving the same amount of dividend.

In the cases where the transferor, the transferee, and the target are all domestic companies, the M&A participants usually prefer to extract profits from the target before transferring the stock of it. Consider a variation of our gain case: shortly after S establishes T with RMB 100, T sells its appreciated assets for RMB 220, earning a profit of RMB 120, on which it pays an income tax of RMB 30. If T pays a dividend of RMB 90 to S, the dividend will be tax-free. The distribution will reduce the value of T to RMB 100. S, therefore, can sell T to P for RMB 100 without recognizing any gain. Upon the completion of the whole arrangement, S receives RMB 190 in total from exiting its investment in T without paying any income tax. If instead, S directly sells T to P without having T make distributions, in order to make RMB 190 after-tax profits, S will charge P RMB 220. The same profits made by T are therefore taxed twice, once in the hands of T and once when S recognizes gain on the sale of T stock.

Admittedly, the current law contains a mechanism that mitigates the above double taxation problem. In our example, after the stock purchase with RMB 220, P can have T distribute an RMB 90 tax-free dividend to it and then sell T for RMB 100. Since the basis of T stock is now RMB 220, P will recognize a loss of RMB 120, which can offset P's gain from other sources and produce an RMB 30 tax benefit, thereby reducing the amount of total tax to RMB 30, just like in the above scenario. However, considering the time gap between the P's purchasing and selling of T, the present value of the RMB 30 tax benefit should be less than that of the additional RMB 30 tax paid by S. Therefore, the tax burden in this scenario is still higher.

If S is an individual and the rest of the assumptions remain the same, S will no doubt prefer to transfer the stock in T before the declaration of dividends. As China has a classical corporate tax system that taxes corporate income twice – once to the company and again to its shareholders, the tax paid by S on the receipt of dividends can never be mitigated. Given that inter-corporate dividends are tax exempted, the taxpayers can avoid the second layer of tax by transferring the T stock from S to P and having T distribute dividends to P. This dividend stripping arrangement severely hampers the integrity of the classical corporate tax system.

Many countries around the world have enacted anti-dividend stripping rules to plug similar loopholes. For example, the US Congress introduced the 'extraordinary dividend' rules in Section 1059 to defeat dividend stripping schemes like the one discussed above. 'Extraordinary dividend' means the dividend whose amount equals or exceeds specified percentages of the recipient's tax basis in the underlying stock.[66] If a company receives an extraordinary dividend from stock held for less than two years, the company must reduce its basis in the stock by the non-taxed portion of such a dividend.

China can learn from the US to close the loophole for dividend stripping. In China, the dividends-received deduction percentage is 100% for corporate shareholders, and the law determines the amount of dividend by subtracting a company's paid-up capital from its liquidating distributions. Hence, a Chinese version of Section 1059 of the IRC will have the same effect as letting the purchasing company's tax basis in the target stock equal the paid-up capital of the target company.

To sum up, we propose a two-prong method to address the disparity problem. The first part of the proposal is that the parties to a stock acquisition may elect to treat the target company as if it first sold all of its assets and liquidated and then purchased back the assets. Due to the election, the target company will have a fair market value basis in its assets. The second part of the proposal is that if the parties make the election provided in part one, the purchasing company's basis in the target stock should be equal to the paid-up capital of the target company. Moreover, whether or not the parties make the part one election, the stock purchased from individual shareholders should always have a basis equal to its corresponding portion of the target company's paid-up capital, with a view to preventing dividend stripping.[67]

66. Internal Revenue Code (US), § 1059(c). The percentage is 5 in the case of stock which is preferred as to dividends and is 10 in the case of any other stock. Such threshold percentages exclude the receipt of minimal dividends from the application scope of § 1059.
67. Here we only provide the key features of the method. It needs additional details to be workable.

[C] Special Tax Treatment and the Disparity Problem

In 1982, the American Law Institute published its study on corporate acquisitions and dispositions,[68] arguing that it would be too hard to eliminate the disparity problem.[69] Our previous analysis perfectly illustrates this point.

Indeed, as Professor Weisbach powerfully argues, the inconsistency between taxing asset acquisitions and stock acquisitions is hard to solve because it results from a fundamental characteristic of the modern business system – an investor can indirectly hold assets through a company. Nevertheless, we can try to mitigate the problem by narrowing the gap between some patterns of asset and stock acquisitions, which is the idea behind this chapter. Up to this point, the discussion adheres to the context of taxable M&A transactions. How the special tax treatment affects the parity in tax treatments of asset and stock acquisitions will be examined in the remaining of this chapter.

A stock acquisition happens between the acquiring company and the target company's shareholders. Under the ordinary tax treatment, a stock acquisition leads to a shareholder-level tax but has no immediate corporate-level tax implications. In a stock acquisition, the tax attributes of the target, such as the tax basis of its assets, get well preserved, even though the ownership of the target company shifts from the original shareholders to the purchasing company. That is to say, regardless of whether the special tax treatment applies, stock acquisitions are always carry-over basis transactions at the corporate level.

In contrast, an asset acquisition aims to change the ownership of the target assets, and therefore, a corporate-level tax arises. Under the ordinary tax treatment, the target company is subject to a current tax on the appreciation of its assets, and the purchasing company obtains a cost basis in the target company's assets. The special tax treatment, however, produces a carry-over basis for the assets in the hands of the purchasing company. As to the shareholder-level tax consequence, regardless of whether the special tax treatment applies, asset acquisitions always do not result in current shareholder level tax unless the target company gets liquidated after the asset acquisition.

The special tax treatment for M&A transactions has the potential to bridge the gap in tax treatments of stock and asset acquisitions. The special tax treatment allows the parties to a stock acquisition to defer the shareholder-level tax, and thus, to that extent, aligning the tax consequence of stock acquisitions with that of asset acquisitions. Furthermore, the special tax treatment mutes the distinction between the corporate-level tax consequences of stock acquisitions and asset acquisitions because, in a tax-deferred asset acquisition, the corporate-level tax gets deferred just like in the case of stock acquisitions.

It thus can be inferred that a possible approach for enhancing the tax neutrality between stock and asset acquisitions is to modify the special tax treatment. When

68. American Law Institute, *Federal Income Tax Project, Subchapter C: Proposals on Corporate Acquisitions and Dispositions* (1982).
69. *Ibid.*, at 36-39.

taxing corporate mergers (which are asset acquisitions followed by the liquidation of the target company in essence), the current law links the corporate-level tax consequence to the shareholder-level tax consequence. A merger leads to an instant tax at the corporate level unless the target company's shareholders are eligible for the special tax treatment and vice versa.[70] Put differently, the parties to a merger cannot defer taxes at one level but recognize gain at another level. The link between the tax consequences at the corporate and the shareholder levels prevents the special tax treatment from playing a more significant role in solving the disparity problem.

Based on the above analysis, this research proposes to break the link between the corporate and the shareholder-level tax consequences when applying the special tax treatment. More specifically, the law should allow the parties to a merger to elect to defer the corporate-level tax irrespective of whether the target shareholders are eligible for the non-recognition tax treatment. To illustrate this, consider an extreme case – a purely cash-financed M&A transaction. According to the current law, a purely cash-financed merger results in current taxes at both the corporate and the shareholder levels, while a purely cash-financed stock acquisition leads to a current tax at the shareholder-level and a deferred tax at the corporate level. However, under the reform proposal, the tax consequence of the purely cash-financed merger could be a deferred corporate-level tax and a current shareholder-level tax, which is the same as the tax consequence of the purely cash-financed stock acquisition.

It is interesting to compare the reform proposal above with the one advanced by Professor Coven. Here this research suggests allowing the parties to a merger to elect to defer the corporate-level tax, while Coven proposes to mandate mergers to be tax-deferred at the corporate level. Coven hopes to eliminate the disparity problem by establishing mandatory uniform rules for taxing different forms of M&A transactions so that his proposal provides many complex tax rules.[71] This research, however, fully acknowledges the difficulty of eliminating the disparity problem and admits that a more practical objective is to mitigate rather than eliminate the problem. Therefore, an elective mechanism should be a better choice.

§7.08 CONCLUSION

The principle of tax neutrality requires tax law to minimize, as far as possible, tax-induced distortions in economic behaviour. The Chinese tax law, however, treats asset acquisitions and stock acquisitions in drastically different manners. A taxable asset acquisition results in immediate taxable gain or loss to the target company and a cost basis in the assets transferred to the purchasing company. By contrast, in a taxable stock acquisition, there is no corporate-level recognition, and the target company keeps the original tax basis in their assets. In the absence of a mechanism dedicated to

70. Caishui (2009) No. 59, Arts. 4(4), 6(4).
71. Coven, *supra* note 18, at 173-191.

coordinating the tax bases of the target company's assets and stock in M&A transactions, China's income tax regime not only distorts the choice between asset acquisitions and stock acquisitions but invites the risk of loss duplication.

In order to mitigate the disparity in the tax treatment of stock and asset acquisitions and the problems associated with it, it is necessary to incorporate into the tax law a set of rules that adjust both the outside and the inside tax bases of the target company in an M&A transaction. Given that the current law has in effect achieved the result of dual basis adjustments in asset acquisitions, the efficient solution aligning the tax treatments of asset and stock acquisitions is to allow the target company in a stock acquisition to adjust the tax basis in its assets.

Following this direction, this chapter examines the US experience in adjusting the tax basis of the target company in an M&A transaction to align the tax treatment of stock acquisitions with that of asset acquisitions and discovers that the US rules are not readily transplantable to China since the Chinese tax rules on corporate distributions differ significantly from its US counterpart. Indeed, the tax treatment of corporate distributions interacts closely with the basis adjustment rules for M&A transactions, and the effort to tackle the disparity problem will be in vain if overlooking how the tax law treats corporate distributions. Taking into account the Chinese tax rules on corporate distributions, a promising approach for China to mitigate the disparity in the tax treatment of stock and asset acquisitions is to first treat the target company in a stock acquisition as if it were liquidated and then have the purchasing company obtain the target company's stock with a basis equal to the amount of the target company's paid-up capital. Furthermore, this research finds that the special tax treatment for M&A transactions has the potential to bridge the gap in the tax treatments of stock and asset acquisitions.

CHAPTER 8
Conclusion

Since the initiation of the economic reform and opening-up policy in the late 1970s, China has experienced enormous economic changes. It is against this background that China's M&A market emerged and against which it has been growing at a dramatic pace. After several decades of development, now China has already become the world's second-largest M&A market behind the US.

However, China's M&A market is still in the early stages of development, and the regulatory rules concerning M&A transactions are far from well-developed. The ambiguities surrounding the income tax treatment of M&A transactions are a clear example of this. This book has reviewed the development of the taxation of M&A transactions in China and then, in the context of the Chinese income taxation system, analysed the features and problems of China's tax rules for M&A transactions.

The tax rules specifically for M&A transactions in China first occurred during the early stages of the development of the Chinese M&A market. Before long, China decided to provide certain M&A transactions with exceptional income tax treatments, which features allowing the selling parties to an M&A transaction to postpone the recognition of gain or loss on disposal of properties. The introduction of the special tax treatment is hardly surprising given the fact that many people regard M&A transactions as beneficial for the economy and that the Chinese government often uses tax incentives to promote economic objectives.

Moreover, foreign experience plays an especially important role in the development of the taxation of M&A transactions in China. Based on the ideas from a range of foreign sources, most notably the US, China has made rapid progress in establishing its M&A taxation system. In a short period of approximately fifteen years, China's income tax rules for M&A transactions have developed from a crude circular that only provided the tax consequences of mergers between foreign-invested enterprises to a relatively comprehensive body of provisions prescribing the tax treatment for M&A transactions in various forms and between different types of enterprises. In order to modernize its taxation system, China has determined to bring its income tax law in line with international standards.

Despite the remarkable progress in the development of income tax rules for M&A transactions, China's income tax rules for M&A transactions have many problems, which hinder the healthy development of China's M&A market and damage the integrity of China's taxation system. One primary reason for this is that China has failed to critically examine foreign experience before inserting it into the local context. The Chinese government has come to believe that a good M&A taxation system should be akin to those in place in developed tax jurisdictions, in particular, the US. This belief has adversely affected the legislative process as it precludes a careful reflection on the rationale and implications of the legislation in the Chinese context.

With a view to building a solid normative foundation for an in-depth examination of and effective reform measures to the incredibly complex income tax regime for M&A, this book has explored the guiding principles for the taxation of M&A by assessing widely recognized taxation principles, including equity, neutrality, administrability, certainty, simplicity, and flexibility. Certainty and simplicity, as well as the principle of flexibility, constitute the second order taxation principles, which are too general and formal to provide guidance on the substantive issues in designing tax rules for M&A. Administrability, although containing substantive criteria that tax design should follow, is in essence a pragmatic concern that should be subordinate to the normative principles of equity and neutrality.

There are two dimensions to the notion of equity – horizontal and vertical. All the possible levels of interpretations of horizontal equity are either not useful because of emptiness or misleading due to the neglect of tax capitalization or replaceable by the principle of tax neutrality. Considering the broader context of China's income tax system, vertical equity – at least for the time being – has very limited weight in guiding how to better tax M&A transactions in China. Thus, the principle of tax neutrality, which basically requires tax law to treat different forms of business activities in a non-partial way so that interference with the market mechanism would not occur, is highlighted as the overarching principle for China's M&A taxation. Since the principle of neutrality requires that tax laws must minimize their effects on a taxpayer's decisions as to whether to engage in an M&A transaction and how to carry out an M&A transaction, the contrasting ordinary and special tax treatments, as well as the distinction in tax consequences between stock and asset acquisitions, stand out as two pivotal issues in the discourse of M&A taxation.

When transplanting the rollover relief for M&A transactions from the US, China's lawmakers did not miss out on the continuity of interest doctrine, under which the selling parties to an M&A transaction can defer their tax liabilities arising from the transaction provided that they receive a quantum of the equity interests in the purchasing company and thus are deemed as continuing interests in their original investment. The development of the special tax treatment regime shows that the Chinese government has spent a considerable amount of effort following the continuity of interest doctrine. Meanwhile, the Chinese government has been continuously attempting to expand the eligibility for the special tax treatment to stimulate M&A transactions. The two tax policies conflict with each other seriously, which has prevented either policy from performing satisfactorily and produced a regime full of inconsistencies and loopholes. The solution to the conflict lies in answer to the question of what counts as an adequate justification for the special tax treatment.

A careful analysis in this regard reveals that the continuity of interest doctrine and the notion behind it fail to justify the special tax treatment. Moreover, other traditional justifications for the special tax treatment, which centre on alleviating the administrative burden on tax authorities and taxpayers, are also unsatisfactory. While counterintuitive at first glance, the principle of tax neutrality supports the practice of granting non-recognition treatment to certain M&A transactions if one takes into account the defect of the current realization-based income tax system. The current tax law creates a severe tax bias between realized and unrealized gains and thus distorts the investment behaviour of taxpayers. Although resulting in new tax biases, the provision of rollover relief for certain M&A transactions helps mitigate the so-called lock-in effect. Overall, the rollover relief for M&A transactions creates more benefits than costs, especially in the Chinese context.

This book has proposed to abandon the continuity of interest doctrine and shift the focus of M&A taxation towards enhancing tax neutrality. There are three possible approaches to making the special tax treatment more accessible to taxpayers, which include reducing the equity consideration ratio threshold, extending the special tax treatment to non-corporate taxpayers, and decoupling the tax treatments of different taxpayers. While all of them can help make the special tax treatment more accessible, cautions are warranted with respect to whether they fit well into the income tax system. Moreover, the flaws of the special tax treatment, in particular, the problematic basis adjustment mechanism, should be addressed to prevent taxpayers from abusing rollover relief for tax avoidance purposes.

The principle of tax neutrality also requires that tax laws ensure various forms of acquisitions are subject to taxes in the same manner. Due to the problem of dual ownership, the current law taxes stock and asset acquisitions inconsistently. A stock acquisition leads to a current tax only at the shareholder level, while an asset acquisition typically results in a current tax at both the corporate level and the shareholder level. The solution to the disparity in the tax treatment of stock and asset acquisitions is to coordinate the outside basis and the inside tax basis of the target company in M&A transactions. Since the Chinese tax law has implicitly mandated a dual basis adjustment mechanism for asset acquisitions, the key to solving the disparity problem is to achieve outside-inside basis coordination in stock acquisitions.

Many Chinese scholars suggest transplanting US tax laws to tackle the disparity problem. However, this book has demonstrated that the historical and existing US laws on this issue are not suited to Chinese conditions. An analysis of the US tax laws reveals that the solution to the disparity problem hinges significantly on how corporate distributions are taxed. This book has further concluded that a promising approach for the Chinese tax law to address the disparity problem is one that takes fully into account the Chinese tax treatments of corporate distributions. Also, this book acknowledges the potential of the special tax treatment for M&A transactions in helping bridge the gap in the tax treatments of stock acquisitions and asset acquisitions.

At last, it is appropriate to conclude this book by pointing out the areas for future study. Due to space and time constraints, this book has not dealt with some specific issues surrounding China's taxation of M&A transactions. For example, one question to address in the future is how to better tackle international tax avoidance schemes in connection with M&A transactions. This line of issues will attract increasing attention, given China's rapidly growing M&A market and the current post-BEPS environment.

Bibliography

Adam Smith, *An Inquiry into the Nature and Causes of the Wealth of Nations* (1791).

Alan J. Auerbach, *Retrospective Capital Gains Taxation*, 81 The American Economic Review 167, (1991).

Alex Raskolnikov, *Accepting the Limits of Tax Law and Economics*, 98 Cornell L. Rev. 523, (2012).

Alfred G. Buehler, *Ability to Pay*, 1 Tax L. Rev. 243, (1945).

American Law Institute, *Federal Income Tax Project, Subchapter C: Proposals on Corporate Acquisitions and Dispositions* (1982).

American Law Institute, *Federal Income Tax Statute (February 1954 Draft)*.

Anonymous, *Woguo Qiye Jianbing You Xinfazhan [An Update on China's Enterprise Mergers and Acquisitions]*, Remin Ribao [People's Daily], 15 June 1990.

Boris Bittker, *Equity, Efficiency, and Income Tax Theory: Do Misallocations Drive Out Inequities?*, 16 San Diego L. Rev. 735, (1979).

Boris Bittker, *Federal Income Taxation of Corporations and Shareholders* (1959).

Cass R. Sunstein, *Problems with Rules*, 83 Cal. L. Rev. 953, (1995).

Charles E. McLure Jr., *Comments, in Do Taxes Matter?: The Impact of the Tax Reform Act of 1986* 332, (J. Slemrod ed., 1990).

Charlotte Crane, *Some Explicit Thinking about Implicit Taxes*, 52 SMU L. Rev. 339, (1999).

Cheryl D. Block, *Corporate Taxation: Examples & Explanations* (4th ed., 2010).

Christine P. W. Wong, *Fiscal Reform and Local Industrialization: The Problematic Sequencing of Reform in Post-Mao China*, 18 Modern China 197, (1992).

Christopher H. Hanna, *Tax Theories and Tax Reform*, 59 SMU L. Rev. 435, (2006).

Chunlai Chen, *Foreign Direct Investment in China: Location Determinants, Investor Differences and Economic Impacts* (2011).

Chunyan Zhang, *Binggou Jiaoyi Suodeshui Falv Zhidu Yanjiu-Jiyu dui Liyi Chixu Yuanze de Kaoliang [Research on the Mergers and Acquisitions Income Tax Law-Based on the Continuity Doctrine]* (2015).

Clinton Alley and Duncan Bentley, *A Remodelling of Adam Smith's Tax Design Principles*, 20 Australian Tax Forum, (2005).

CPC Central Committee, *Zhonggong Zhongyang Guanyu Jianli Shehui Zhuyi Shichang Jingji Tizhi Ruogan Wenti de Jueding [Decision of the CPC Central Committee on Some Issues Concerning the Establishment of a Socialist Market Economic Structure]* (14 November 1993).

CPC Central Committee, *Zhonggong Zhongyang Guanyu Quanmian Shenhua Gaige Ruogan Zhongda Wenti de Jueding [Decision of the CPC Central Committee on Some Major Issues Concerning Comprehensively Deepening the Reform]* (12 November 2013).

CSRC, *Shangshi Gongsi Binggou Chongzu Fuwu Shiti Jingji Zhuanfanshi Tiaojiegou Qude Mingxian Chengxiao [Listed Company M&A Transactions Help Restructure the Economy]*, CSRC (5 October 2021), http://www.csrc.gov.cn/pub/newsite/gjb/dyxc/201708/t20170815_322153.html.

Cynthia Blum, *Rollover: An Alternative Treatment of Capital Gains*, 41 Tax L. Rev. 383, (1985).

Dahong Liu and Jianhui Zhang, *Neutrality and the Regulatory Function of Taxation*, Zhongnan Caijing Zhengfa Daxue Xuebao [Journal of Zhongnan University of Finance and Economics], no. 4, 2002, at 94.

Daniel M. Schneider, *Groman – Or Namorg – Revisited; The Persisting Problem of Remote Continuity of Interest*, 61 Denv. L.J. 469, (1983).

Daniel N. Shaviro, *An Efficiency Analysis of Realization and Recognition Rules under the Federal Income Tax*, 48 Tax L. Rev. 1, (1992).

Daniel Q. Posin, *A Case Study in Income Tax Complexity: The Type A Reorganization*, 47 Ohio St. L.J. 627, (1986).

Daniel Q. Posin, *Taxing Corporate Reorganizations: Purging Penelope's Web*, 133 U. Pa. L. Rev. 1335, (1984).

David A. Weisbach, *Implications of Implicit Taxes*, 52 SMU Law Review 373, (1999).

David A. Weisbach, *The Irreducible Complexity of Firm-Level Income Taxes: Theory and Doctrine in the Corporate Tax*, 60 Tax L. Rev. 215, (2006).

David A. Weisbach, *A Partial Mark-to-Market Tax System*, 53 Tax L. Rev. 95, (1999).

David F. Shores, *Continuity of Business Enterprise: A Concept Whose Time Has Passed*, 63 Tax Law. 471, (2009).

David F. Shores, *Reexamining Continuity of Shareholder Interest in Corporate Reorganizations*, 17 Va. Tax Rev. 419, (1997).

David G. Levere, *Remote Continuity of Interest: The Problem Persists*, 49 Tax Law. 795, (1995).

David J. Shakow, *Taxation without Realization: A Proposal for Accrual Taxation*, 134 U. Pa. L. Rev. 1111, (1986).

David M. Schizer, *Realization as Subsidy*, 73 New York University Law Review 1549, (1998).

David S. Miller, *The Devolution and Inevitable Extinction of the Continuity of Interest Doctrine*, 3 Fla. Tax Rev. 187, (1996).

David W. Pearce (ed.), *The MIT Dictionary of Modern Economics* (4th ed., 1992).

Deborah H. Schenk, *A Positive Account of the Realization Rule*, 57 Tax L. Rev. 355, (2003).

Deborah H. Schenk, *Taxation of Equity Derivatives: A Partial Integration Proposal* 50 Tax L. Rev. 571, (1994).

Department of Household Surveys of the National Bureau of Statistics of China, *Zhongguo Zhuhu Diaocha Nianjian 2017 [China Yearbook of Household Survey 2017]* (2017).

Dong Zhang and Owen Freestone, *China's Unfinished State-owned Enterprise Reforms*, Economic Round-up, no. 2, 2013, at 77.

Douglas A. Kahn, *The Two Faces of Tax Neutrality: Do They Interact or Are They Mutually Exclusive* 18 N. Ky. L. Rev. 1, (1990).

Douglas A. Kahn and Jeffrey H. Kahn, *Prevention of Double Deductions of a Single Loss: Solutions in Search of a Problem*, 26 Va. Tax Rev. 1, (2006).

Duoqi Xu, *On the Ability to Pay Principle of Taxation*, Zhongguo Faxue [China Legal Science], no. 5, 2013, at 65.

Editorial Board of China Township and Village Enterprises Yearbook, *Zhongguo Xiangzhen Qiye Nianjian 1978-1987 [China Township and Village Enterprises Yearbook 1978-1987]* (1989).

Edward A. Zelinsky, *Efficiency and Income Taxes: The Rehabilitation of Tax Incentives*, 64 Tex. L. Rev. 973, (1986).

Edward A. Zelinsky, *For Realization: Income Taxation, Sectoral Accretionism, and the Virtue of Attainable Virtues*, 19 Cardozo L. Rev. 861, (1997).

Erwin Chemerinsky, *In Defense of Equality: A Reply to Professor Westen*, 81 Mich. L. Rev. 575, (1983).

Feng Li and Deyin Yang, *M&A Tax Policies and Continuity of Shareholder Interest*, Shuiwu Yanjiu [Taxation Research], no. 8, 2015, at 37.

Feng Shen, *The Evolution of M&A Tax Policy and Reform Proposals*, Shuishou Jingji Yanjiu [Tax and Economic Research], no. 5, 2016, at 31.

Frans Vanistendael, *Legal Framework for Taxation, in* 1 *Tax Law Design and Drafting* 15, (V. Thuronyi ed., 1996).

Frans Vanistendael, *Taxation of Corporate Reorganizations, in* 2 *Tax Law Design and Drafting* 895, (V. Thuronyi ed., 1998).

General Office of the CPC Central Committee and General Office of the State Council, *Shenhua Guoshui Dishui Zhengguan Tizhi Gaige Fang'an [Blueprint for Deepening the Reform of Tax Collection and Administrative Systems of State and Local Tax Administrations]* (24 December 2015).

Glenn E. Coven, *Taxing Corporate Acquisitions: A Proposal for Mandatory Uniform Rules*, 44 Tax L. Rev. 145, (1988).

Guo Feng, *Rethinking and Reconstruction: Tax Aspects of Corporate M&A in China*, Gansu Zhengfa Xueyuan Xuebao [Journal of Gansu Institute of Political Science and Law], no. 4, 2007, at 105.

Haiyong Wang, *Improving M&A Tax Policies to Promote Economic Structural Reform*, Guoji Shuishou [International Taxation in China], no. 2, 2015, at 39.

Harold Dubroff and Robert L. Daileader Jr., *Kimbell-Diamond Revisited: A Critique of Judicial Analysis of the Exclusivity of Section 334(b)(2)*, 43 Alb. L. Rev. 739, (1978).

Harvey S. Rosen and Ted Gayer, *Public Finance* (9th ed., 2010).
Henry C. Simons, *Personal Income Taxation: The Definition of Income as a Problem of Fiscal Policy* (1938).
Henry G. Manne, *Mergers and the Market for Corporate Control*, 73 Journal of Political Economy 110, (1965).
H. L. A. Hart, *The Concept of Law* (3d ed., 2012).
Holley H. Ulbrich, *Public Finance in Theory and Practice* (2nd ed., 2011).
Huai Kou, *Zhongguo Guoyou Qiye Binggou Qushi yu Zhanlue Yanjiu [China's SOE Reorganization: Trend and Strategy]* (2008).
Hugh J. Ault and Brian J. Arnold, *Comparative Income Taxation: A Structural Analysis* (3rd ed., 2010).
Hui Huang, *China's Takeover Law: A Comparative Analysis and Proposals for Reform*, 30 Del. J. Corp. L. 145, (2005).
Hui Huang, *The New Takeover Regulation in China: Evolution and Enhancement*, 42 The International Lawyer 153, (2008).
Hui Li, *M&A and Individual Income Tax Policy: Theoretical Examination and Reform Proposal*, Shuiwu Yanjiu [Taxation Research], no. 4, 2017, at 108.
Hui Li and Xiuyao Wu, *Application of the Special Tax Treatment to Cross-border Intra-group Reorganizations*, Shuiwu Yanjiu [Taxation Research], no. 8, 2015, at 26.
Hui Li and Yudong Zhou, *The Special Tax Treatment and Neutral Principle of Taxation: Questions and Solutions of Taxation for China Enterprise Reorganizations by Way of Stock Payment*, Zhongyang Caijing Daxue Xuebao [Journal of Central University of Finance & Economics], no. 4, 2014, at 18.
Huiman Yi, *Yi Huiman Zai 2021 Jinrongjie Luntan Nianhui Shang de Zhuti Yanjiang [Keynote Speech by Chairman Yi Huiman at the 2021 Annual Meeting of Financial Street Forum]*, (20 October 2021).
Ilan Benshalom and Kenda Stead, *Realization and Progressivity*, 3 Colum. J. Tax L. 43, (2011).
Irving Fisher, *Are Savings Income?*, 9 American Economic Association Quarterly 21, (1908).
Irving Fisher, *The Nature of Capital and Income* (1906).
James Repetti and Diane Ring, *Horizontal Equity Revisited*, 13 Fla. Tax Rev. 135, (2012).
James W. Wetzler, *The Role of Fairness in State Tax Policy*, 47 Rec. Ass'n B. City N.Y. 38, (1992).
Jerome Hellerstein, *Mergers, Taxes, and Realism*, 71 Harv. L. Rev. 254, (1957).
Jianfu Chen, *Securitisation of State-Owned Enterprises and the Ownership Controversy in the PRC*, 15 Sydney L. Rev. 59, (1993).
Jintao Hu, *Hu Jintao Zai Zhongguo Gongchandang Di Shiba Ci Quanguo Daibiao Dahui Shang de Baogao [Hu Jintao's Report to the 18th National Congress of the CPC]*, (8 November 2012).
Jinyan Li, *The Rise and Fall of Chinese Tax Incentives an Implications for International Tax Debates*, 8 Fla. Tax Rev. 669, (2006).

Jinyan Li, *Tax Transplants and the Critical Role of Processes: A Case Study of China*, 3 Journal of Chinese Tax and Policy 85, (2013).

Joel Slemrod and Jon Bakija, *Taxing Ourselves: A Citizen's Guide to the Debate over Taxes* (4th ed., 2008).

John A. Busterud, *The Liquidation of Subsidiaries under Section 112(b)(6)*, 58 Yale L. J. 1050, (1948).

John Andrew Simpson and Eva S. Weiner, *Oxford English Dictionary* (2nd ed., 1989).

John Whalley and Xian Xin, *China's FDI and Non-FDI Economies and the Sustainability of Future High Chinese Growth*, 21 China Economic Review 123, (2010).

John Whalley and Weimin Zhou, *Technology Upgrading and China's Growth Strategy to 2020, in China's Integration into the World Economy* 35, (J. Whalley ed., 2011).

Jon R. Neill, *The Benefit and Sacrifice Principles of Taxation: A Synthesis*, 17 Soc Choice Welfare 117, (2000).

Joseph Bankman and David A. Weisbach, *The Superiority of an Ideal Consumption Tax Over an Ideal Income Tax*, 58 Stan. L. Rev. 1413, (2005).

Joshua D. Blank, *Confronting Continuity: A Tradition of Fiction in Corporate Reorganizations*, 2006 Colum. Bus. L. Rev. 1, (2006).

Jun Wang, *Guotou Zhonglu Chongzu Gaochui Buneng Guijiu yu Shuifa [Tax Law is not to Blame for the Failure of the Reorganization of Guotou Zhonglu]*, ZhongGuo Shuiwu Bao [China Taxation News], 10 April 2015, at B02

Justin Yifu Lin, *The Household Responsibility System Reform in China: A Peasant's Institutional Choice*, 69 American Journal of Agricultural Economics 410, (1987).

Kent Greenawalt, *How Empty Is the Idea of Equality?*, 83 Colum. L. Rev. 1167, (1983).

Kevin Holmes, *The Concept of Income: A Multi-Disciplinary Analysis* (2001).

Kim Woodard, *Acquisitions in China: A View of the Field*, 31 China Business Review 34, (2004).

Lanxiang Zhou, *Continuity of Interest and Equity Consideration*, Caikuai Yuekan [Finance and Accounting Monthly], no. 5, 2015, at 90.

Lee Burns and Richard Krever, *Individual Income Tax, in* 2 *Tax Law Design and Drafting* 495, (V. Thuronyi ed., 1998).

Lei Yin, *A Research on the Effects of the Enterprise Income Tax Policies on Mergers and Acquisitions in China: An Empirical Test Based on A-share Listed Companies*, Shuiwu Yanjiu [Taxation Research], no. 7, 2021, at 104.

Lifen An, *Shuishou Cheng Binggou Chongzu Lanluhu [Taxation Becomes an Obstacle to M&A Transactions]* (12 March 2015), http://m.21jingji.com/article/20150312/34bf0ea0a7a6dad9b5450e1f293e8312.html.

Li Guo, *Revisiting the Chinese Styled Board of Supervisors-How It Gets Failed? An International Comparative Perspective*, Bijiaofa Yanjiu [Journal of Comparative Law], no. 2, 2016, at 74.

Lon L. Fuller, *The Morality of Law* (rev. ed., 1969).

Lori Farnan, *A Mandatory Section 338: Can It Be Implemented*, 42 Fla. L. Rev. 679, (1990).

Louis Kaplow, *Horizontal Equity: Measures in Search of a Principle*, 42 National Tax Journal 139, (1989).

Lucian A. Bebchuk, Reinier Kraakman and George G. Triantis, *Stock Pyramids, Cross-Ownership, and Dual Class Equity-The Mechanisms and Agency Costs of Separating Control from Cash-Flow Rights, in Concentrated Corporate Ownership* (R. K. Morck ed., 2000).

Mai Lu and Mingliang Feng, *The Evolution of China's Reform and Development Process, in Thirty Years of China's Reform* 28, (M. Wang ed., 2012).

Marina Martynova and Luc Renneboog, *A Century of Corporate Takeovers: What Have We Learned and Where Do We Stand?*, 32 Journal of Banking and Finance 2148, (2008).

Martin Feldstein, *Compensation in Tax Reform*, 29 National Tax Journal 123, (1976).

Mary Louise Fellows, *A Comprehensive Attack on Tax Deferral*, 88 Mich. L. Rev. 722, (1989).

Meredith R. Conway, *With or Without You: Debt and Equity and Continuity of Interest*, 15 Stan. J.L. Bus. & Fin. 261, (2009).

Michael J. Graetz and Rachael Doud, *Technological Innovation, International Competition, and the Challenges of International Income Taxation*, 113 Colum. L. Rev. 347, (2013).

Michael J. Waggoner, *Eliminating the Capital Gains Preference – Part I: The Problems of Inflation, Bunching and Lock-In*, 48 U. Colo. L. Rev. 313, (1976).

Munawer Sultan Khwaja, *Overview, in Risk-Based Tax Audits: Approaches and Country Experiences* 1, (M. S. Khwaja, R. Awasthi and J. Loeprick eds., 2011).

Myron S. Scholes and Mark A. Wolfson, *The Effects of Changes in Tax Laws on Corporate Reorganization Activity*, 63 The Journal of Business S141, (1990).

Ningbo Local Taxation Bureau, *Qiye Suodeshui Redian Zhengce Wen Da (2014 Nian Di Yi Qi) [Answers to Frequently Asked Questions Concerning the Enterprise Income Tax (Issue 1 of 2014)]* (2014).

Noam Noked, *Integrated Tax Policy Approach to Designing Research & Development Tax Benefits*, 34 Va. Tax Rev. 109, (2014).

Noel B. Cunningham and Deborah H. Schenk, *The Case for a Capital Gains Preference* 48 Tax L. Rev. 319, (1992).

OECD, *Addressing the Tax Challenges of the Digital Economy, Action 1 – 2015 Final Report* (2015).

OECD, *Compliance Risk Management: Managing and Improving Tax Compliance*, (2004).

OECD, *Taxation of Capital Gains of Individuals: Policy Considerations and Approaches* (2006).

Paul Kenny, *The 1999 Review of Business Taxation: Should We Fast Track Small Business Tax Reform?*, Revenue L.J. 138, (2008).

Paul Kenny, *Business Tax Reform Down Under: The 1999 Ralph Report* (18 October 2013), https://ssrn.com/abstract=2340891.

Paul R. McDaniel and James R. Repetti, *Horizontal and Vertical Equity: The Musgrave/Kaplow Exchange*, 1 Fla. Tax Rev. 607, (1993).

Peng Li, *Zhengfu Gongzuo Baogao [Report on the Work of the Government]*, (25 March 1988).

Peter L. Faber, *Continuity of Interest and Business Enterprise: Is It Time to Bury Some Sacred Cows*, 34 Tax Law. 239, (1980).

Peter Westen, *The Empty Idea of Equality*, 95 Harv. L. Rev. 537, (1982).

PwC, *M&A 2015 Review and 2016 Outlook* (26 January 2016), https://www.pwccn.com/en/services/deals-m-and-a/publications/ma-2015-review-and-2016-outlook.html.

Reuven S. Avi-Yonah, *The Three Goals of Taxation*, 60 Tax L. Rev. 1, (2006).

Review of Business Taxation, *An International Perspective* (1998).

Review of Business Taxation, *A Platform for Consultation* (1999).

Review of Business Taxation, *A Strong Foundation* (1998).

Review of Business Taxation, *A Tax System Redesigned* (1999).

R. G. Lipsey and Kelvin Lancaster, *The General Theory of Second Best*, 24 The Review of Economic Studies 11, (1956).

Richard A. Musgrave, *Horizontal Equity, Once More*, 43 National Tax Journal 113, (1990).

Richard A. Musgrave, *The Theory of Public Finance: A Study in Public Economy* (1959).

Richard Krever, *Structural Issues in the Taxation of Capital Gains*, 1 Australian Tax Forum, (1984).

R. Lawrence Heinkel, *Section 338 – An Analysis and Proposals for Reform*, 59 Notre Dame L. Rev. 158, (1983).

Roberta Romano, *A Guide to Takeovers: Theory, Evidence, and Regulation*, 9 Yale J. on Reg. 119, (1992).

Robert Murray Haig, *The Concept of Income-Economic and Legal Aspects, in The Federal Income Tax* 1, (R. M. Haig ed., 1921).

Robert S. Summers, *The Principles of the Rule of Law*, 74 Notre Dame L. Rev. 1691, (1999).

Roberto Galbiati and Pietro Vertova, *Horizontal Equity*, 75 Economica 384, (2008).

Roscoe Pound, *Interpretations of Legal History* (1923).

Ru-yin Hu, *The Evolution of China's Capital Markets* (2012).

Shukui Dong, Jianhua Chen, Baozhu Liu, Youwang You and Kaining Dong, *Shuiqian Kouchu yu Touzi Gaizu Yewu Suodeshui Wenti Jiexi [Explanations of Income Tax Tax Issues Concerning Before-Tax Deductions and Reorganizations]* (2001).

Shusong Ba and Yafang Yu, *Coordination of Market-Oriented M&A and Government Policy to Address Overcapacity*, Shuiwu Yanjiu [Taxation Research], no. 11, 2013, at 3.

Silvia Appelt, Matej Bajgar, Chiara Criscuolo and Fernando Galindo-Rueda, *R&D Tax Incentives: Evidence on Design, Incidence and Impacts*, OECD Science, Technology and Industry Policy Papers, No. 32, (2016).

Stanley S. Surrey, *Supreme Court and the Federal Income Tax: Some Implications of the Recent Decisions*, 35 Ill. L. Rev. 779, (1940).

Stanley S. Surrey, *Tax Incentives as a Device for Implementing Government Policy: A Comparison with Direct Government Expenditures*, 83 Harv. L. Rev. 705, (1969).

Stanley S. Surrey and Paul R. McDaniel, *The Tax Expenditure Concept: Current Developments and Emerging Issues*, 20 B.C. L. Rev. 225, (1978).

Stèphane Dees, *Foreign Direct Investment in China: Determinants and Effects*, 31 Economics of Planning 175, (1998).

Stephanie Hoffer and Dale A. Oesterle, *Tax-Free Reorganizations: The Evolution and Revolution of Triangular Mergers*, 108 Nw. U. L. Rev. 1083, (2014).

Stephen Utz, *Ability to Pay*, 23 Whittier L. Rev. 867, (2001).

Steven A. Bank, *Federalizing the Tax-Free Merger: Toward an End to the Anachronistic Reliance on State Corporation Laws*, 77 N.C. L. Rev. 1307, (1998).

Steven A. Bank, *Mergers, Taxes, and Historical Realism*, 75 Tul. L. Rev. 1, (2000).

Steven J. Burton, *Comment on 'Empty Ideas': Logical Positivist Analyses of Equality and Rules*, 91 Yale L.J. 1136, (1982).

Tao Zhang, *Utilization of Foreign Capital and Economic Growth in China*, 37 The Chinese Economy 62, (2004).

Tax Commission of Japan, *Tax Commission Paper of Japan* (2000).

Tax Science Research Institute of the STA, *Qiye Chongzu Qiye Suodeshui Wenti Yanjiu [On Enterprise Income Tax Issues in M&A], in Zhongguo Shuishou Yanjiu Baogao 2012-2013 [Report on Taxation in China, 2012-2013]* (T. S. R. I. o. t. STA ed., 2014).

Terrence R. Chorvat, *Perception and Income: The Behavioral Economics of the Realization Doctrine*, 36 Conn. L. Rev. 75, (2003).

Tetsuya Watanabe, *Tax-Free Treatment for Corporate Reorganizations in Japan* (Sho Sato Conference on Tax Law, Social Policy, and the Economy, UC Berkeley, 9-10 March 2009), https://www.law.berkeley.edu/files/sho_sato_tax_conf_web_paper--watanabe.pdf.

Thomas N. Tarleau, *Continuity of the Business Enterprise in Corporate Reorganizations and Other Corporate Readjustments*, 60 Colum. L. Rev. 792, (1960).

Tianyong Liu, *Jianxi Qiye Chongzu Shiyong Teshuxing Shuiwu Chuli Wei Jishi Bei'an de Falv Houguo [A Brief Analysis on the Consequence of Failure to Filing Documentation for the Special Tax Treatment on Time]* (24 October 2021), http://www.xingtao.cn/news/1325.html.

Timothy A. Kearney, *An Overview of the EC Merger Directive and Its Implementation by Member States*, 21 Int'l Tax J. 26, (1995).

Tyrrell Levine and Kim Woodard, *The New Face of Chinese M&A*, 169 Far Eastern Economic Review 18, (2006).

Ulysses S. Crockett Jr., *Federal Taxation of Corporate Unifications: A Review of Legislative Policy*, 15 Duq. L. Rev. 1, (1976).

US Congress Joint Committee on Internal Revenue Taxation, *Summary of the New Provisions of the Internal Revenue Code of 1954 (H.R. 8300)* (1955).

US Senate Committee on Finance, S. REP. No. 617, 65th Cong., 3d Sess. 5 (US) (1918).

Uwe E. Reinhardt, *Reflections on the Meaning of Efficiency: Can Efficiency Be Separated from Equity?*, 10 Yale L. & Pol'y Rev. 302, (1992).

Valentine Brookes, *The Continuity of Interest Test in Reorganizations – A Blessing or a Curse*, 34 Cal. L. Rev. 1, (1946).

Victor Thuronyi, *The Concept of Income*, 46 Tax L. Rev. 45, (1990).

Vivienne Bath, *Reducing the Role of Government – The Chinese Experiment*, 3 Asian Journal of Comparative Law 1, (2008).

Walter J. Blum, *A Handy Summary of the Capital Gains Arguments*, 35 Taxes 247, (1957).

Wei Cui, *Qiye Chongzu Shuiwu Guize Qicao Guocheng de Fansi [Reflections on the Making of the Income Tax Rules for Enterprise Reorganizations], in* 1 *Shuifa Jieshi yu Panli Pingzhu [Tax Law and Case Review]* 163, (W. Xiong ed., 2010).

Wei Cui, *Taxing Indirect Transfers: Improving an Instrument for Stemming Tax and Legal Base Erosion*, 33 Virginia Tax Review 653, (2014).

Wei Cui, *'Ultra Special' Tax Treatment for Restructuring of SOEs: Legal Background and Comments*, Zhongwai Faxue [Peking University Law Journal], no. 6, 2010, at 944.

Wei Cui, *What is the 'Law' in Chinese Tax Administration?*, 19 Asia Pacific Law Review 73, (2011).

Wei Cui and Richard Krever, *The Tax Consequences of Corporate Reorganisations in China*, British Tax Review, no. 3, 2011, at 340.

Weiping Li, *The Incentive Effect of the Tax System on M&A Activities*, Caijing Wenti Yanjiu [Research on Financial and Economic Issues], no. 4, 2007, at 72.

Wei Zheng, *Guotou Zhonglu Hungai Qiake huo Lingyou Yinqing [Possible Hidden Cause of the Failure of Guotou Zhonglu Reorganization]* (12 April 2015), http://www.changjiangtimes.com/2015/04/500261.html.

William A. Lovett, *Tax Subsidies for Merger: Should Mergers be Made to Meet a Market Test for Efficiency*, 45 N.Y.U. L. Rev. 844, (1970).

William D. Andrews, *A Consumption-Type or Cash Flow Personal Income Tax*, 87 Harv. L. Rev. 1113, (1973).

William J. Turnier, *Continuity of Interest – Its Application to Shareholders of the Acquiring Corporation*, 64 Calif. L. Rev. 902, (1976).

Wind Info, *Binggou Langchao Xingqi: 2015 Nian Zhongguo Binggou Guimo Chuang Lishi Xingao [The Rising Tide of M&A: China's M&A Activities Hit A New Record in 2015]* (18 February 2016), http://money.163.com/16/0218/19/BG4LPIE700254UB4.html.

World Bank, *SOE Dividends: How Much and to Whom*, World Bank (17 October 2005), https://documents1.worldbank.org/curated/en/961421468243568454/pdf/566510WP0SOE1E10Box353729B01PUBLIC1.pdf.

Xiaoguang Zhou, *Tax Deferral and Anti-Avoidance in M&A Taxation*, Shuiwu Yanjiu [Taxation Research], no. 4, 2015, at 64.

Xiaohui Hong, *The Problem of Double Taxation in M&A Transactions*, Xin Kuaiji [Modern Accounting], no. 7, 2015, at 69.

Xiaoping Deng, *Zai Wuchang, Shenzhen, Zhuhai, Shanghai Dengdi de Tanhua Yaodian [Excerpts from Talks Given in Wuchang, Shenzhen, Zhuhai and Shanghai], in* 3 *The Selected Works of Deng Xiaoping* 370, (1993).

Xiaosun Gui, *Guotou Zhonglu Hungai Pengshang Heitiane-Chongzufang Jiaobuqi Geshui Chongzu Gaochui [The Restructuring of Guotou Zhonglu Failed Because of a Black Swan Event–One Party Cannot Afford Income Taxes]*, Zhengquan Ribao [Securities Daily], 3 April 2015, at C04.

Xiaowei Hao, Chun Hu and Lingshuang Chen, *On Improving M&A Tax Policies*, Shuishou Jingji Yanjiu [Tax and Economic Research], no. 4, 2015, at 42.

Xinhua News Agency, *Li Keqiang Zongli deng Huijian Caifang Lianghui de Zhongwai Jizhe bing Huida Tiwen [Premier Li Keqiang's Press Conference and Q&A Session]* (17 March 2013), http://www.xinhuanet.com//2013lh/2013-03/17/c_124469054_2.htm.

Yariv Brauner, *A Good Old Habit, or Just an Old One? Preferential Tax Treatment for Reorganizations*, 2004 BYU L. Rev. 1, (2004).

Yong Zhen, *China's Capital Markets* (2013).

Yunbin Gao, *Does the Special Tax Treat Lead to Double Taxation?*, Caiwu yu Kuaiji [Finance & Accounting], no. 6, 2013, at 34.

Yu Xie and Xiang Zhou, *Income Inequality in Today's China*, 111 Proceedings of the National Academy of Sciences of the United States of America 6928, (2014).

Zemin Jiang, *Jiang Zemin Zai Zhongguo Gongchandang Di Shisi Ci Quanguo Daibiao Dahui Shang de Baogao [Jiang Zemin's Report to the 14th National Congress of the CPC]*, (12 October 1992).

Zemin Jiang, *Jiang Zemin Zai Zhongguo Gongchandang Di Shiwu Ci Quanguo Daibiao Dahui Shang de Baogao [Jiang Zemin's Report to the 15th National Congress of the CPC]*, (12 September 1997).

Zemin Jiang, *Jiang Zemin Zai Zhongguo Gongchandang Di Shiliu Ci Quanguo Daibiao Dahui Shang de Baogao [Jiang Zemin's Report to the 16th National Congress of the CPC]*, (8 November 2002).

Zhengwen Shi, *Distributive Justice and Individual Income Tax Law Reform*, Zhongguo Faxue [China Legal Science], no. 5, 2011, at 32.

Ziyang Zhao, *Zhao Ziyang Zai Zhongguo Gongchandang Di Shisan Ci Quanguo Daibiao Dahui Shang de Baogao [Zhao Ziyang's Report to the 13th National Congress of the CPC]*, (25 October 1987).

Zongtao Wang, *The Regulation of Tax Incentives in China*, 23 Henan Shehui Kexue [Henan Social Sciences] 52, (2015).

Table of Cases

US Cases

Table of Statutes

Chinese Statutes

Overseas Statutes

Index

D

T

SERIES ON INTERNATIONAL TAXATION

1. Alberto Xavier, *The Taxation of Foreign Investment in Brazil,* 1980 (ISBN 90-200-0582-0).
2. Hugh J. Ault & Albert J. Rädler, *The German Corporation Tax Law with 1980 Amendments,* 1981 (ISBN 90-200-0642-8).
3. Paul R. McDaniel & Hugh J. Ault, *Introduction to United States International Taxation,* 1981 (ISBN 90-6544-004-6).
4. Albert J. Rädler, *German Transfer Pricing/Prix de Transfer en Allemagne,* 1984 (ISBN 90-6544-143-3).
5. Paul R. McDaniel & Stanley S. Surrey, *International Aspects of Tax Expenditures: A Comparative Study,* 1985 (ISBN 90-654-4163-8).
6. Kees van Raad, *Nondiscrimination in International Tax Law,* 1986 (ISBN 90-6544-266-9).
7. Sijbren Cnossen (ed.), *Tax Coordination in the European Community,* 1987 (ISBN 90-6544-272-3).
8. Ben Terra, *Sales Taxation. The Case of Value Added Tax in the European Community,* 1989 (ISBN 90-6544-381-9).
9. Rutsel S.J. Martha, *The Jurisdiction to Tax in International Law: Theory and Practice of Legislative Fiscal Jurisdiction,* 1989 (ISBN 90-654-4416-5).
10. Paul R. McDaniel & Hugh J. Ault, *Introduction to United States International Taxation* (3rd revised edition), 1989 (ISBN 90-6544-423-8).
11. Manuel Pires, *International Juridicial Double Taxation of Income,* 1989 (ISBN 90-6544-426-2).
12. A.H.M. Daniels, *Issues in International Partnership Taxation,* 1991 (ISBN 90-654-4577-3).
13. Arvid A. Skaar, *Permanent Establishment: Erosion of a Tax Treaty Principle,* 1992 (ISBN 90-6544-594-3).
14. Cyrille David & Geerten M.M. Michielse (eds), *Tax Treatment of Financial Instruments,* 1996 (ISBN 90-654-4666-4).
15. Herbert H. Alpert & Kees van Raad (eds), *Essays on International Taxation,* 1993 (ISBN 90-654-4781-4).
16. Wolfgang Gassner, Michael Lang & Eduard Lechner (eds), *Tax Treaties and EC Law,* 1997 (ISBN 90-411-0680-4).
17. Glória Teixeira, *Taxing Corporate Profits in the EU,* 1997 (ISBN 90-411-0703-7).
18. Michael Lang et al. (eds), *Multilateral Tax Treaties,* 1998 (ISBN 90-411-0704-5).
19. Stef van Weeghel, *The Improper Use of Tax Treaties,* 1998 (ISBN 90-411-0737-1).

20. Klaus Vogel (ed.), *Interpretation of Tax Law and Treaties and Transfer Pricing in Japan and Germany,* 1998 (ISBN 90-411-9655-2).
21. Bertil Wiman (ed.), *International Studies in Taxation: Law and Economics; Liber Amicorum Leif Mutén,* 1999 (ISBN 90-411-9692-7).
22. Alfonso J. Martín Jiménez, *Towards Corporate Tax Harmonization in the European Community,* 1999 (ISBN 90-411-9690-0).
23. Ramon J. Jeffery, *The Impact of State Sovereignty on Global Trade and International Taxation,* 1999 (ISBN 90-411-9703-6).
24. A.J. Easson, *Taxation of Foreign Direct Investment,* 1999 (ISBN 90-411-9741-9).
25. Marjaana Helminen, *The Dividend Concept in International Tax Law: Dividend Payments Between Corporate Entities,* 1999 (ISBN 90-411-9765-6).
26. Paul Kirchhof, Moris Lehner, Kees van Raad, Arndt Raupach & Michael-Rodi (eds), *International and Comparative Taxation: Essays in Honour of Klaus Vogel,* 2002 (ISBN 90-411-9841-5).
27. Krister Andersson, Peter Melz & Christer Silfverberg (eds), *Liber Amicorum Sven-Olof Lodin,* 2001 (ISBN 90-411-9850-4).
28. Juan Martín Jovanovich, *Customs Valuation and Transfer Pricing: Is It Possible to Harmonize Customs and Tax Rules?,* Second Edition, 2018 (ISBN 978-90-411-6134-5).
29. Stefano Simontacchi, *Taxation of Capital Gains under the OECD Model Convention: With Special Regard to Immovable Property,* 2007 (ISBN 978-90-411-2549-1).
30. Michael Lang, Josef Schuch, & Claus Staringer (eds), *Tax Treaty Law and EC Law,* 2007 (ISBN 978-90-411-2629-0).
31. Duncan Bentley, *Taxpayers' Rights: Theory Origin and Implementation,* 2007 (ISBN 978-90-411-2650-4).
32. Sergio André Rocha, *Interpretation of Double Taxation Conventions: General Theory and Brazilian Perspective,* 2008 (ISBN 978-90-411-2822-5).
33. Robert F. van Brederode, *Systems of General Sales Taxation: Theory, Policy and Practice,* 2009 (ISBN 978-90-411-2832-4).
34. John G. Head & Richard Krever (eds), *Tax Reform in the 21st Century: A Volume in Memory of Richard Musgrave,* 2009 (ISBN 978-90-411-2829-4).
35. Jens Wittendorff, *Transfer Pricing and the Arm's Length Principle in International Tax Law,* 2010 (ISBN 978-90-411-3270-3).
36. Marjaana Helminen, *The International Tax Law Concept of Dividend,* Second Edition, 2017 (ISBN 978-90-411-8394-1).
37. Robert F. van Brederode (ed.), *Immovable Property under VAT: A Comparative Global Analysis,* 2011 (ISBN 978-90-411-3126-3).
38. Dennis Weber & Stef van Weeghel, *The 2010 OECD Updates: Model Tax Convention & Transfer Pricing Guidelines - A Critical Review,* 2011 (ISBN 978-90-411-3812-5).
39. Yariv Brauner & Martin James McMahon, Jr. (eds), *The Proper Tax Base: Structural Fairness from an International and Comparative Perspective— Essays in Honour of Paul McDaniel,* 2012 (ISBN 978-90-411-3286-4).
40. Robert F. van Brederode (ed.), *Science, Technology and Taxation,* 2012 (ISBN 978-90-411-3125-6).

41. Oskar Henkow, *The VAT/GST Treatment of Public Bodies*, 2013 (ISBN 978-90-411-4663-2).
42. Jean Schaffner, *How Fixed Is a Permanent Establishment?*, 2013 (ISBN 978-90-411-4662-5).
43. Miguel Correia, *Taxation of Corporate Groups*, 2013 (ISBN 978-90-411-4841-4).
44. Veronika Daurer, *Tax Treaties and Developing Countries*, 2014 (ISBN 978-90-411-4982-4).
45. Claire Micheau, *State Aid, Subsidy and Tax Incentives under EU and WTO Law*, 2014 (ISBN 978-90-411-4555-0).
46. Robert F. van Brederode & Richard Krever (eds), *Legal Interpretation of Tax Law*, 2014 (ISBN 978-90-411-4945-9).
47. Radhakishan Rawal, *Taxation of Cross-border Services*, 2014 (ISBN 978-90-411-4947-3).
48. João Dácio Rolim, *Proportionality and Fair Taxation*, 2014 (ISBN 978-90-411-5838-3).
49. Paulo Rosenblatt, *General Anti-avoidance Rules for Major Developing Countries*, 2015 (ISBN 978-90-411-5839-0).
50. Gaspar Lopes Dias V.S., *Tax Arbitrage through Cross-Border Financial Engineering*, 2015 (ISBN 978-90-411-5875-8).
51. Geerten M.M. Michielse & Victor Thuronyi (eds), *Tax Design Issues Worldwide*, 2015 (ISBN 978-90-411-5610-5).
52. Oktavia Weidmann, *Taxation of Derivatives*, 2015 (ISBN 978-90-411-5977-9).
53. Chris Evans, Richard Krever & Peter Mellor (eds), *Tax Simplification*, 2015 (ISBN 978-90-411-5976-2).
54. Reuven Avi-Yonah & Joel Slemrod (eds), *Taxation and Migration*, 2015 (ISBN 978-90-411-6136-9).
55. Alexander Bosman, *Other Income under Tax Treaties: An Analysis of Article 21 of the OECD Model Convention*, 2015 (ISBN 978-90-411-6610-4).
56. John Abrahamson, *International Taxation of Manufacturing and Distribution*, 2016 (ISBN 978-90-411-6664-7).
57. Frederik Boulogne, *Shortcomings in the EU Merger Directive*, 2016 (ISBN 978-90-411-6713-2).
58. Angelika Meindl-Ringler, *Beneficial Ownership in International Tax Law*, 2016 (ISBN 978-90-411-6833-7).
59. Andreas Waltrich, *Cross-Border Taxation of Permanent Establishments: An International Comparison*, 2016 (ISBN 978-90-411-6832-0).
60. Sergio André Rocha & Allison Christians (eds), *Tax Sovereignty in the BEPS Era*, 2017 (ISBN 978-90-411-6707-1).
61. Peter Antony Wilson, *BRICS and International Tax Law*, 2018 (ISBN 978-90-411-9435-0).
62. Louise Otis, Brigitte Alepin & Blanca Moreno-Dodson (eds), *Winning the Tax Wars: Tax Competition and Cooperation*, 2018 (ISBN 978-90-411-9460-2).
63. Marta Castelon, *International Taxation of Income from Services under Double Taxation Conventions: Development, Practice and Policy*, 2018 (ISBN 978-90-411-9594-4).

64. D.M. Broekhuijsen, *A Multilateral Tax Treaty: Designing an Instrument to Modernise International Tax Law*, 2018 (ISBN 978-90-411-9872-3).
65. John Abrahamson, *International Taxation of Energy Production and Distribution*, 2018 (ISBN 978-90-411-9101-4).
66. Leopoldo Parada, *Double Non-taxation and the Use of Hybrid Entities: An Alternative Approach in the New Era of BEPS*, 2018 (ISBN 978-90-411-9991-1).
67. Richard Snoeij, *International Tax Aspects of Sovereign Wealth Investors: A Source State Perspective*, 2018 (ISBN 978-90-411-9431-2).
68. Aleksandra Bal, *Taxation, Virtual Currency and Blockchain*, 2019 (ISBN 978-94-035-0103-1).
69. Werner Haslehner, Georg Kofler, Katerina Pantazatou & Alexander Rust (eds), *Tax and the Digital Economy: Challenges and Proposals for Reform*, 2019 (ISBN 978-94-035-0361-5).
70. Eva Escribano, *Jurisdiction to Tax Corporate Income Pursuant to the Presumptive Benefit Principle: A Critical Analysis of Structural Paradigms Underlying Corporate Income Taxation and Proposals for Reform*, 2019 (ISBN 978-94-035-0640-1).
71. Jérôme Monsenego & Jan Bjuvberg (eds), *International Taxation in a Changing Landscape: Liber Amicorum in Honour of Bertil Wiman*, 2019 (ISBN 978-90-411-9234-9).
72. Kasper Dziurdź, *Non-discrimination in Tax Treaty Law and World Trade Law: The Impact of Formal, Substantive and Subjective Approaches*, 2019 (ISBN 978-94-035-0904-4).
73. Félix Daniel Martínez Laguna, *Hybrid Financial Instruments, Double Nontaxation and Linking Rules*, 2019 (ISBN 978-94-035-1074-3).
74. Jan Gooijer, *Tax Treaty Residence of Entities*, 2019 (ISBN 978-94-035-1301-0).
75. John Abrahamson, *International Taxation of Banking*, 2020 (ISBN 978-94-035-1094-1).
76. Richard Krever & François Vaillancourt (eds), *The Allocation of Multinational Business Income: Reassessing the Formulary Apportionment Option*, 2020 (ISBN 978-94-035-0614-2).
77. Ajit Kumar Singh, *Exploring the Nexus Doctrine in International Tax Law*, 2021 (ISBN 978-94-035-3363-6).
78. Galya Savir, *Regulation and Tax in Space*, 2021 (ISBN 978-94-035-3393-3).
79. Rita Julien, *Credit Method Compatibility and Constraints under EU Law: An Analysis of the Case Law of the CJEU*, 2022 (ISBN 978-94-035-2363-7).
80. Sergio André Rocha & Allison Christians (eds), *A Multilateral Convention for Tax: From Theory to Implementation*, 2022 (ISBN 978-90-411-9428-2).
81. Brigitte Alepin, Lyne Latulippe & Louise Otis (eds), *Coordination and Cooperation: Tax Policy in the 21st Century*, 2022 (ISBN 978-94-035-3740-5).
82. Chunyang Zhang, *The Role of Tax Law in Mergers and Acquisitions: A Chinese Perspective*, 2022 (ISBN 978-94-035-3741-2).